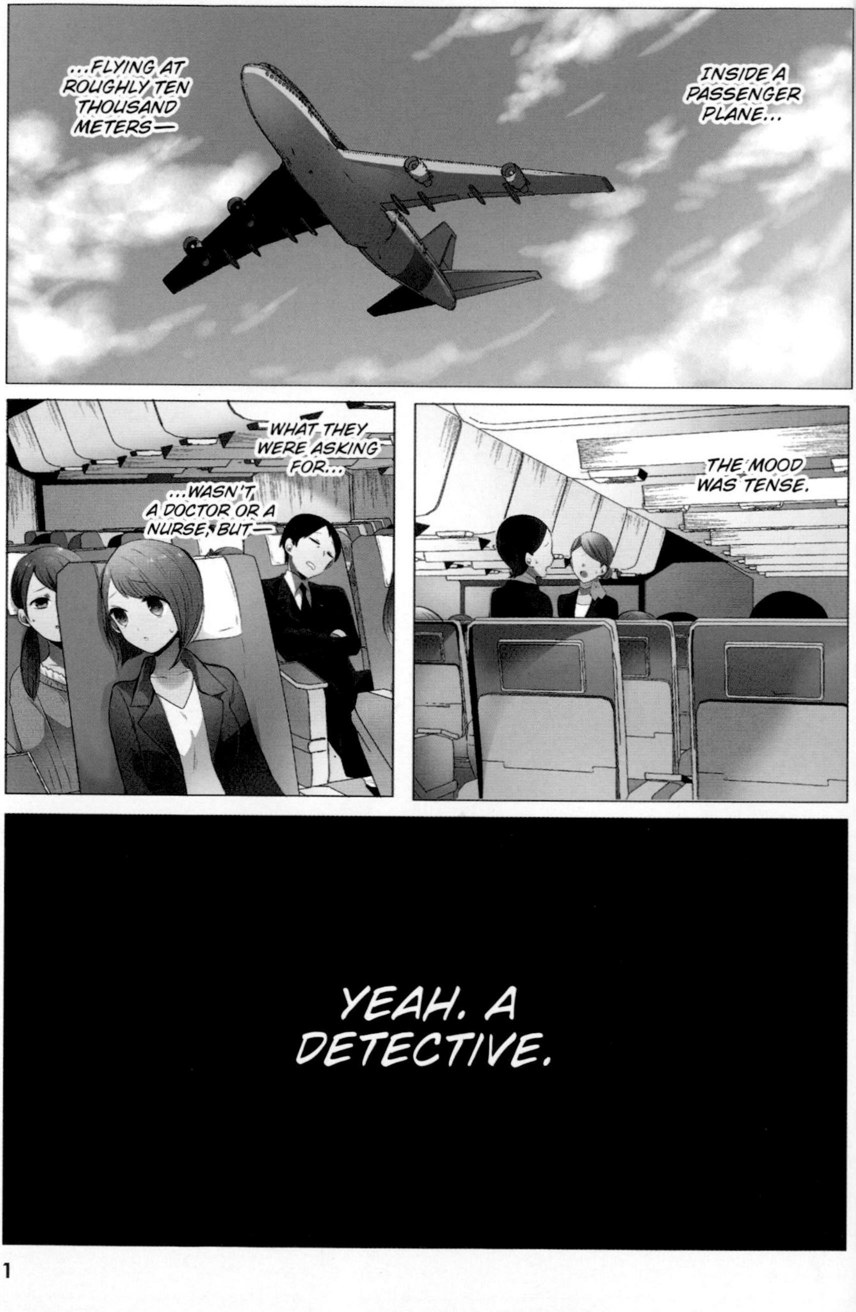
INSIDE A PASSENGER PLANE...
...FLYING AT ROUGHLY TEN THOUSAND METERS—
THE MOOD WAS TENSE.
WHAT THEY WERE ASKING FOR...
...WASN'T A DOCTOR OR A NURSE, BUT—
YEAH. A DETECTIVE.

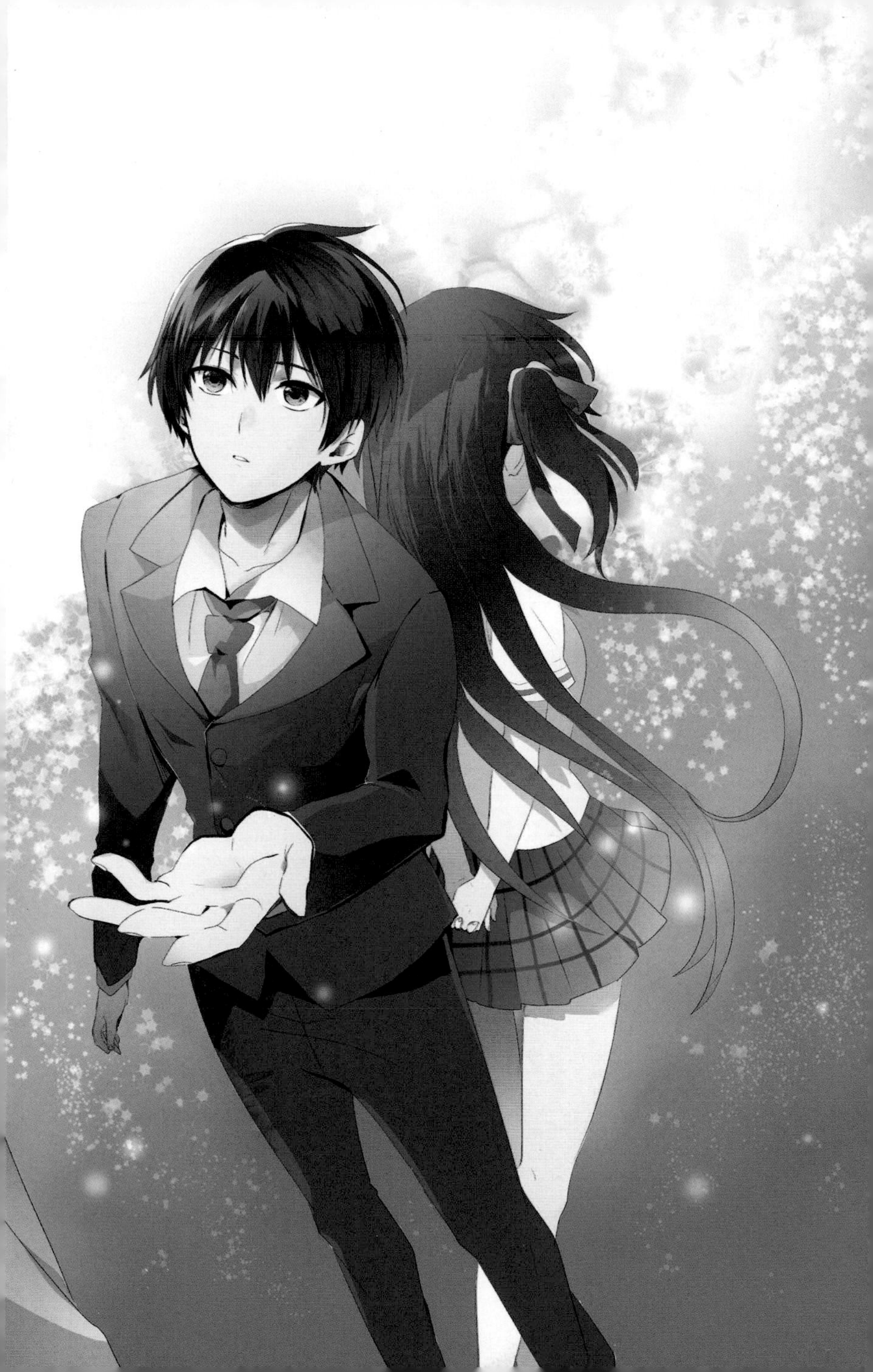

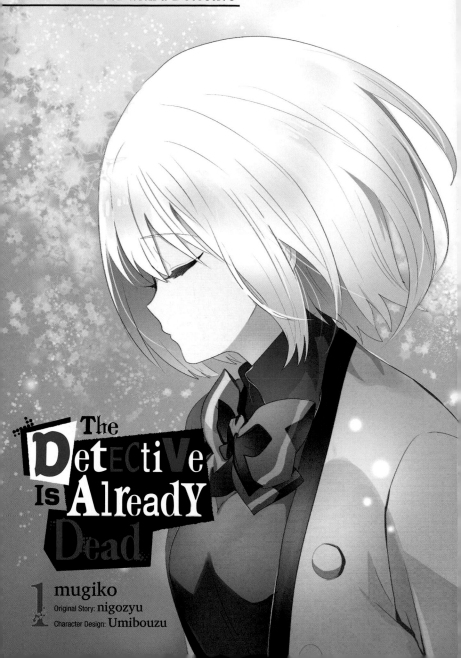

Episode. **0**
An Encounter with a Detective

The
Detective
Is Already
Dead

1 mugiko
Original Story: **nigozyu**
Character Design: **Umibouzu**

Contents

Episode.0　**An Encounter with a Detective** ·························· 001

Episode.1　**The Detective Is Out** ································· 021

Episode.2　**Whose Heart Is This?** ······························· 049

Episode.3　**I'll Blow Your Head Off** ······················· 081

Episode.4　**Heart, Bat** ·· 111

Episode.5　**The Detective on the Plane** ···················· 137

Afterword ·· 162

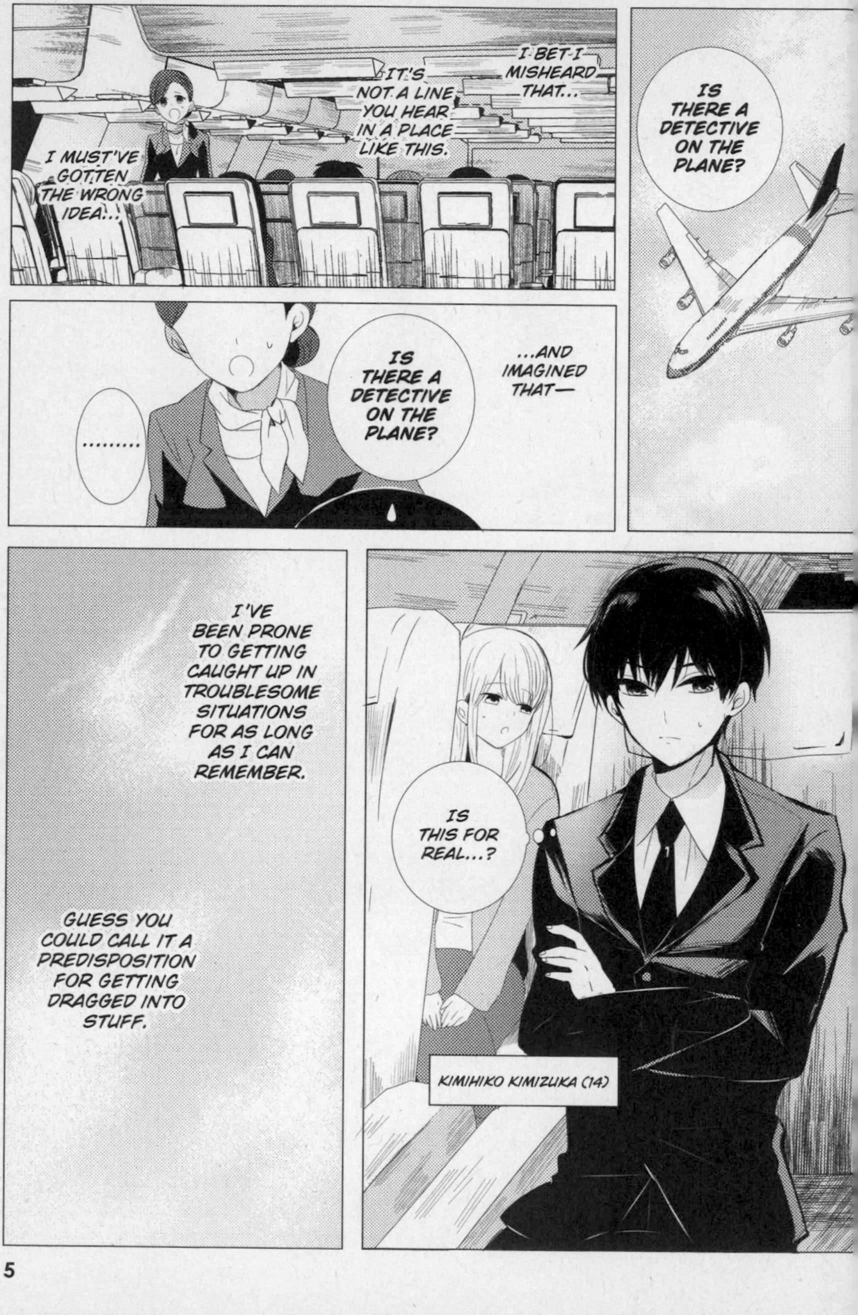
IS THERE A DETECTIVE ON THE PLANE?
I BET I MISHEARD THAT...
IT'S NOT A LINE YOU HEAR IN A PLACE LIKE THIS.
I MUST'VE GOTTEN THE WRONG IDEA...
...AND IMAGINED THAT—
IS THERE A DETECTIVE ON THE PLANE?
....
IS THIS FOR REAL...?
KIMIHIKO KIMIZUKA (14)
I'VE BEEN PRONE TO GETTING CAUGHT UP IN TROUBLESOME SITUATIONS FOR AS LONG AS I CAN REMEMBER.
GUESS YOU COULD CALL IT A PREDISPOSITION FOR GETTING DRAGGED INTO STUFF.

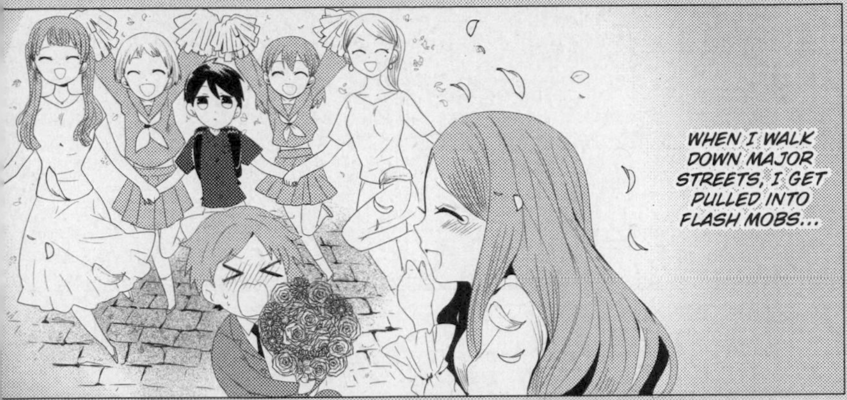
WHEN I WALK DOWN MAJOR STREETS, I GET PULLED INTO FLASH MOBS...
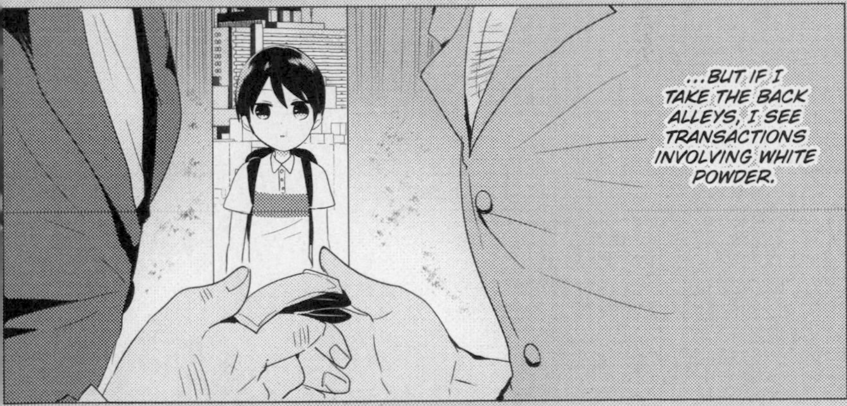
...BUT IF I TAKE THE BACK ALLEYS, I SEE TRANSACTIONS INVOLVING WHITE POWDER.
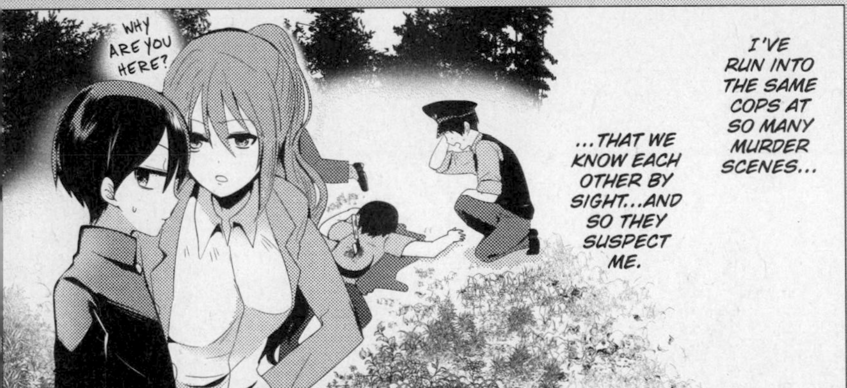
I'VE RUN INTO THE SAME COPS AT SO MANY MURDER SCENES...
...THAT WE KNOW EACH OTHER BY SIGHT...AND SO THEY SUSPECT ME.
WHY ARE YOU HERE?

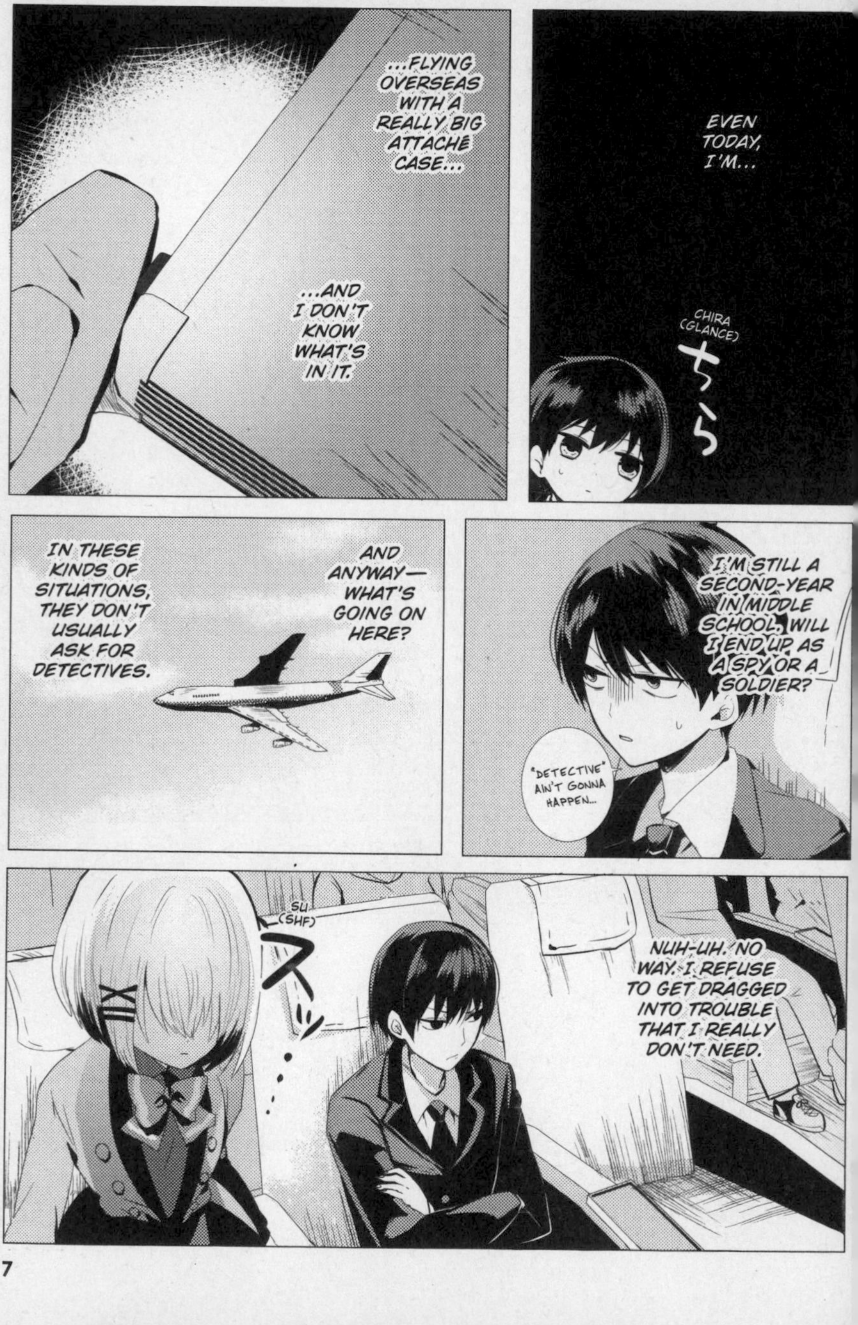
EVEN TODAY, I'M...
CHIRA (GLANCE)
ちら
...FLYING OVERSEAS WITH A REALLY BIG ATTACHE CASE...
...AND I DON'T KNOW WHAT'S IN IT.
I'M STILL A SECOND-YEAR IN MIDDLE SCHOOL. WILL I END UP AS A SPY OR A SOLDIER?
"DETECTIVE" AIN'T GONNA HAPPEN...
AND ANYWAY— WHAT'S GOING ON HERE?
IN THESE KINDS OF SITUATIONS, THEY DON'T USUALLY ASK FOR DETECTIVES.
NUH-UH. NO WAY. I REFUSE TO GET DRAGGED INTO TROUBLE THAT I REALLY DON'T NEED.
SU (SHF)
スッ

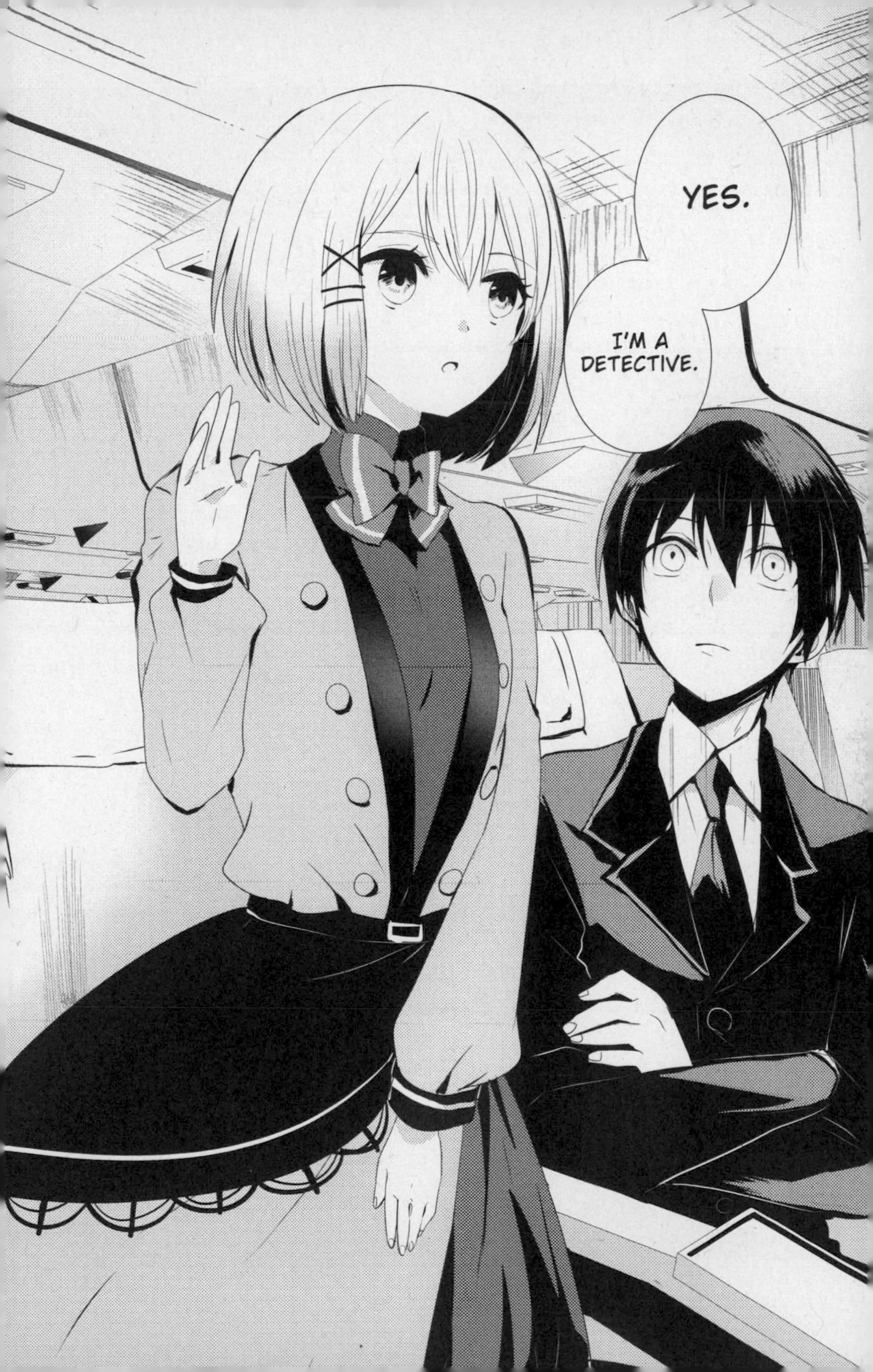
YES.
I'M A DETECTIVE.

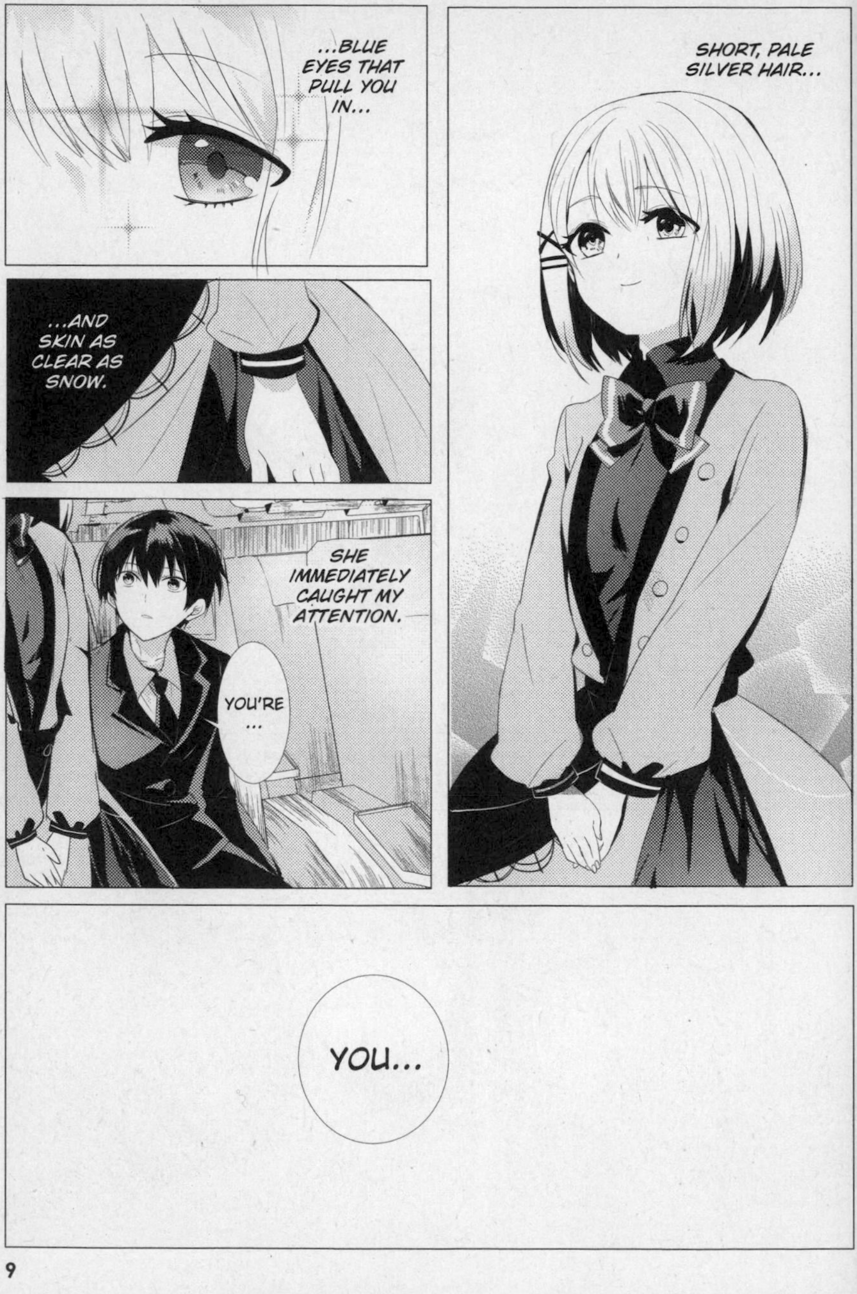
SHORT, PALE SILVER HAIR...
...BLUE EYES THAT PULL YOU IN...
...AND SKIN AS CLEAR AS SNOW.
SHE IMMEDIATELY CAUGHT MY ATTENTION.
YOU'RE ...
YOU...

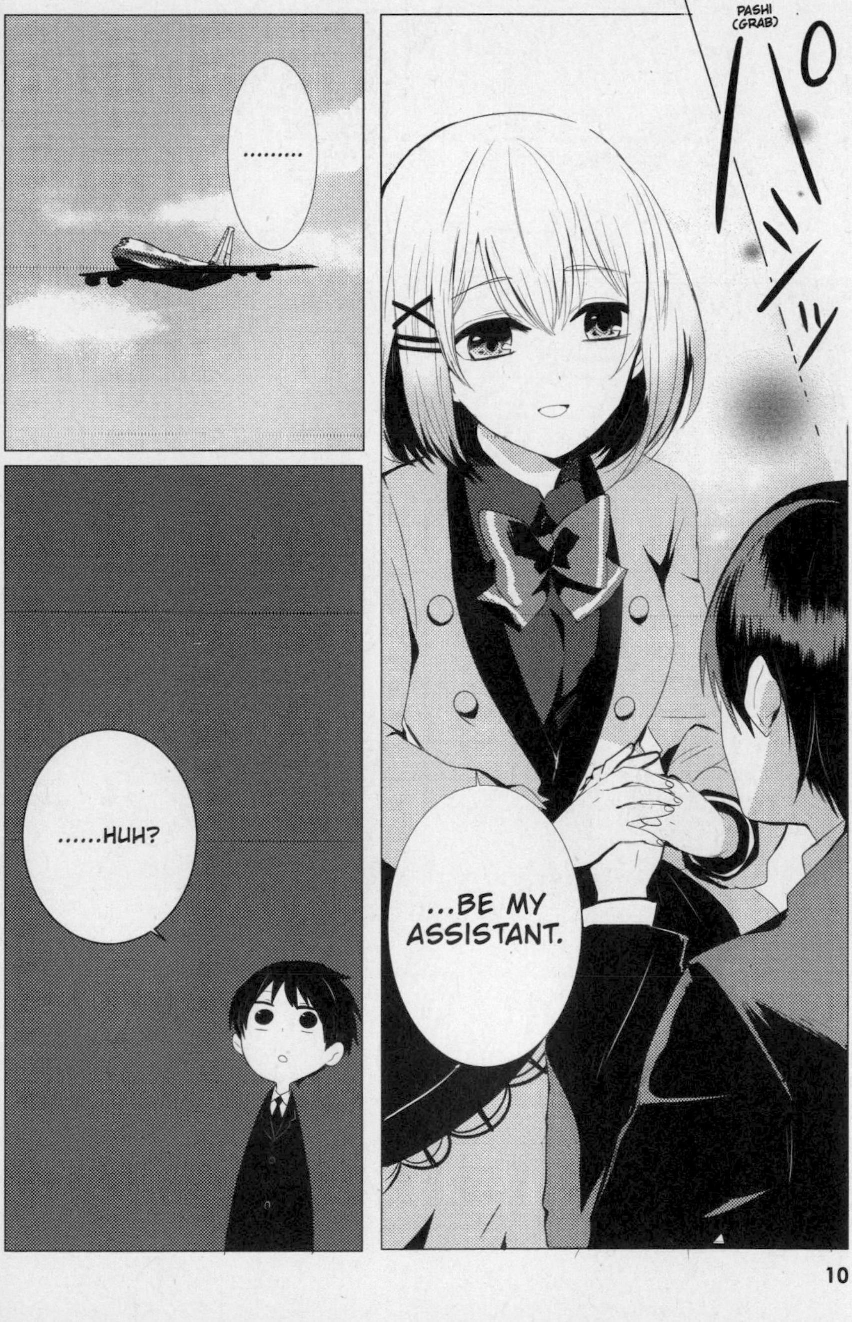
PASHI (GRAB)
...BE MY ASSISTANT.
....
......HUH?

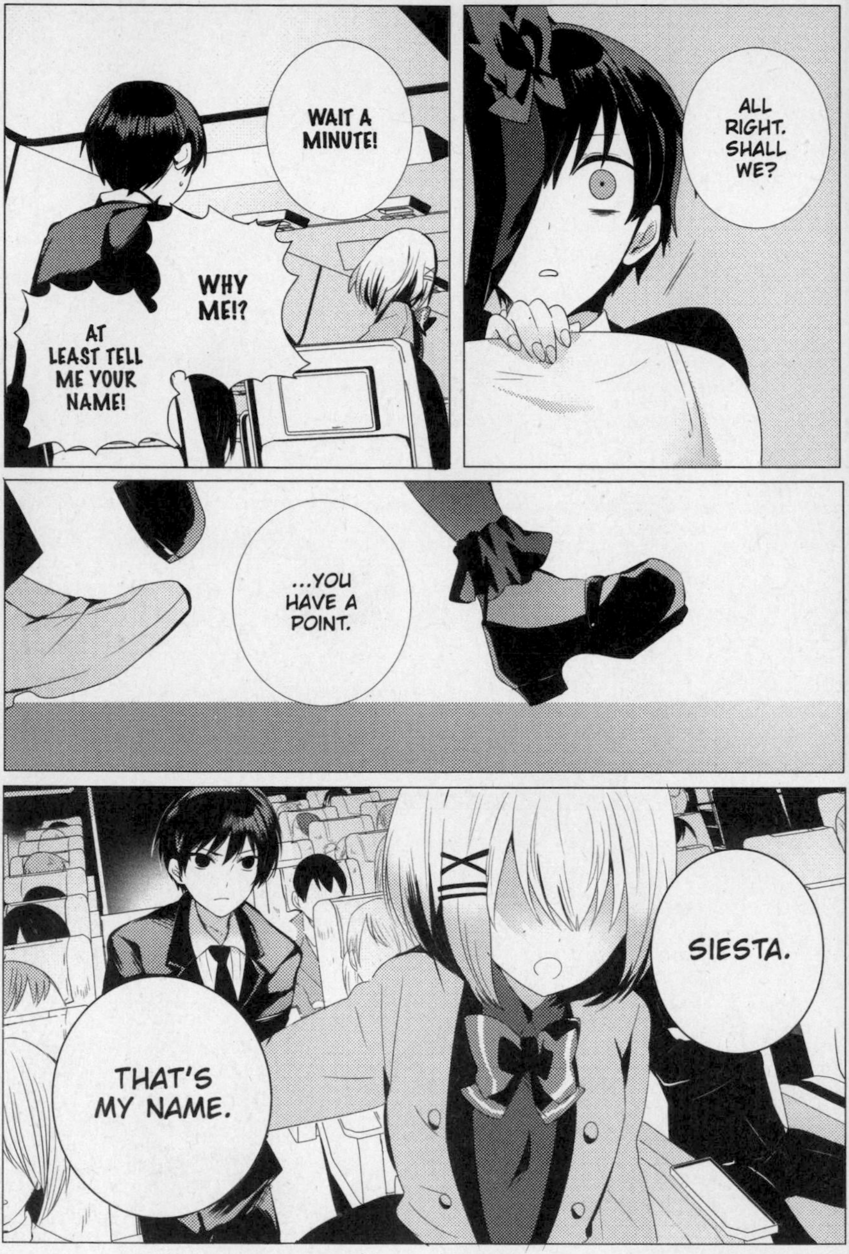
ALL RIGHT. SHALL WE?
WAIT A MINUTE!
WHY ME!?
AT LEAST TELL ME YOUR NAME!
...YOU HAVE A POINT.
SIESTA.
THAT'S MY NAME.

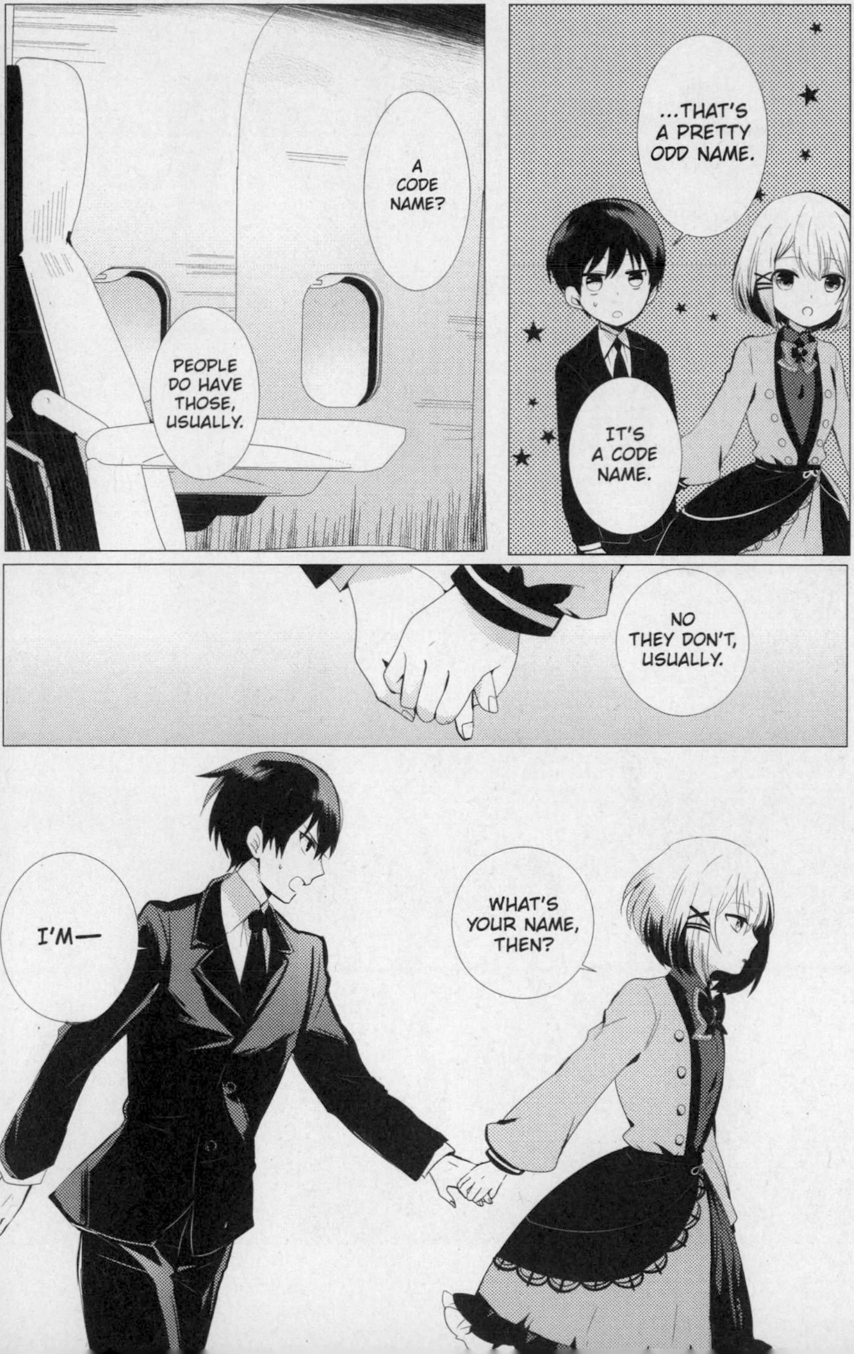
...THAT'S A PRETTY ODD NAME.
IT'S A CODE NAME.
A CODE NAME?
PEOPLE DO HAVE THOSE, USUALLY.
NO THEY DON'T, USUALLY.
WHAT'S YOUR NAME, THEN?
I'M—

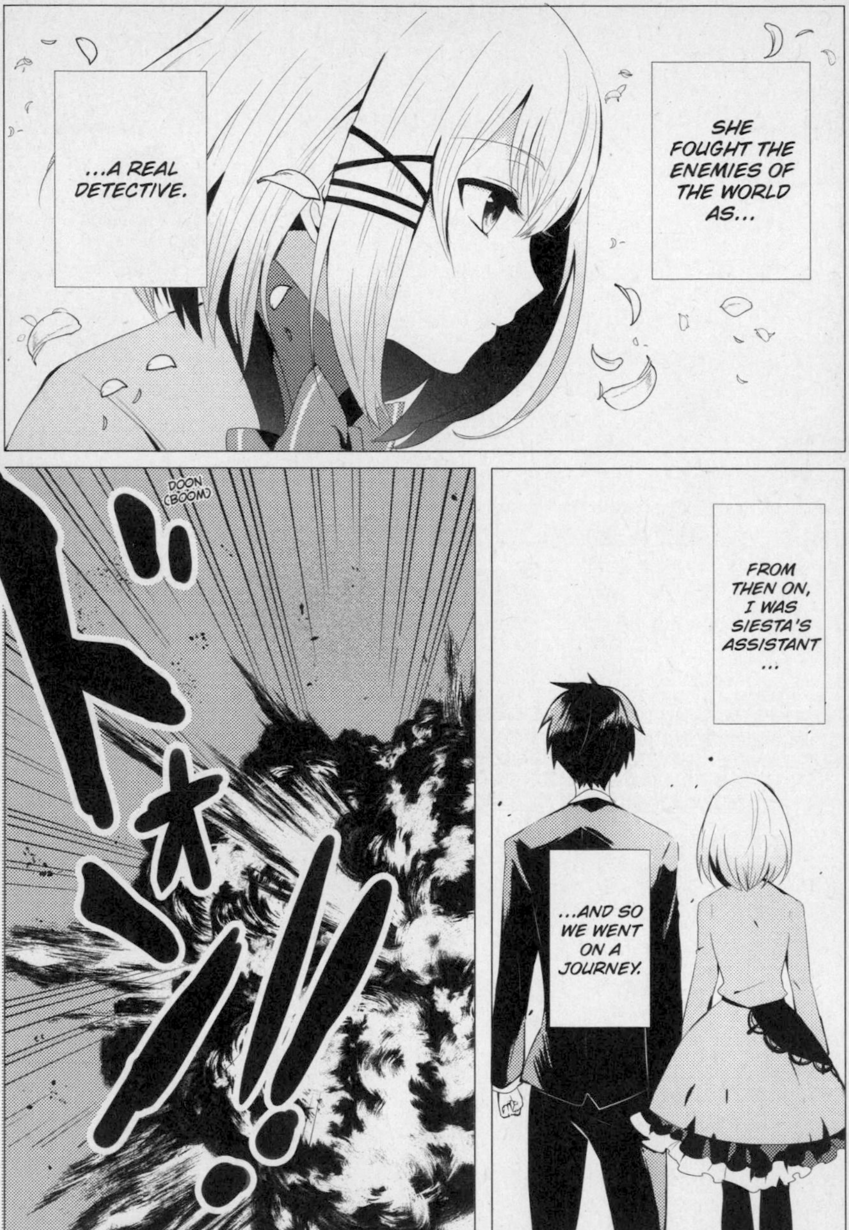
SHE FOUGHT THE ENEMIES OF THE WORLD AS...
...A REAL DETECTIVE.
FROM THEN ON, I WAS SIESTA'S ASSISTANT ...
...AND SO WE WENT ON A JOURNEY.
DOON (BOOM)

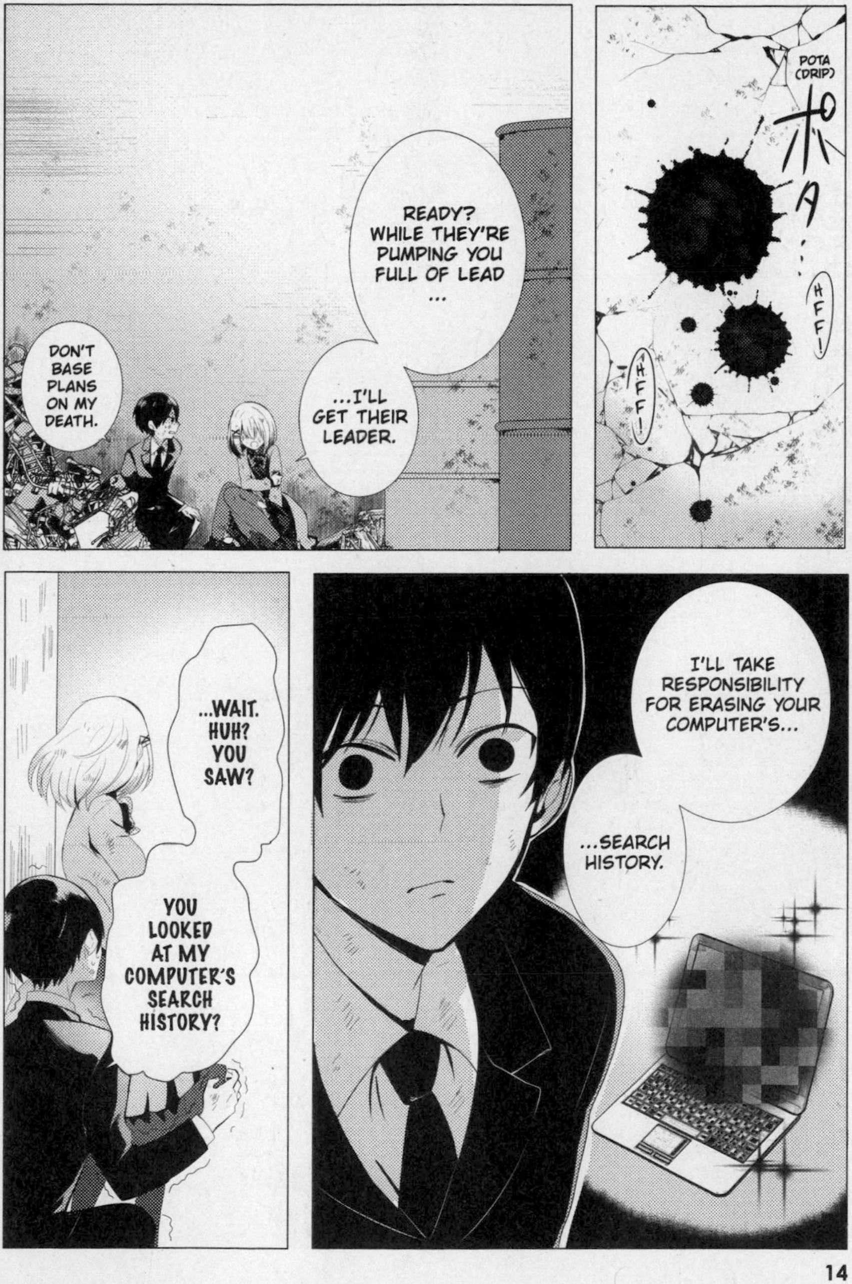
POTA (DRIP)
ポタ…
HFF!
HFF!
READY? WHILE THEY'RE PUMPING YOU FULL OF LEAD ...
...I'LL GET THEIR LEADER.
DON'T BASE PLANS ON MY DEATH.
I'LL TAKE RESPONSIBILITY FOR ERASING YOUR COMPUTER'S...
...SEARCH HISTORY.
...WAIT. HUH? YOU SAW?
YOU LOOKED AT MY COMPUTER'S SEARCH HISTORY?

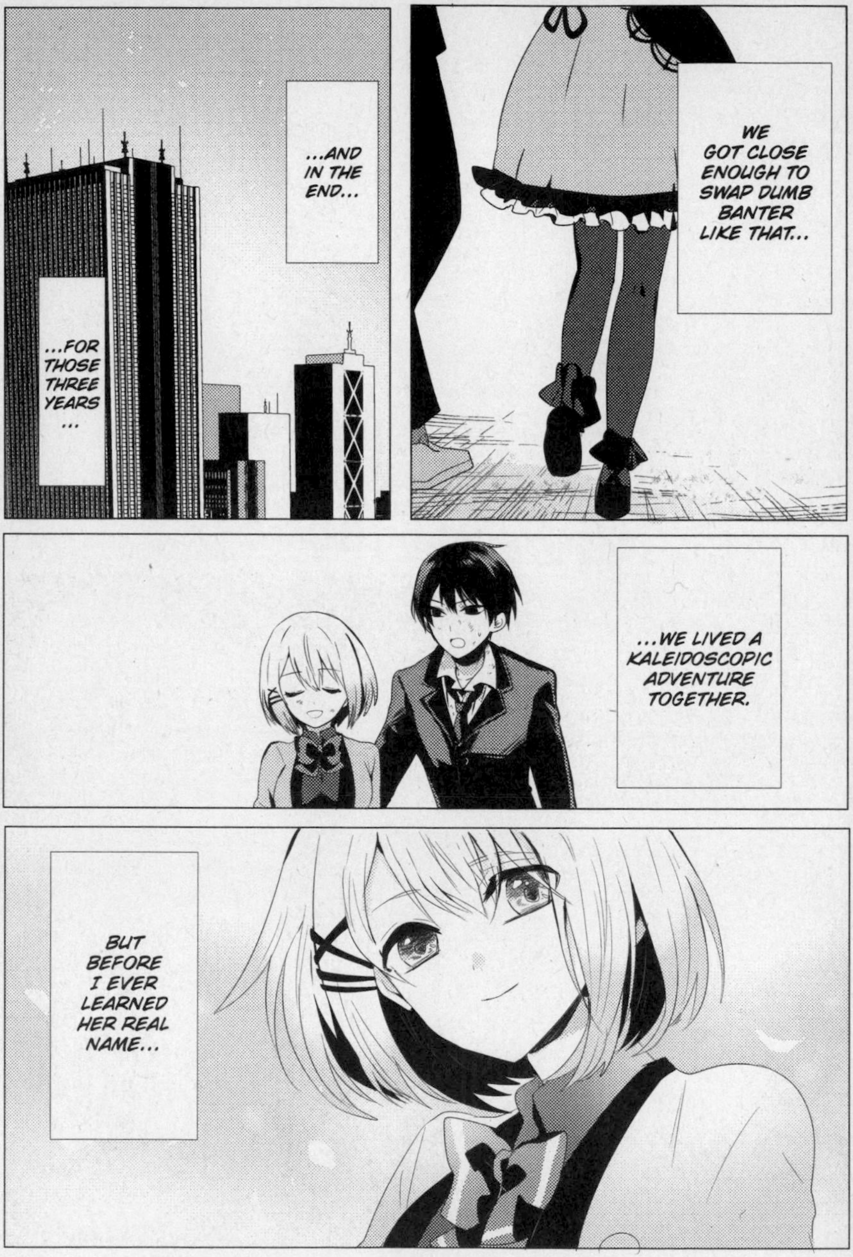
WE GOT CLOSE ENOUGH TO SWAP DUMB BANTER LIKE THAT...
...AND IN THE END...
...FOR THOSE THREE YEARS...
...WE LIVED A KALEIDOSCOPIC ADVENTURE TOGETHER.
BUT BEFORE I EVER LEARNED HER REAL NAME...

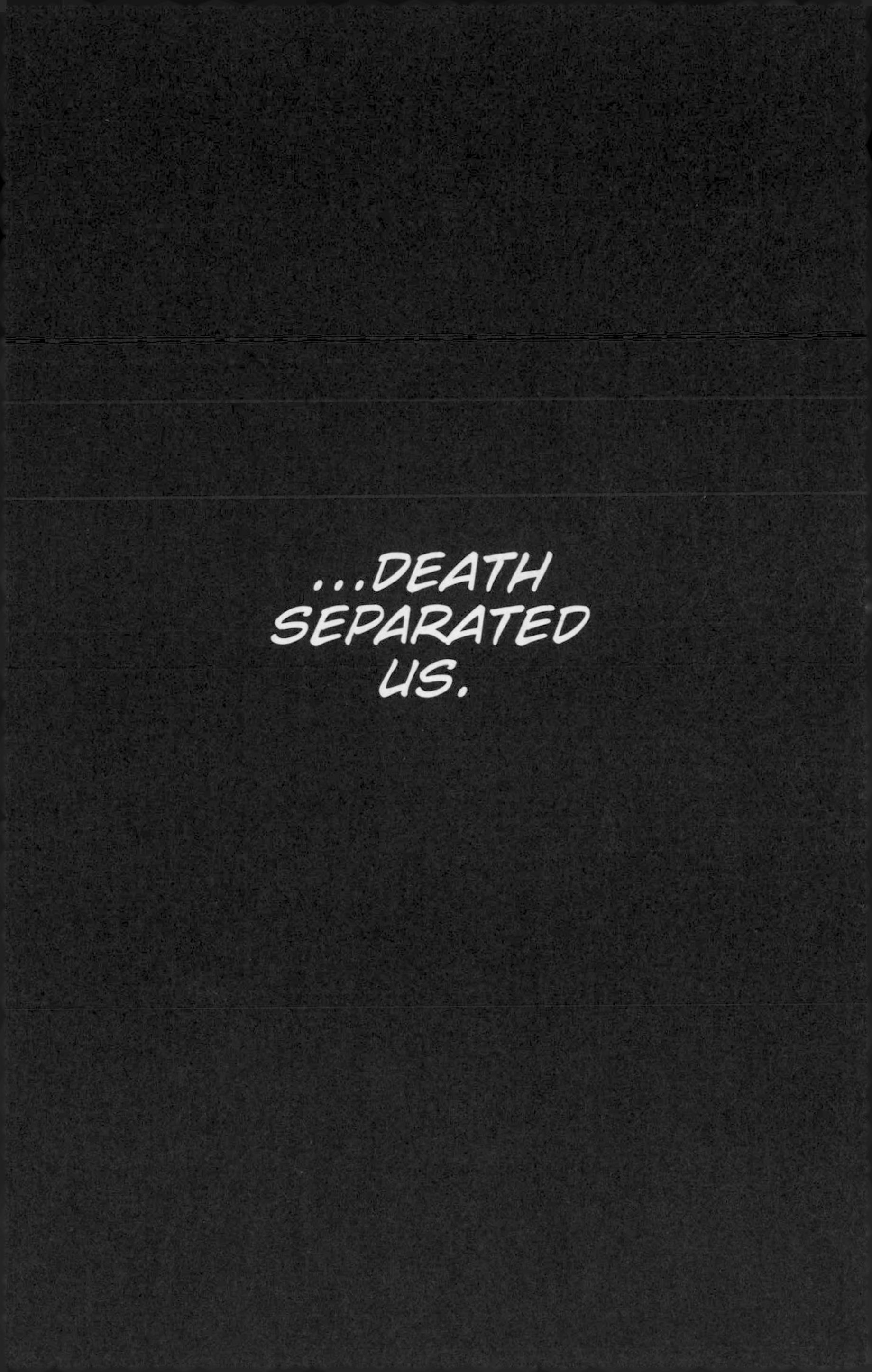
...DEATH SEPARATED US.

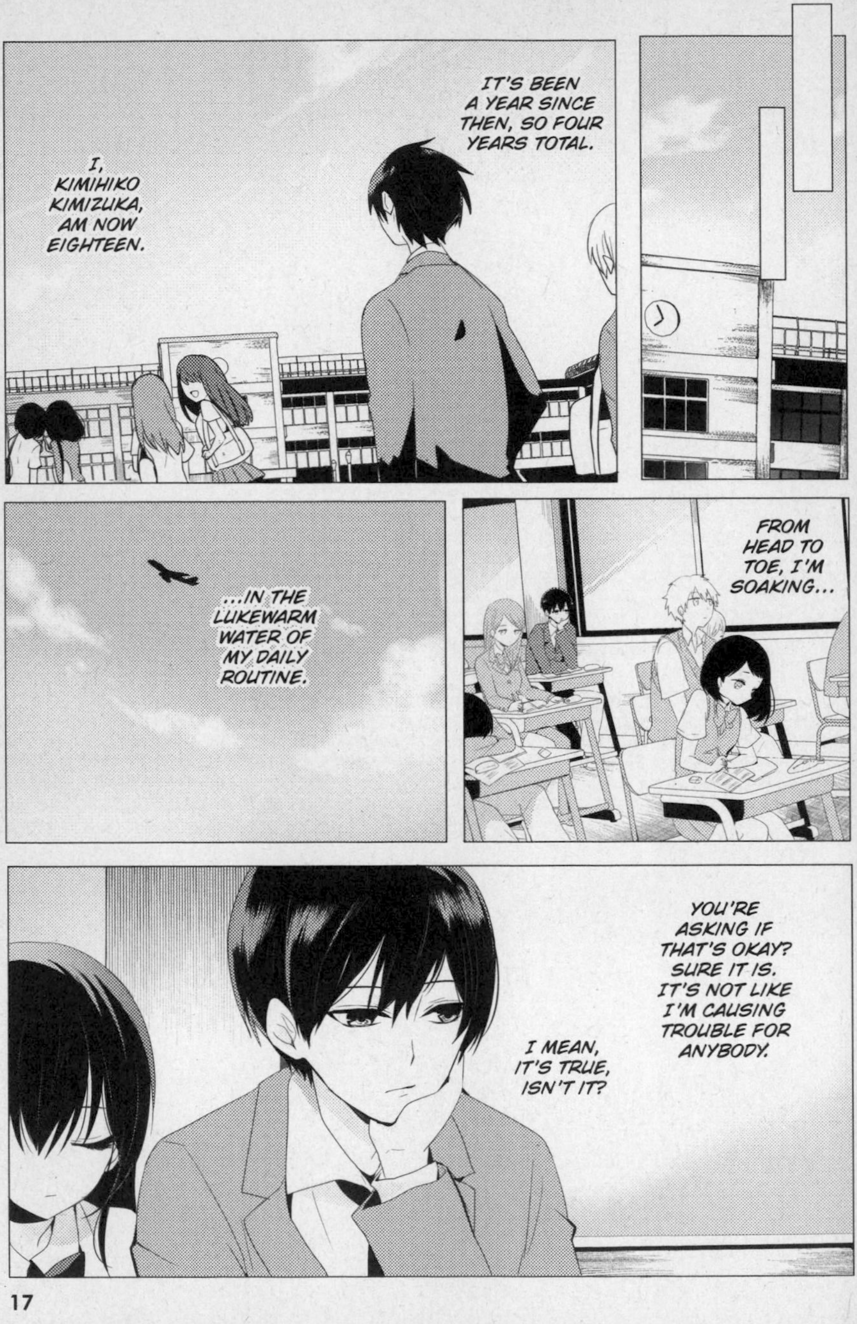
IT'S BEEN A YEAR SINCE THEN, SO FOUR YEARS TOTAL.
I, KIMIHIKO KIMIZUKA, AM NOW EIGHTEEN.
FROM HEAD TO TOE, I'M SOAKING...
...IN THE LUKEWARM WATER OF MY DAILY ROUTINE.
YOU'RE ASKING IF THAT'S OKAY? SURE IT IS. IT'S NOT LIKE I'M CAUSING TROUBLE FOR ANYBODY.
I MEAN, IT'S TRUE, ISN'T IT?

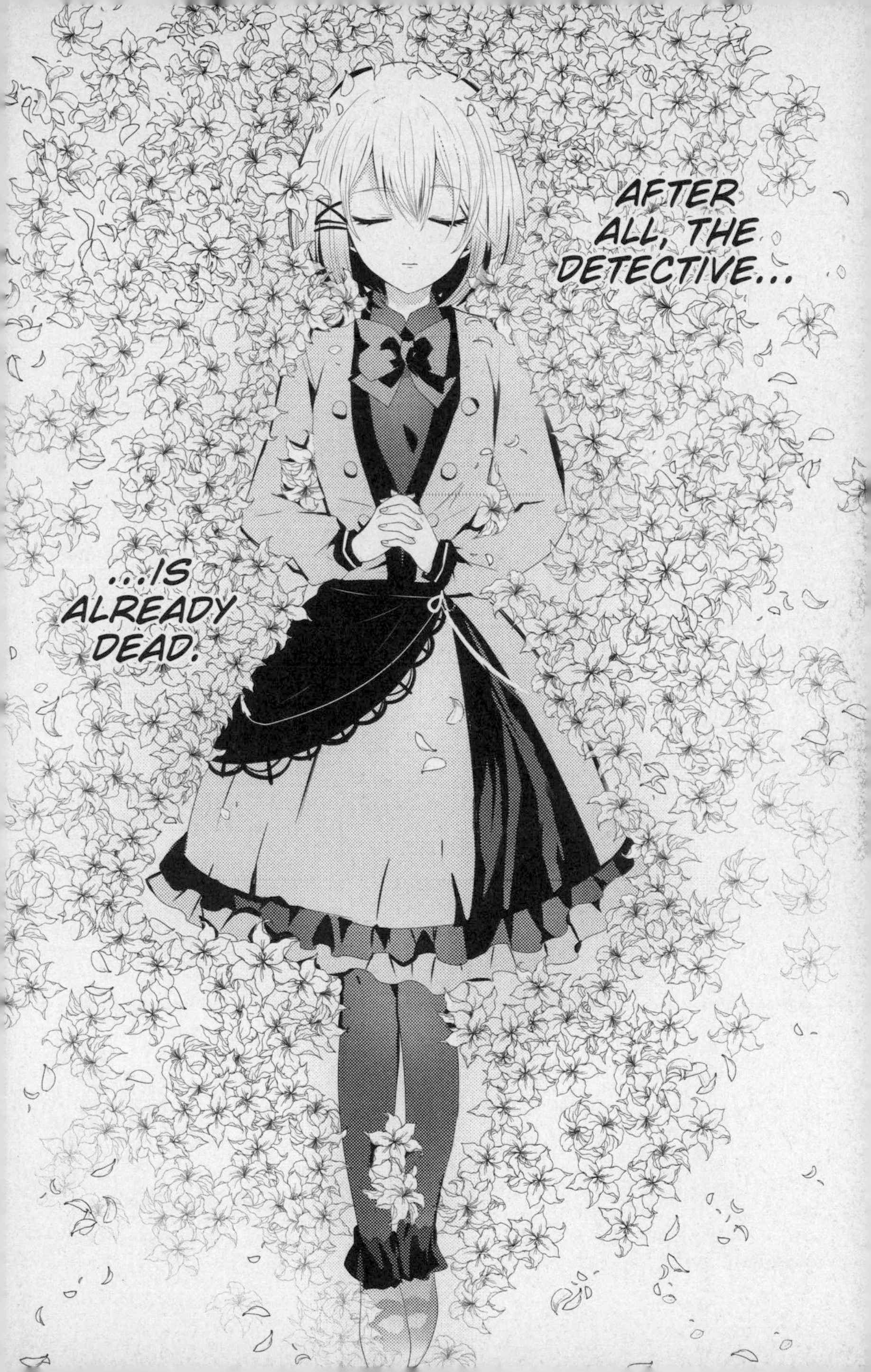
AFTER ALL, THE DETECTIVE...
...IS ALREADY DEAD.

The Detective Is Already Dead

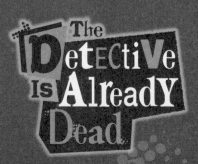

The Detective Is Already Dead

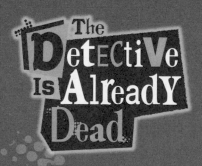

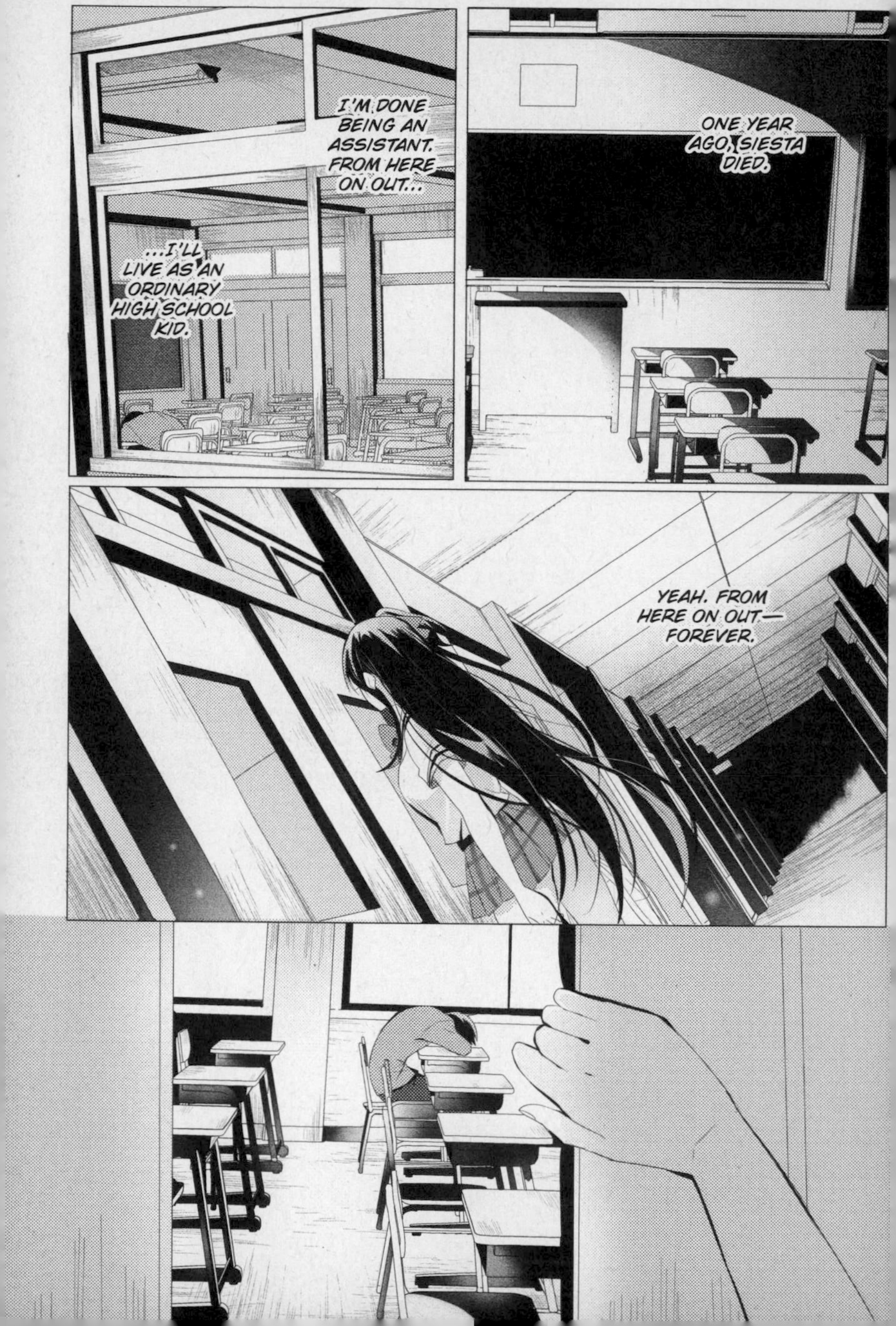
ONE YEAR AGO, SIESTA DIED.
I'M DONE BEING AN ASSISTANT. FROM HERE ON OUT...
...I'LL LIVE AS AN ORDINARY HIGH SCHOOL KID.
YEAH. FROM HERE ON OUT— FOREVER.

Episode. 1 The Detective Is Out

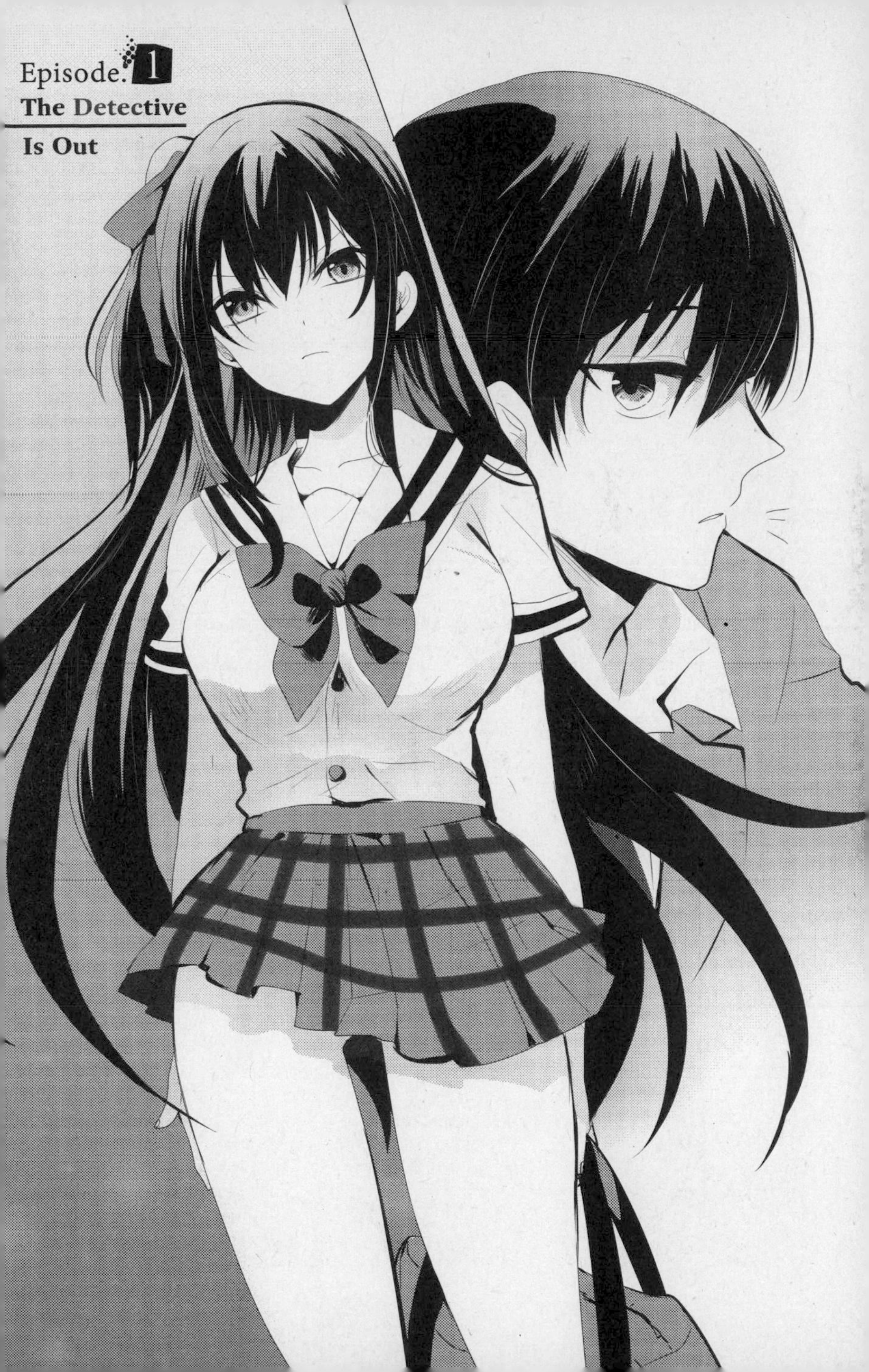

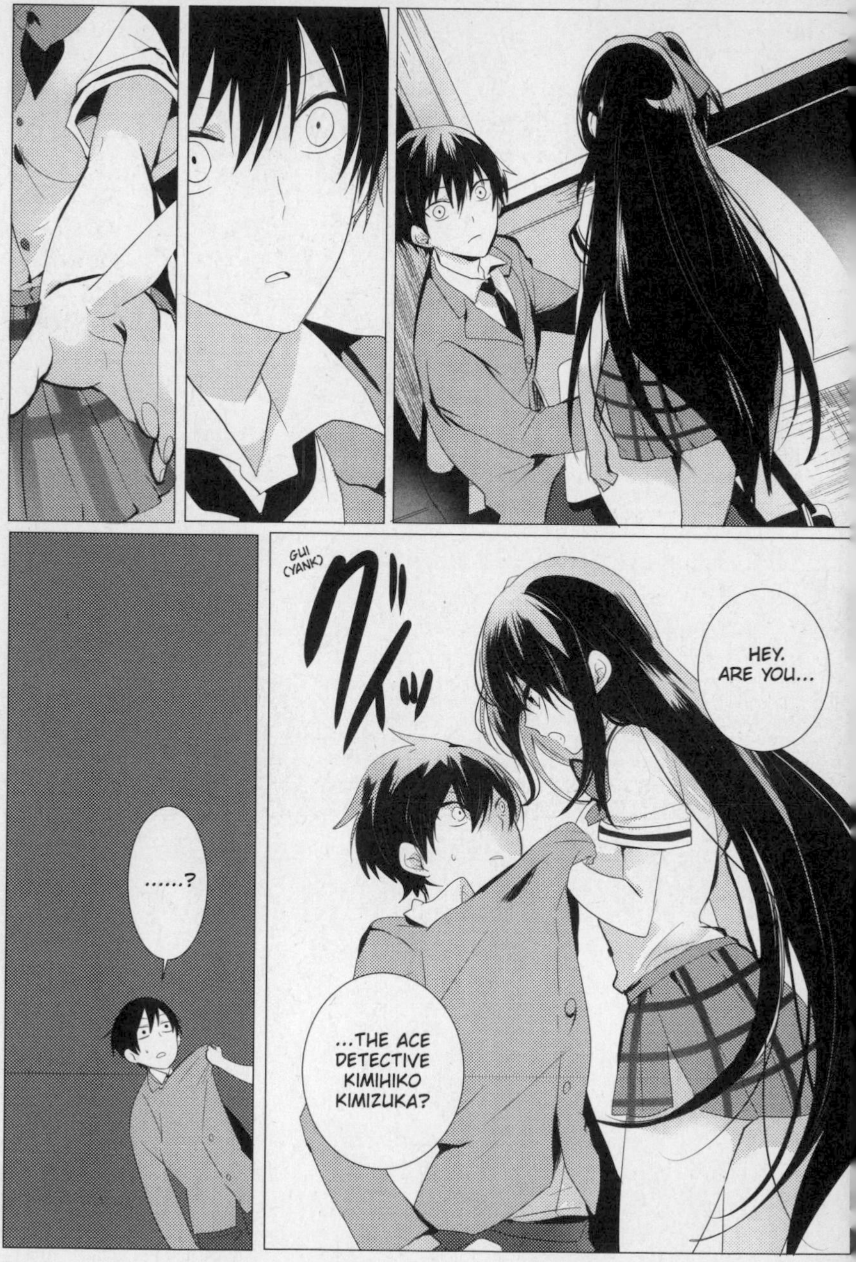
GUI (YANK)
HEY. ARE YOU...
...THE ACE DETECTIVE KIMIHIKO KIMIZUKA?
......?

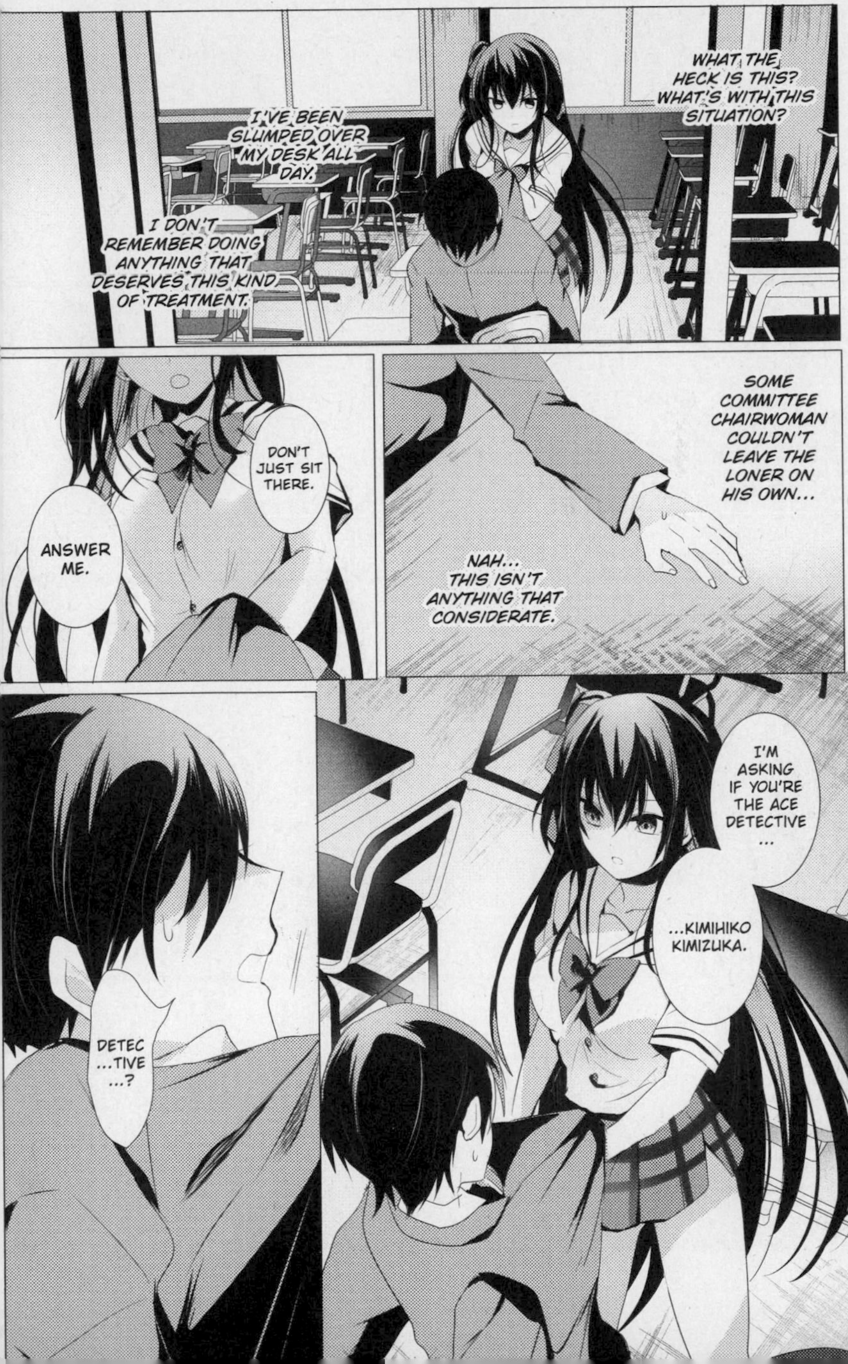
WHAT THE HECK IS THIS? WHAT'S WITH THIS SITUATION?
I'VE BEEN SLUMPED OVER MY DESK ALL DAY.
I DON'T REMEMBER DOING ANYTHING THAT DESERVES THIS KIND OF TREATMENT.
SOME COMMITTEE CHAIRWOMAN COULDN'T LEAVE THE LONER ON HIS OWN...
NAH... THIS ISN'T ANYTHING THAT CONSIDERATE.
DON'T JUST SIT THERE.
ANSWER ME.
I'M ASKING IF YOU'RE THE ACE DETECTIVE ...
...KIMIHIKO KIMIZUKA.
DETEC ...TIVE ...?

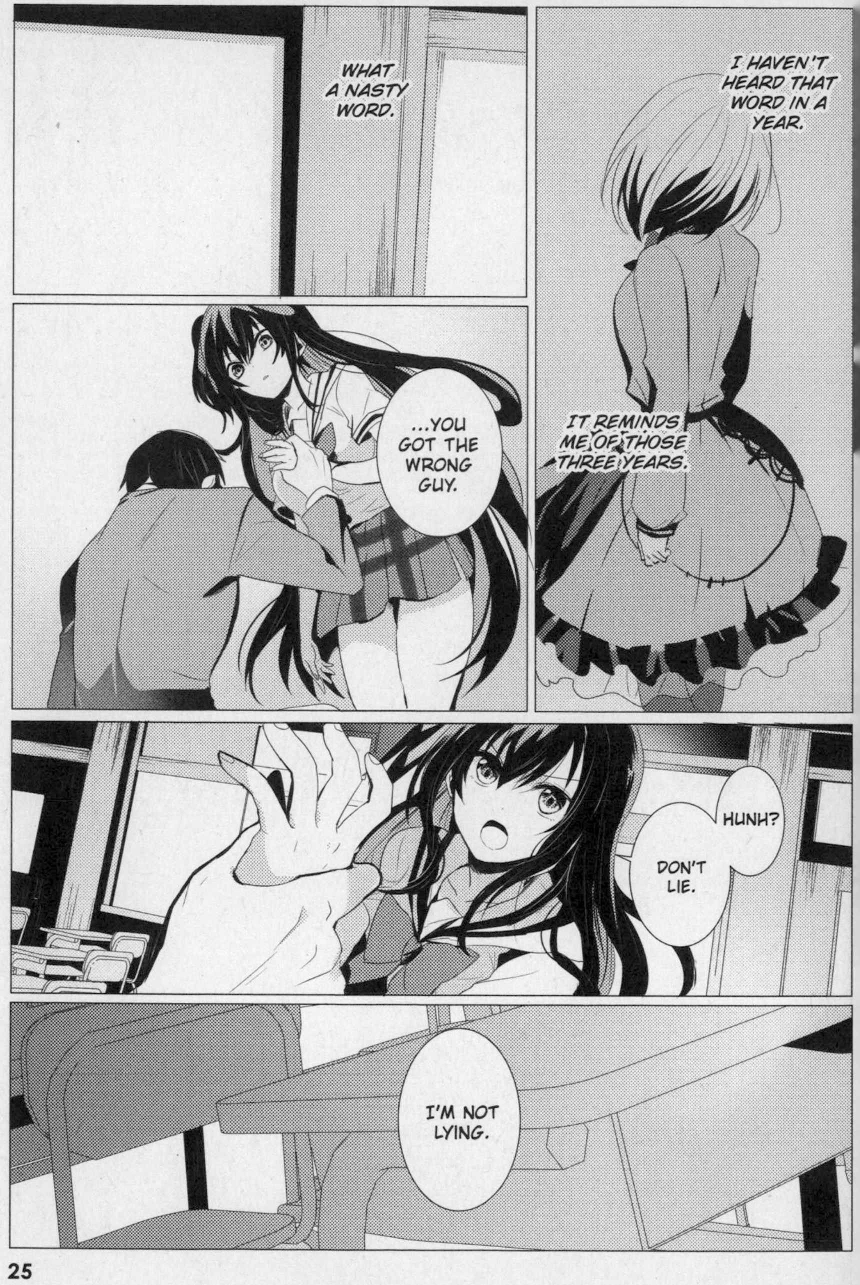
I HAVEN'T HEARD THAT WORD IN A YEAR.
IT REMINDS ME OF THOSE THREE YEARS.
WHAT A NASTY WORD.
...YOU GOT THE WRONG GUY.
HUNH?
DON'T LIE.
I'M NOT LYING.

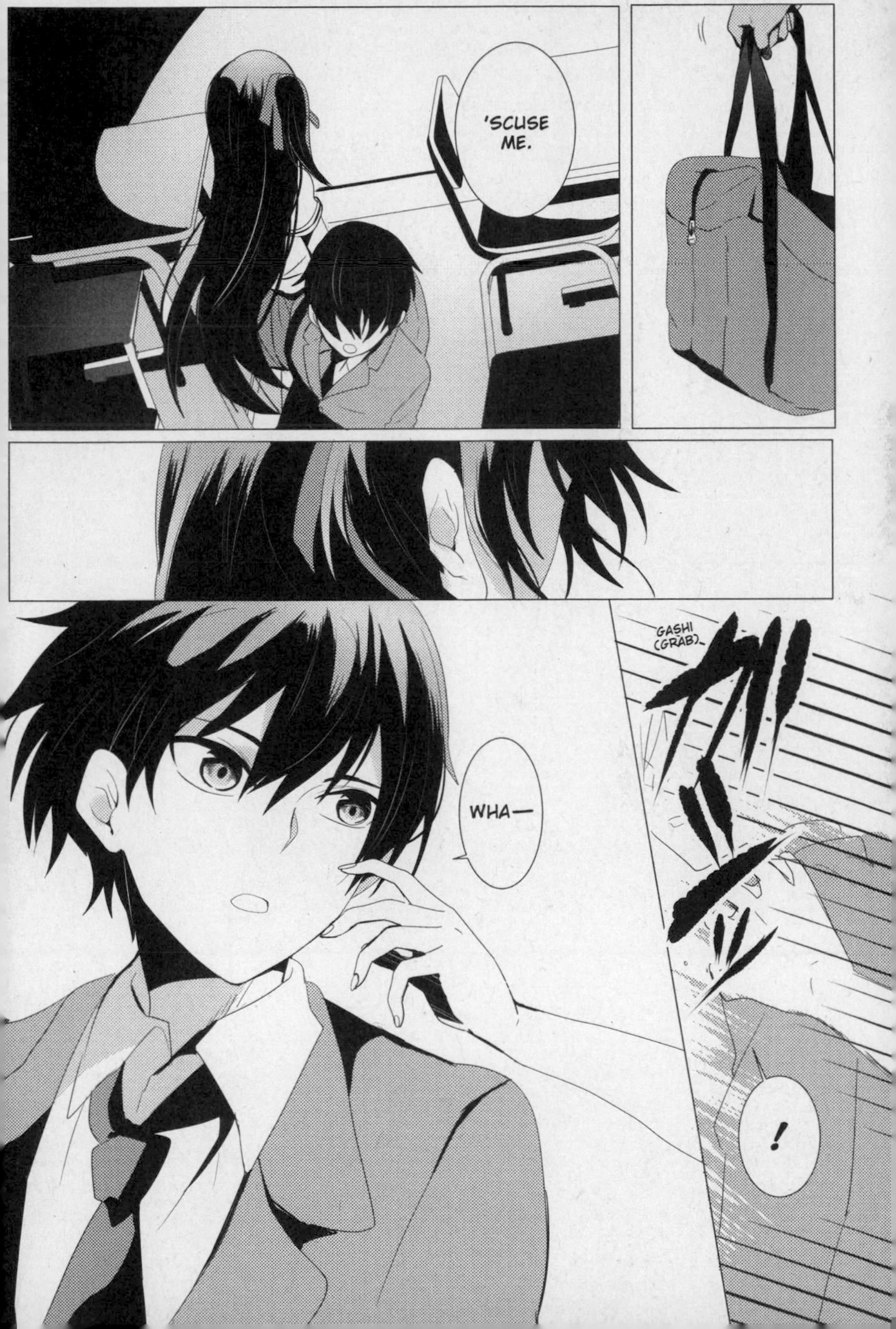
'SCUSE ME.
GASHI (GRAB)
!
WHA—

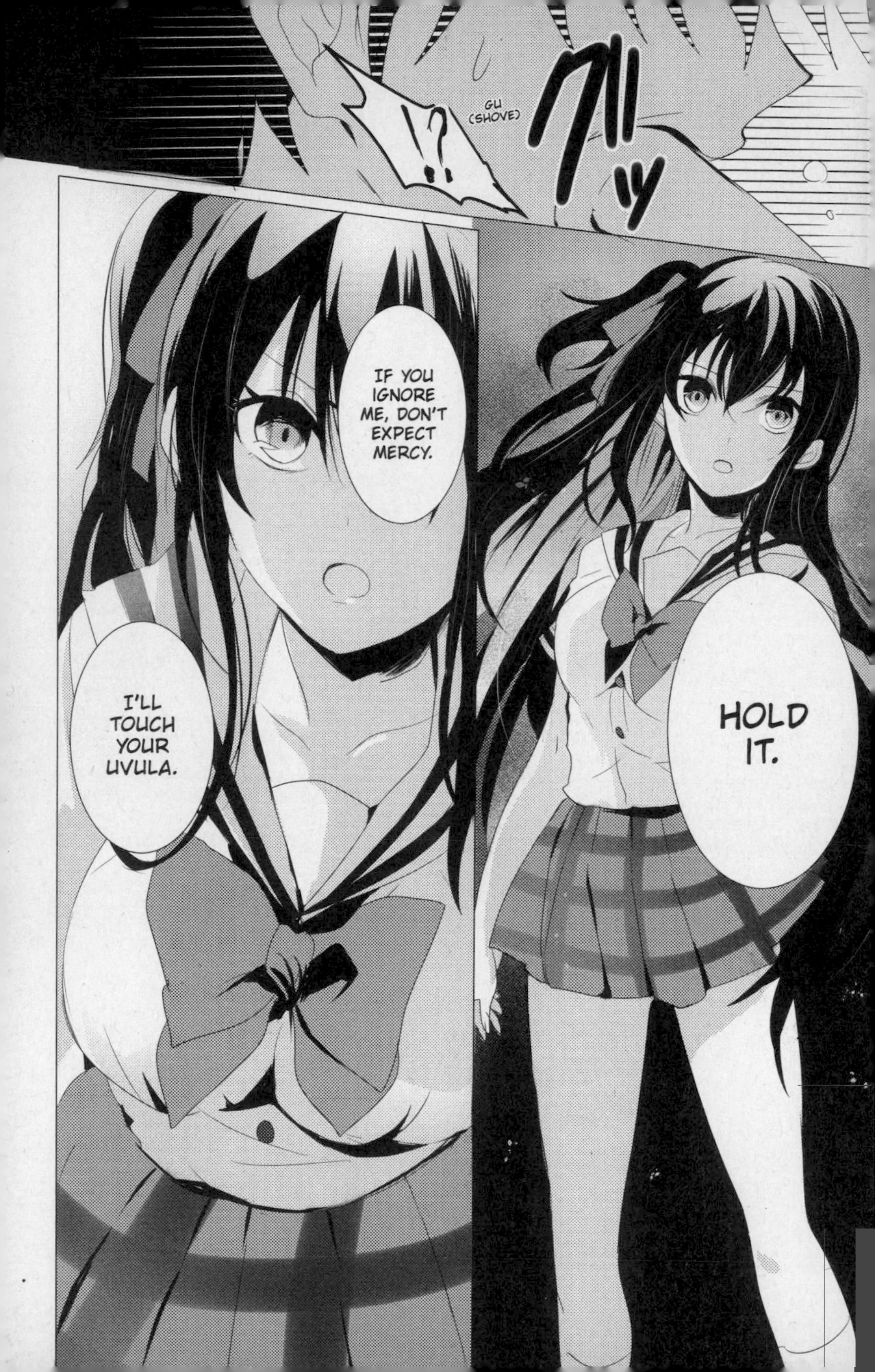
グッ
GU (SHOVE)
!?
HOLD IT.
IF YOU IGNORE ME, DON'T EXPECT MERCY.
I'LL TOUCH YOUR UVULA.

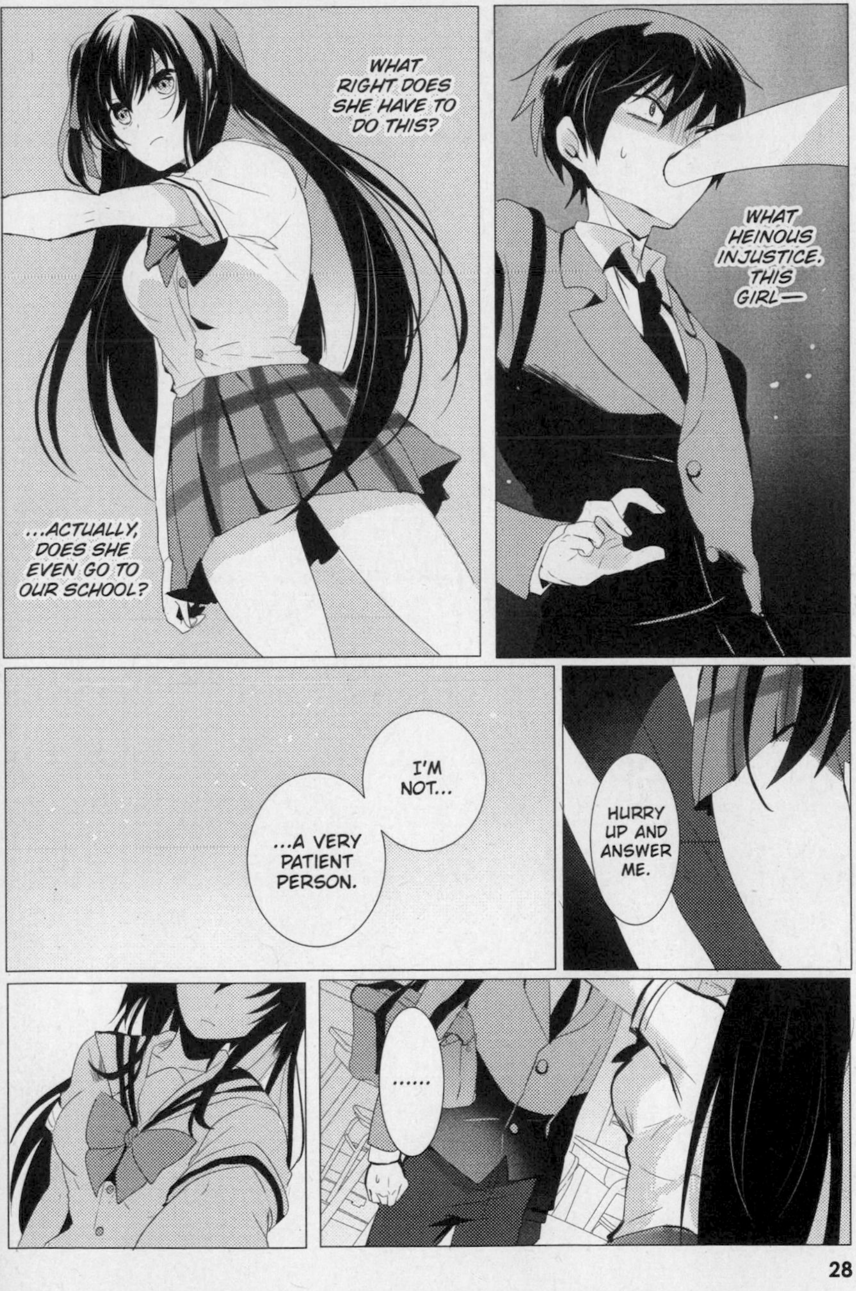
WHAT HEINOUS INJUSTICE. THIS GIRL—
WHAT RIGHT DOES SHE HAVE TO DO THIS?
...ACTUALLY, DOES SHE EVEN GO TO OUR SCHOOL?
HURRY UP AND ANSWER ME.
I'M NOT...
...A VERY PATIENT PERSON.
......

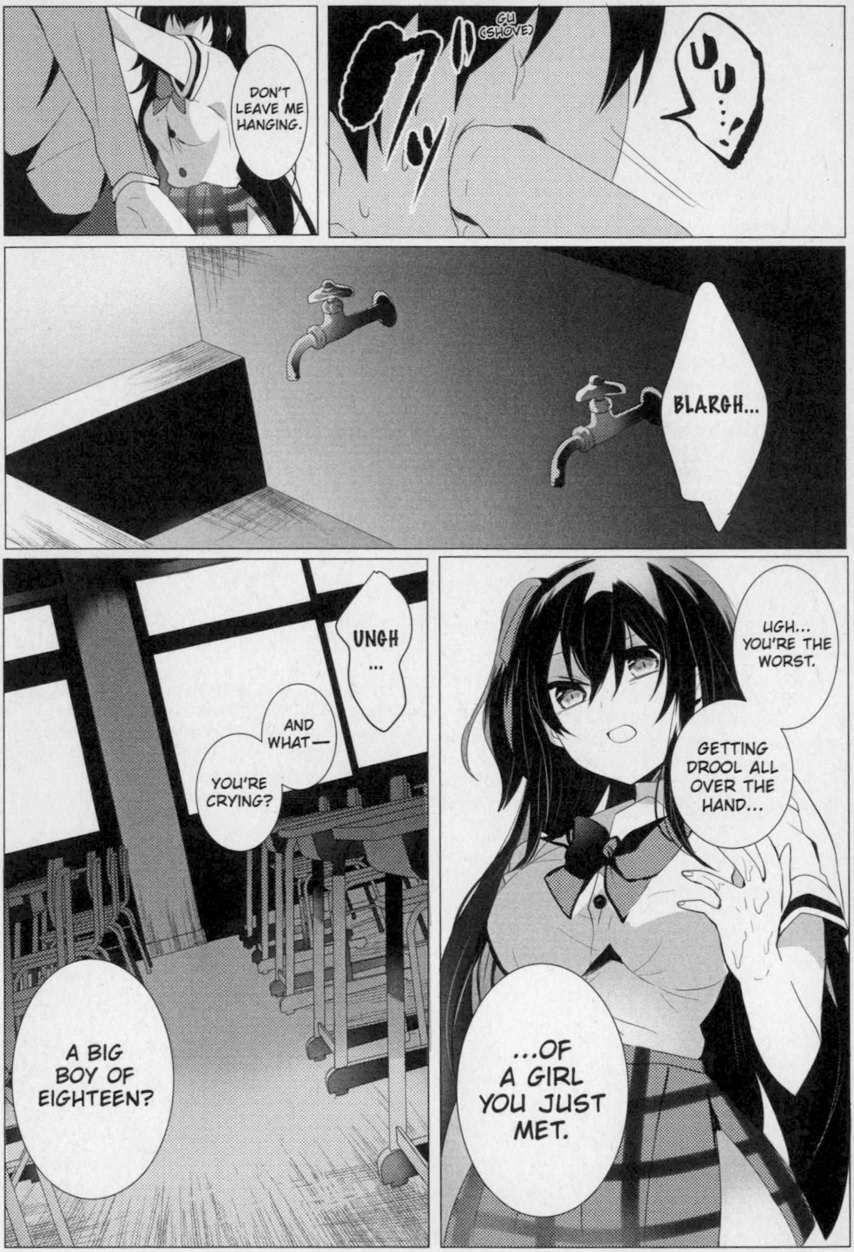
UU...!
GU (SHOVE)
DON'T LEAVE ME HANGING.
BLARGH...
UGH... YOU'RE THE WORST.
GETTING DROOL ALL OVER THE HAND...
...OF A GIRL YOU JUST MET.
UNGH ...
AND WHAT—
YOU'RE CRYING?
A BIG BOY OF EIGHTEEN?

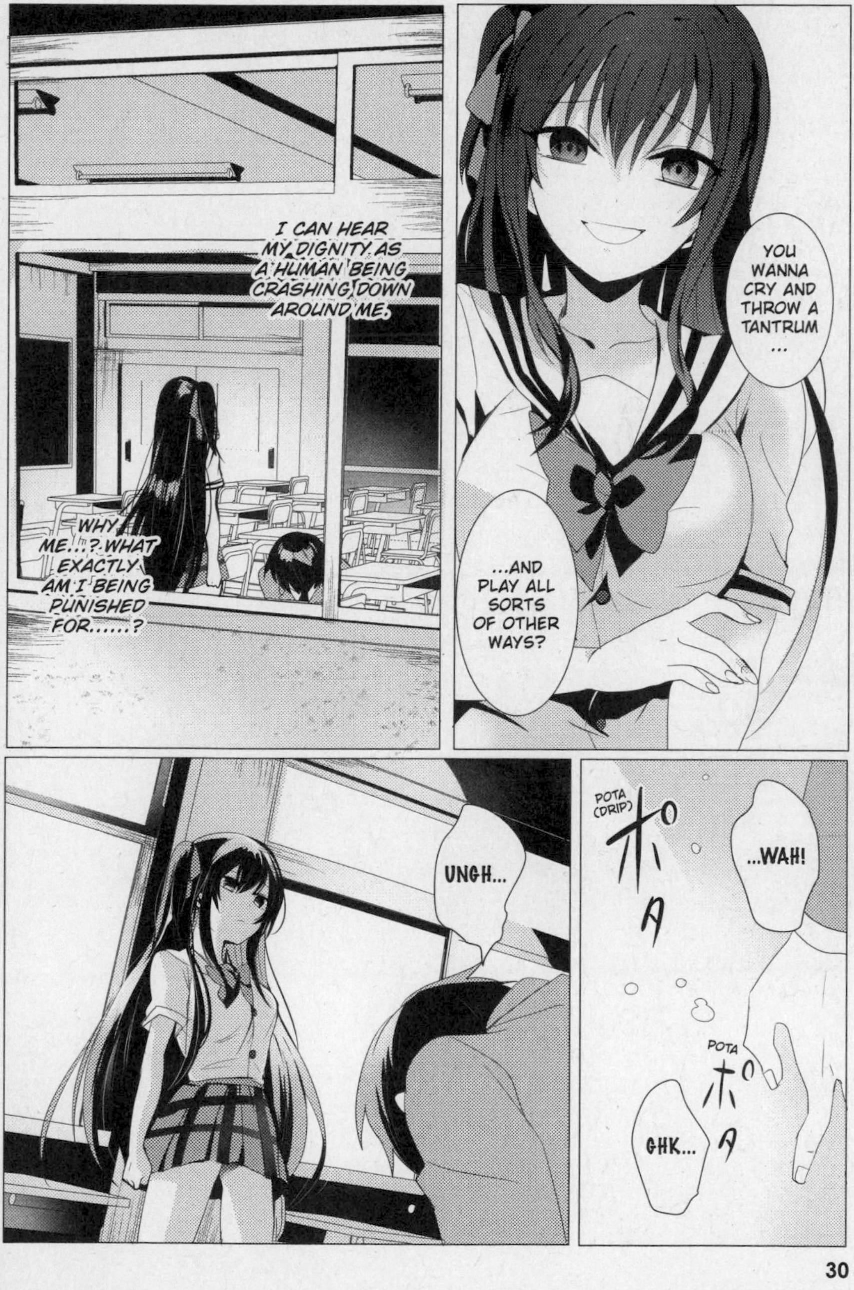
YOU WANNA CRY AND THROW A TANTRUM ...
...AND PLAY ALL SORTS OF OTHER WAYS?
I CAN HEAR MY DIGNITY AS A HUMAN BEING CRASHING DOWN AROUND ME.
WHY ME...? WHAT EXACTLY AM I BEING PUNISHED FOR......?
POTA (DRIP)
ポタ
...WAH!
POTA
ポタ
GHK...
UNGH...

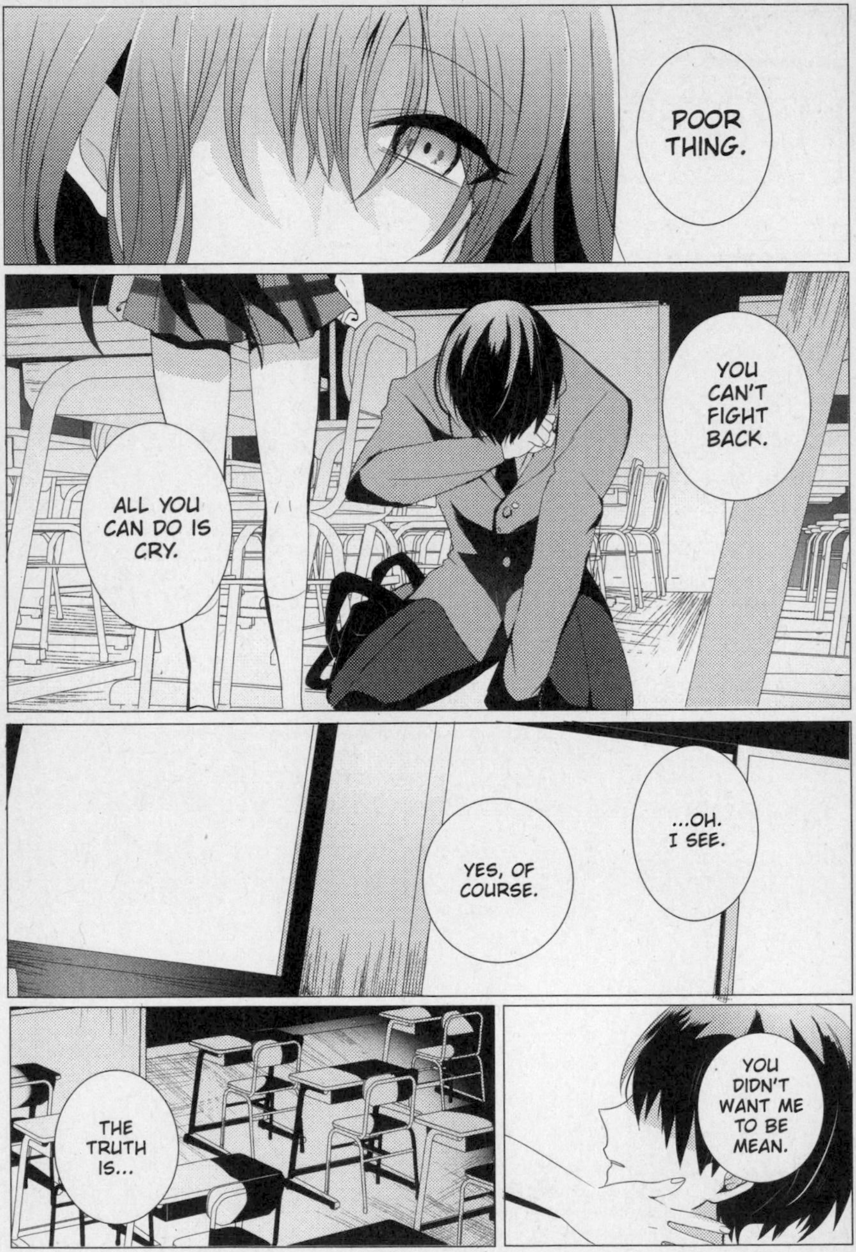
POOR THING.
YOU CAN'T FIGHT BACK.
ALL YOU CAN DO IS CRY.
...OH. I SEE.
YES, OF COURSE.
YOU DIDN'T WANT ME TO BE MEAN.
THE TRUTH IS...

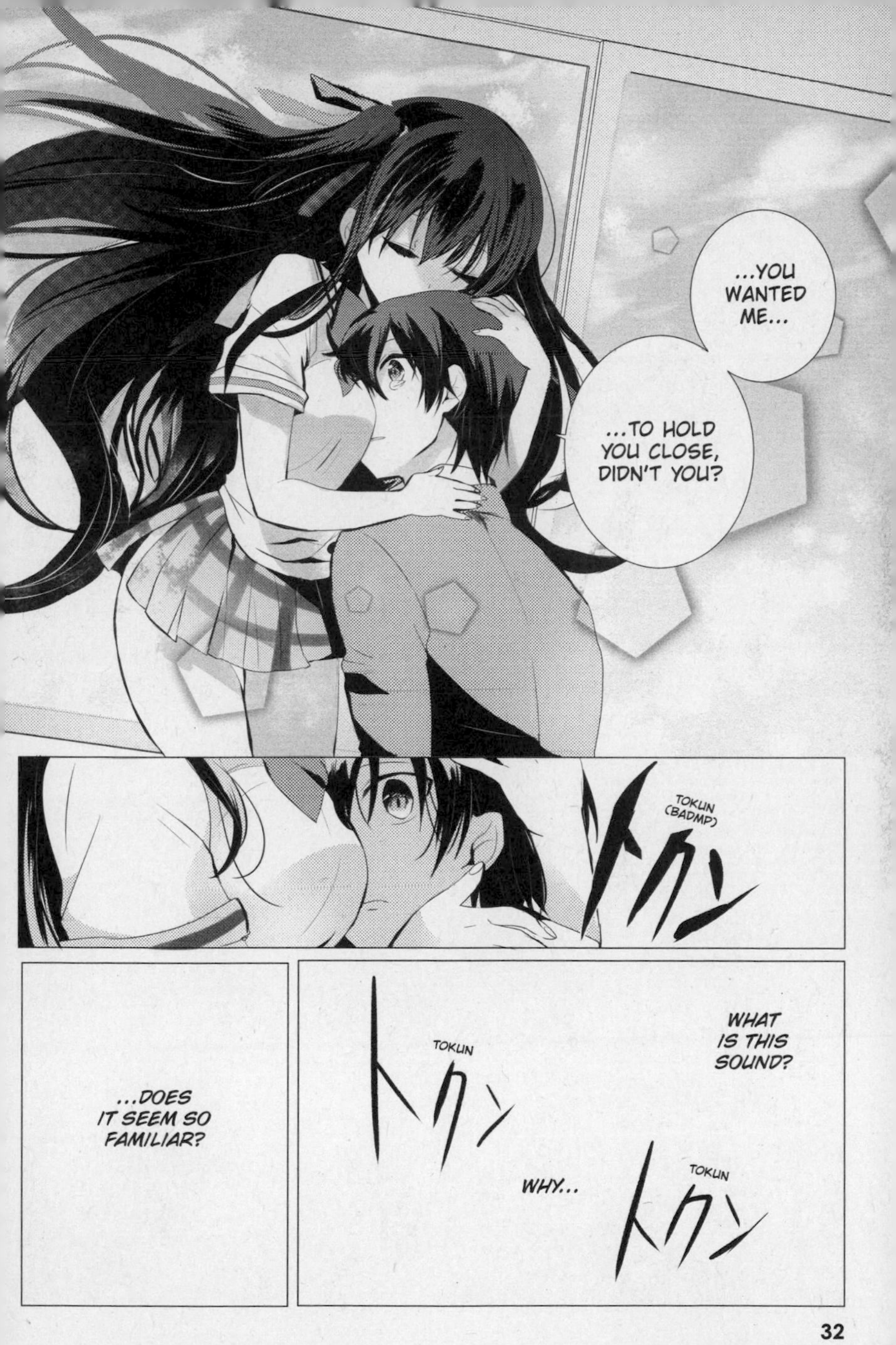
...YOU WANTED ME...
...TO HOLD YOU CLOSE, DIDN'T YOU?
TOKUN (BADMP)
WHAT IS THIS SOUND?
TOKUN
TOKUN
WHY...
...DOES IT SEEM SO FAMILIAR?

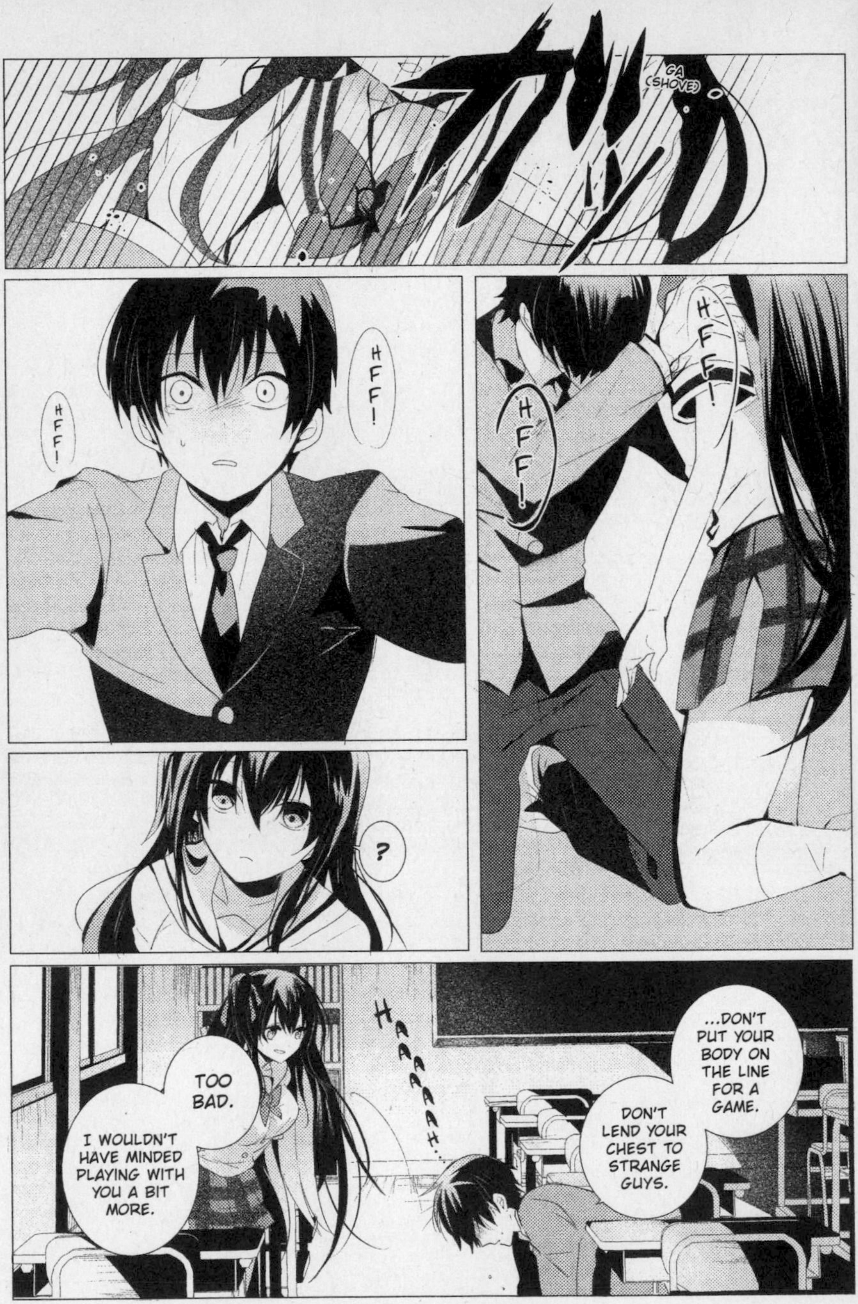
GA (SHOVE)
HFF!
HFF!
HFF!
HFF!
?
...DON'T PUT YOUR BODY ON THE LINE FOR A GAME.
DON'T LEND YOUR CHEST TO STRANGE GUYS.
HAAAAAAH...
TOO BAD.
I WOULDN'T HAVE MINDED PLAYING WITH YOU A BIT MORE.

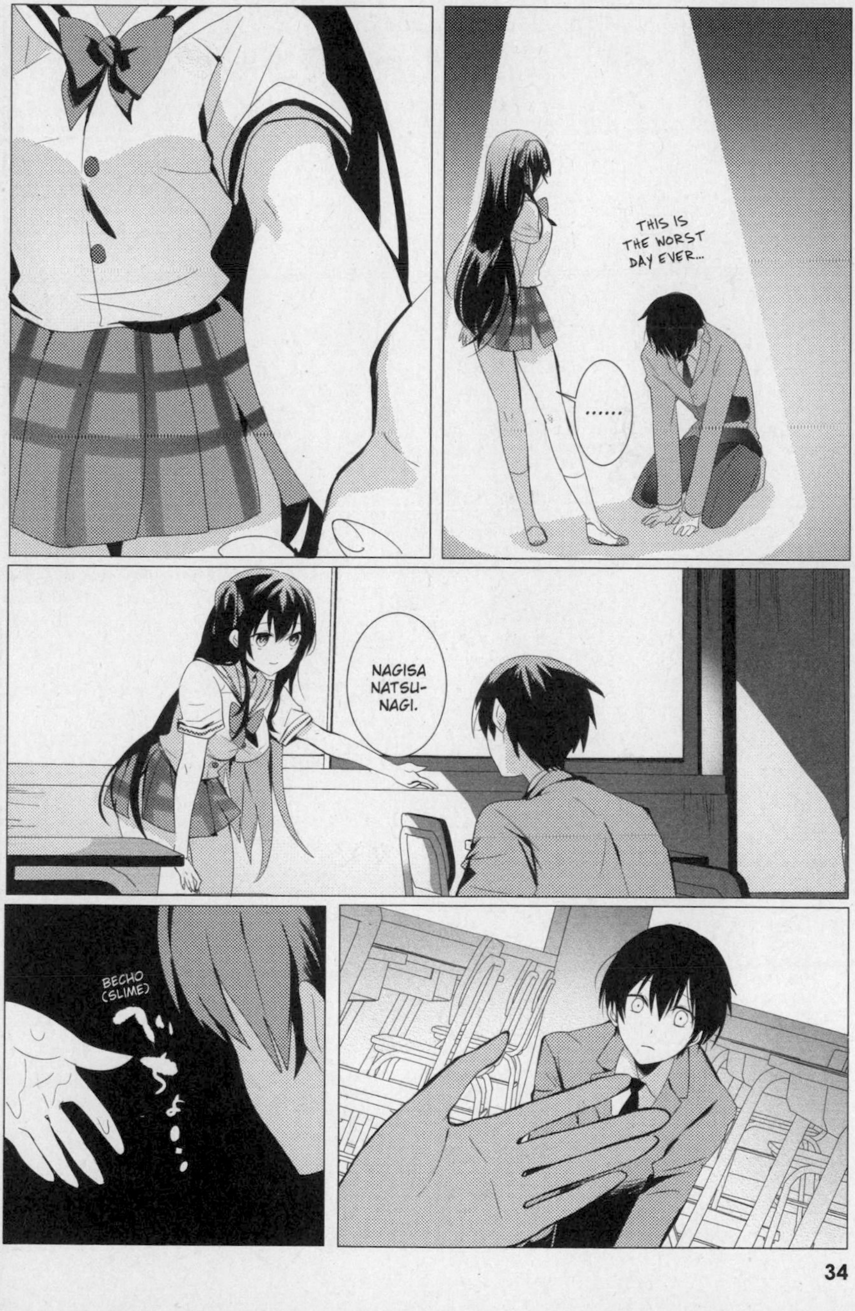
THIS IS THE WORST DAY EVER...
......
NAGISA NATSU-NAGI.
BECHO (SLIME)

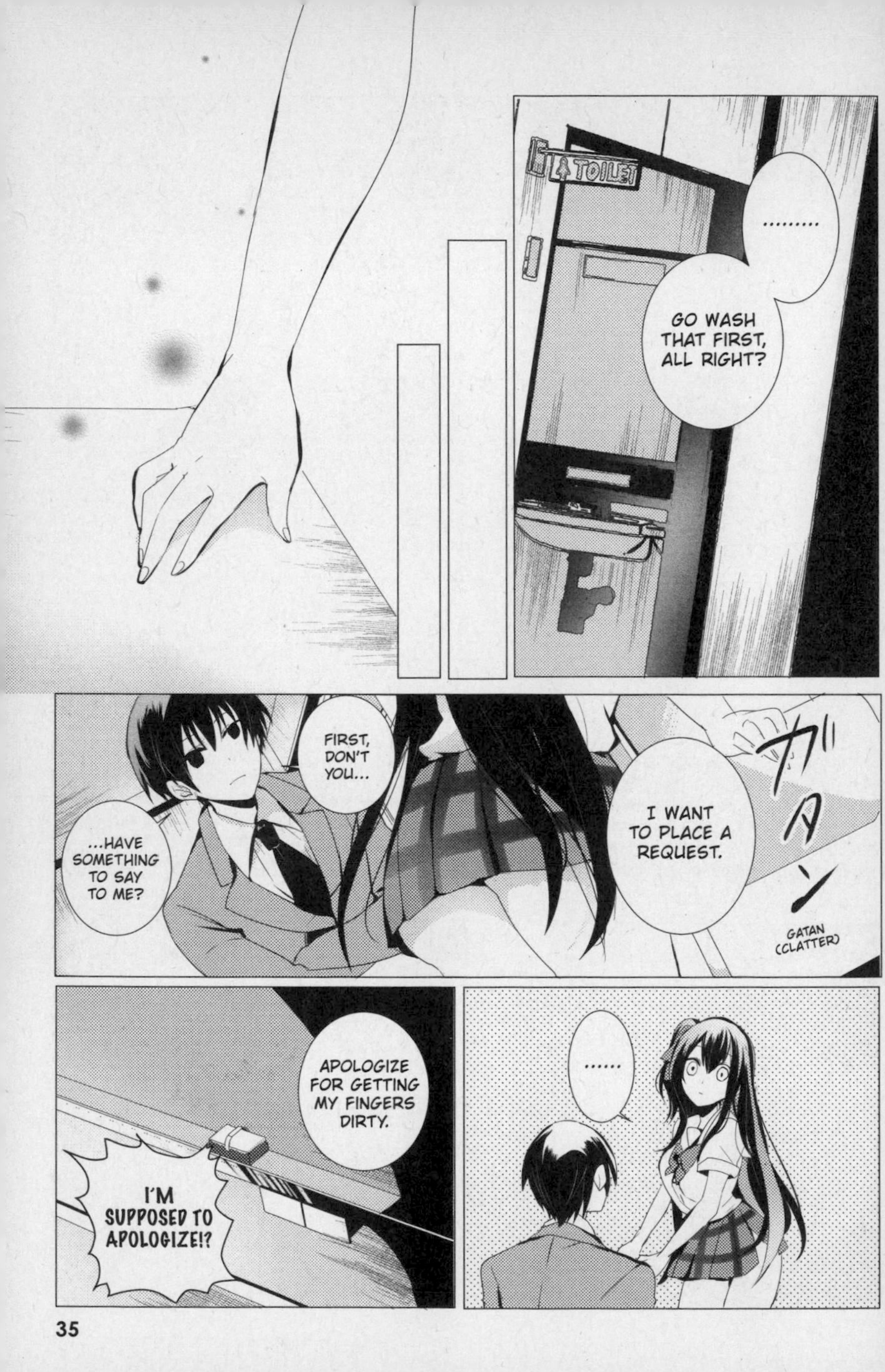
....
GO WASH THAT FIRST, ALL RIGHT?
ガタン
GATAN (CLATTER)
I WANT TO PLACE A REQUEST.
FIRST, DON'T YOU...
...HAVE SOMETHING TO SAY TO ME?
......
APOLOGIZE FOR GETTING MY FINGERS DIRTY.
I'M SUPPOSED TO APOLOGIZE!?

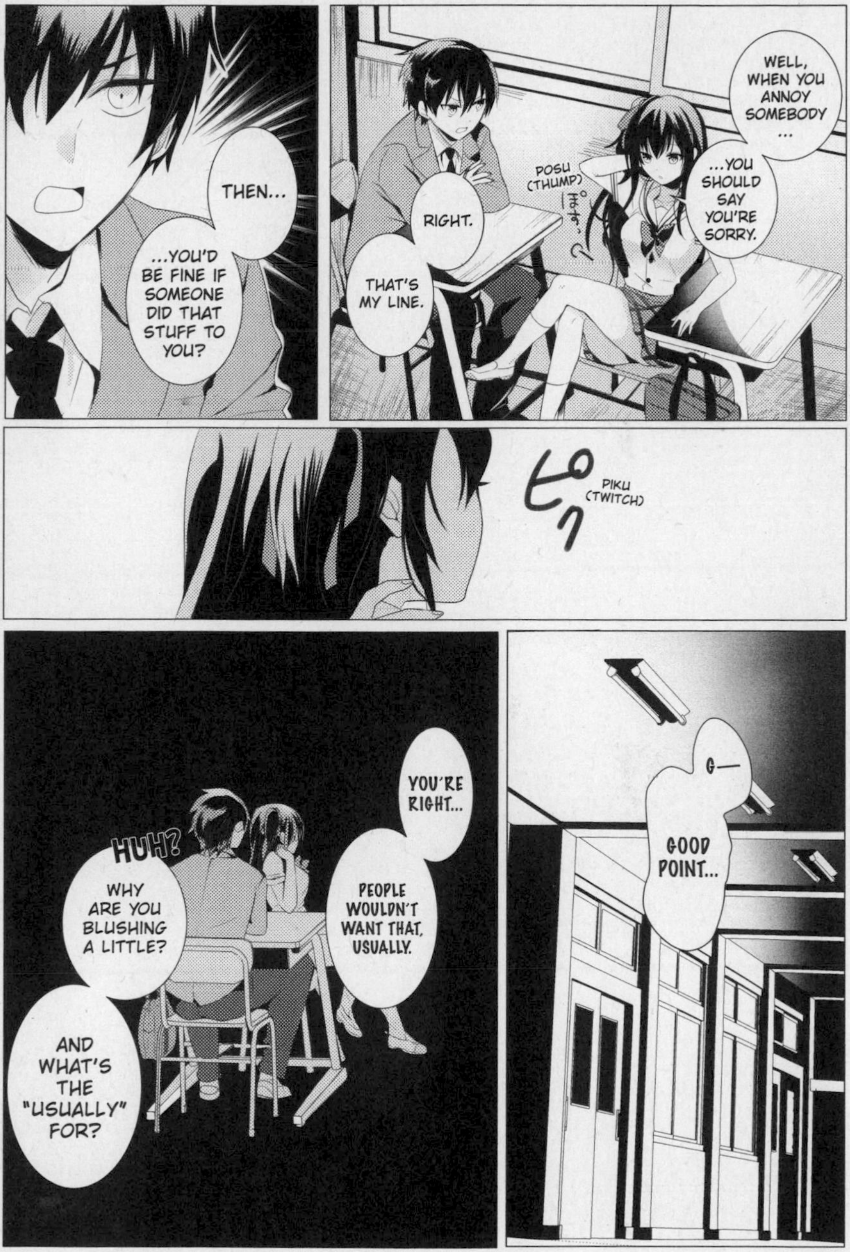
WELL, WHEN YOU ANNOY SOMEBODY ...
...YOU SHOULD SAY YOU'RE SORRY.
POSU (THUMP)
ぽす
RIGHT.
THAT'S MY LINE.
THEN...
...YOU'D BE FINE IF SOMEONE DID THAT STUFF TO YOU?
ピク
PIKU (TWITCH)
G—
GOOD POINT...
YOU'RE RIGHT...
PEOPLE WOULDN'T WANT THAT, USUALLY.
HUH?
WHY ARE YOU BLUSHING A LITTLE?
AND WHAT'S THE "USUALLY" FOR?

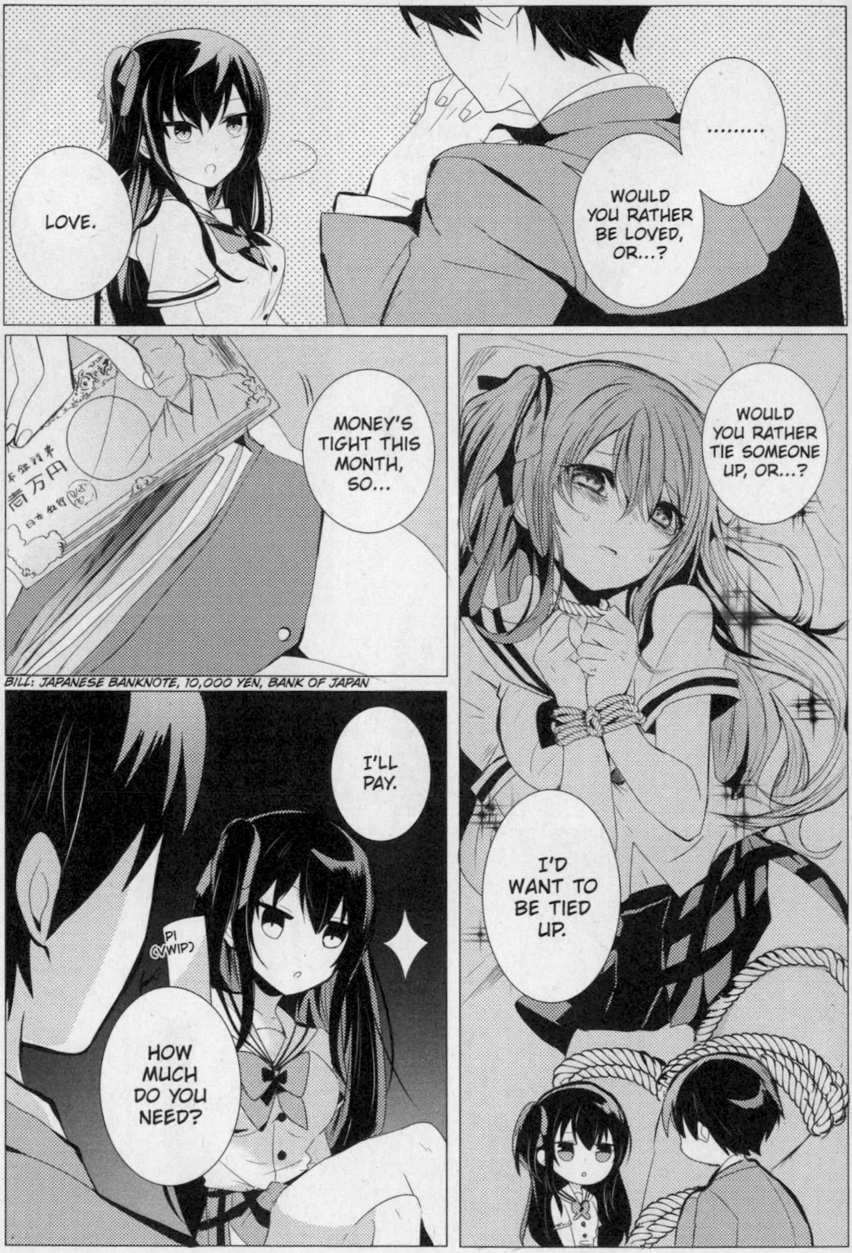
....
WOULD YOU RATHER BE LOVED, OR...?
LOVE.
WOULD YOU RATHER TIE SOMEONE UP, OR...?
I'D WANT TO BE TIED UP.
MONEY'S TIGHT THIS MONTH, SO...
I'LL PAY.
PI (VWIP)
HOW MUCH DO YOU NEED?

BILL: JAPANESE BANKNOTE, 10,000 YEN, BANK OF JAPAN

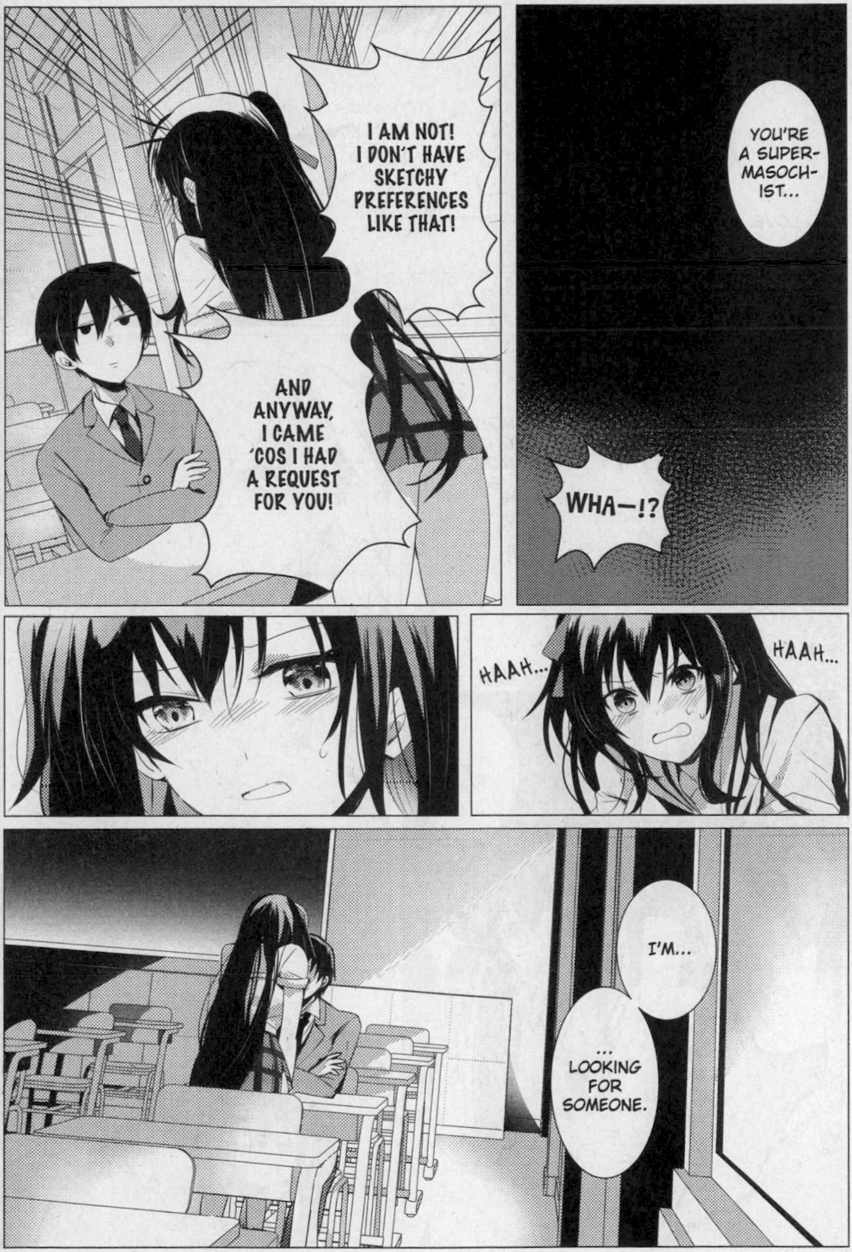
YOU'RE A SUPER-MASOCH-IST...
WHA—!?
I AM NOT! I DON'T HAVE SKETCHY PREFERENCES LIKE THAT!
AND ANYWAY, I CAME 'COS I HAD A REQUEST FOR YOU!
HAAH...
HAAH...
I'M...
... LOOKING FOR SOMEONE.

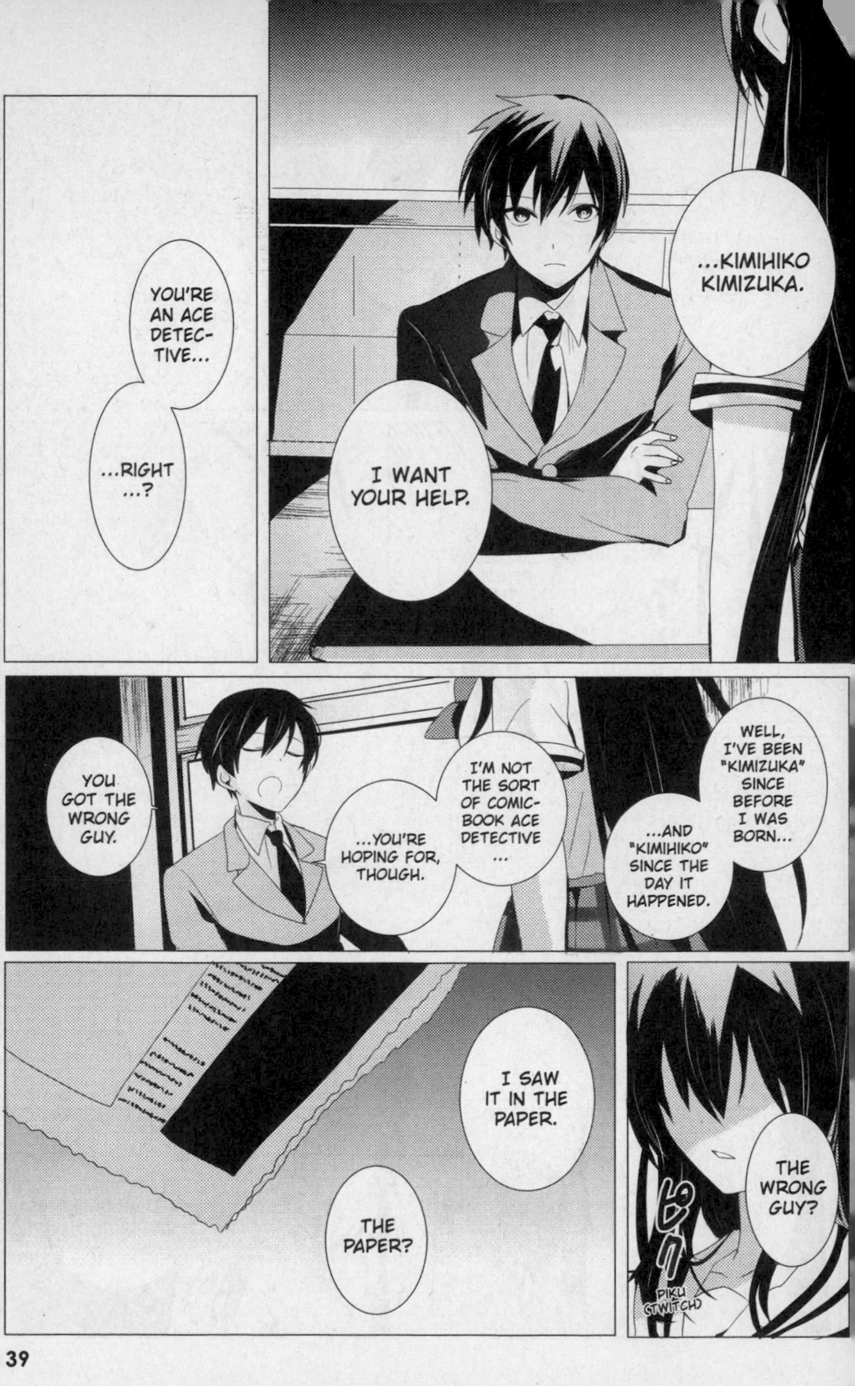
...KIMIHIKO KIMIZUKA.
I WANT YOUR HELP.
YOU'RE AN ACE DETECTIVE...
...RIGHT ...?
WELL, I'VE BEEN "KIMIZUKA" SINCE BEFORE I WAS BORN...
...AND "KIMIHIKO" SINCE THE DAY IT HAPPENED.
I'M NOT THE SORT OF COMIC-BOOK ACE DETECTIVE ...
...YOU'RE HOPING FOR, THOUGH.
YOU GOT THE WRONG GUY.
THE WRONG GUY?
PIKU (TWITCH)
I SAW IT IN THE PAPER.
THE PAPER?

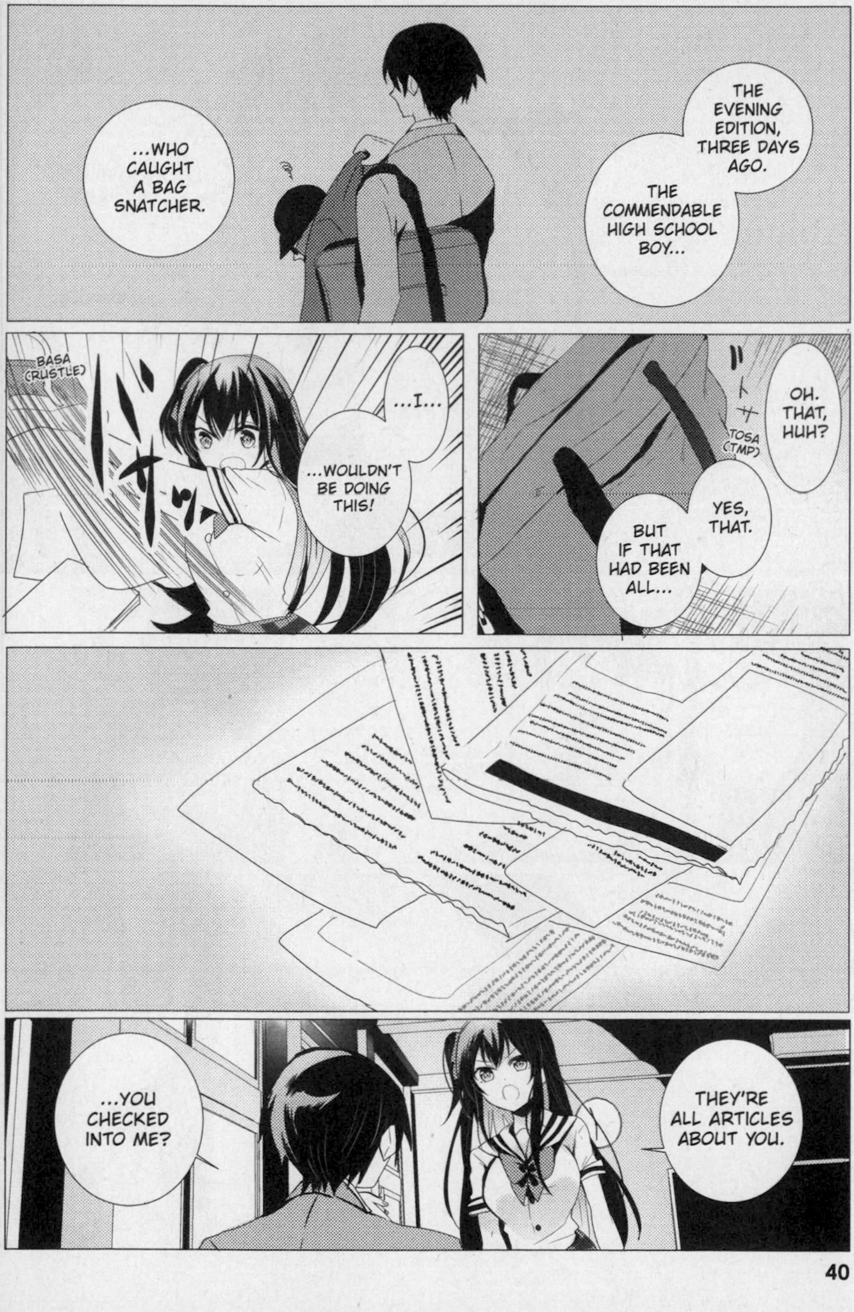
THE EVENING EDITION, THREE DAYS AGO.
THE COMMENDABLE HIGH SCHOOL BOY...
...WHO CAUGHT A BAG SNATCHER.
TOSA (TMP)
OH. THAT, HUH?
YES, THAT.
BUT IF THAT HAD BEEN ALL...
BASA (RUSTLE)
...I...
...WOULDN'T BE DOING THIS!
THEY'RE ALL ARTICLES ABOUT YOU.
...YOU CHECKED INTO ME?

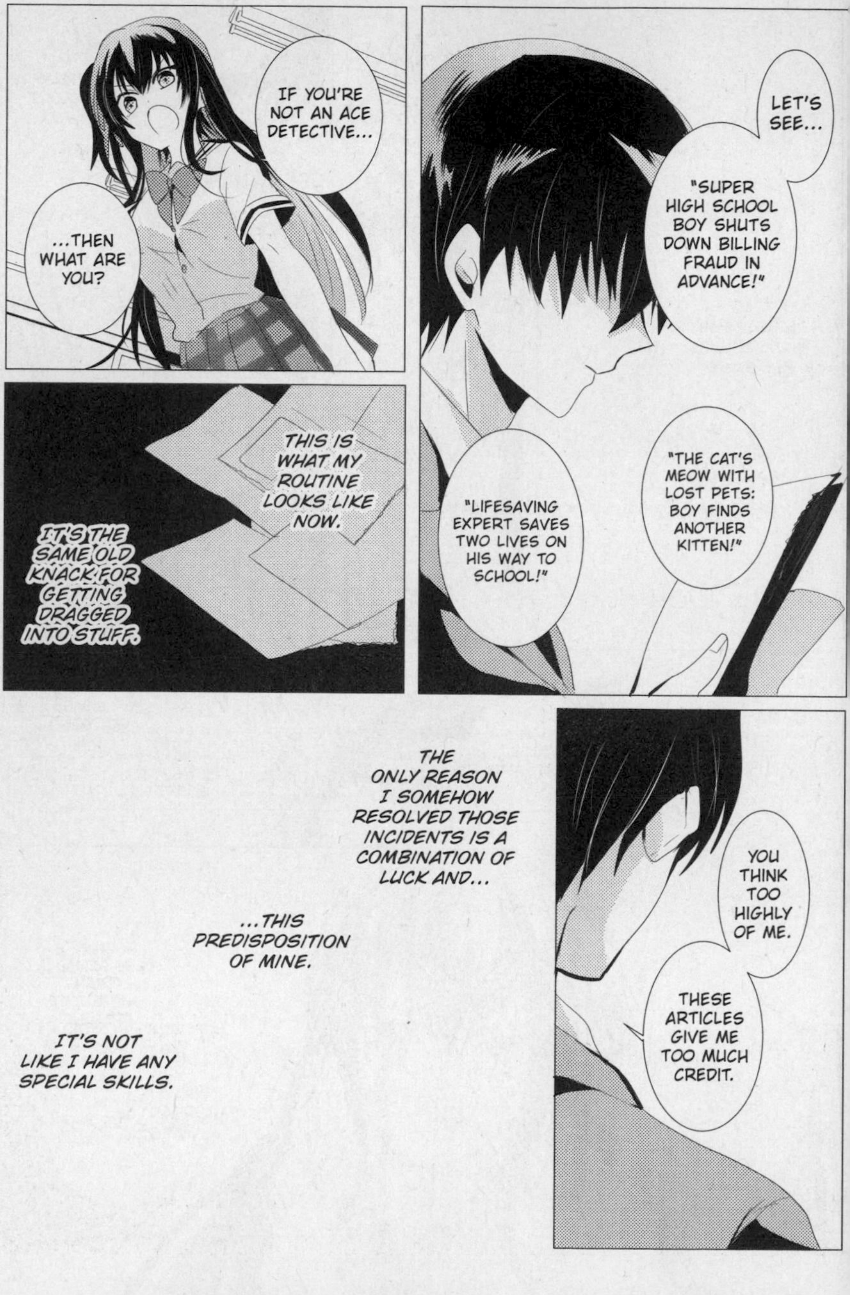
IF YOU'RE NOT AN ACE DETECTIVE...
...THEN WHAT ARE YOU?
LET'S SEE...
"SUPER HIGH SCHOOL BOY SHUTS DOWN BILLING FRAUD IN ADVANCE!"
"THE CAT'S MEOW WITH LOST PETS: BOY FINDS ANOTHER KITTEN!"
"LIFESAVING EXPERT SAVES TWO LIVES ON HIS WAY TO SCHOOL!"
THIS IS WHAT MY ROUTINE LOOKS LIKE NOW.
IT'S THE SAME OLD KNACK FOR GETTING DRAGGED INTO STUFF.
YOU THINK TOO HIGHLY OF ME.
THESE ARTICLES GIVE ME TOO MUCH CREDIT.
THE ONLY REASON I SOMEHOW RESOLVED THOSE INCIDENTS IS A COMBINATION OF LUCK AND...
...THIS PREDISPOSITION OF MINE.
IT'S NOT LIKE I HAVE ANY SPECIAL SKILLS.

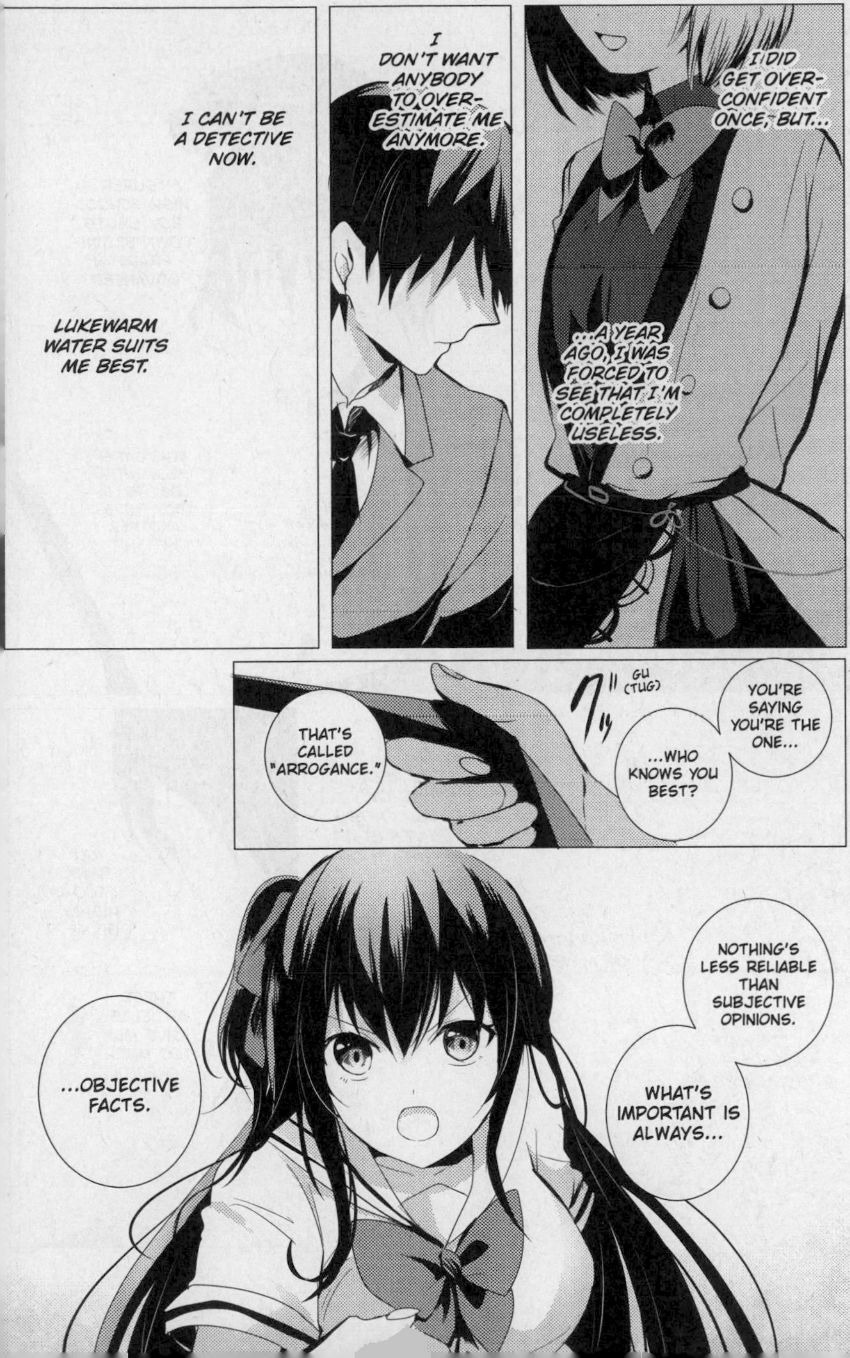
I DID GET OVER-CONFIDENT ONCE, BUT...
...A YEAR AGO, I WAS FORCED TO SEE THAT I'M COMPLETELY USELESS.
I DON'T WANT ANYBODY TO OVER-ESTIMATE ME ANYMORE.
I CAN'T BE A DETECTIVE NOW.
LUKEWARM WATER SUITS ME BEST.
GU (TUG)
YOU'RE SAYING YOU'RE THE ONE...
...WHO KNOWS YOU BEST?
THAT'S CALLED "ARROGANCE."
NOTHING'S LESS RELIABLE THAN SUBJECTIVE OPINIONS.
WHAT'S IMPORTANT IS ALWAYS...
...OBJECTIVE FACTS.

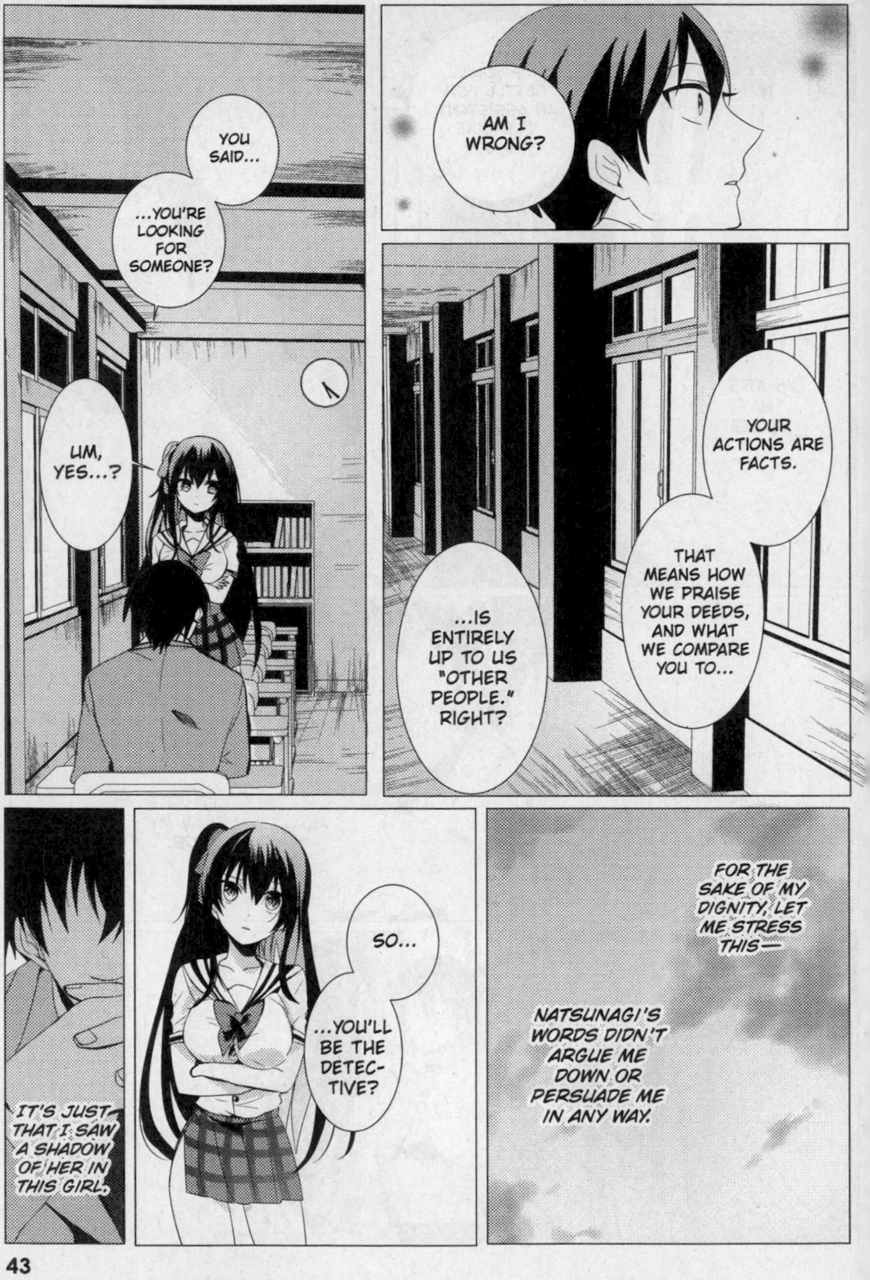
AM I WRONG?
YOUR ACTIONS ARE FACTS.
THAT MEANS HOW WE PRAISE YOUR DEEDS, AND WHAT WE COMPARE YOU TO...
...IS ENTIRELY UP TO US "OTHER PEOPLE." RIGHT?
YOU SAID...
...YOU'RE LOOKING FOR SOMEONE?
UM, YES...?
FOR THE SAKE OF MY DIGNITY, LET ME STRESS THIS—
NATSUNAGI'S WORDS DIDN'T ARGUE ME DOWN OR PERSUADE ME IN ANY WAY.
SO...
...YOU'LL BE THE DETEC-TIVE?
IT'S JUST THAT I SAW A SHADOW OF HER IN THIS GIRL.

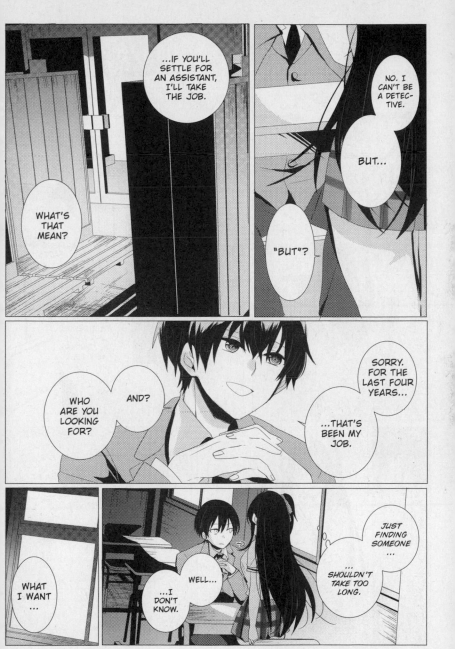

NO. I CAN'T BE A DETECTIVE.
BUT...
"BUT"?
...IF YOU'LL SETTLE FOR AN ASSISTANT, I'LL TAKE THE JOB.
WHAT'S THAT MEAN?
SORRY. FOR THE LAST FOUR YEARS...
...THAT'S BEEN MY JOB.
AND?
WHO ARE YOU LOOKING FOR?
JUST FINDING SOMEONE...
...SHOULDN'T TAKE TOO LONG.
WELL...
...I DON'T KNOW.
WHAT I WANT...

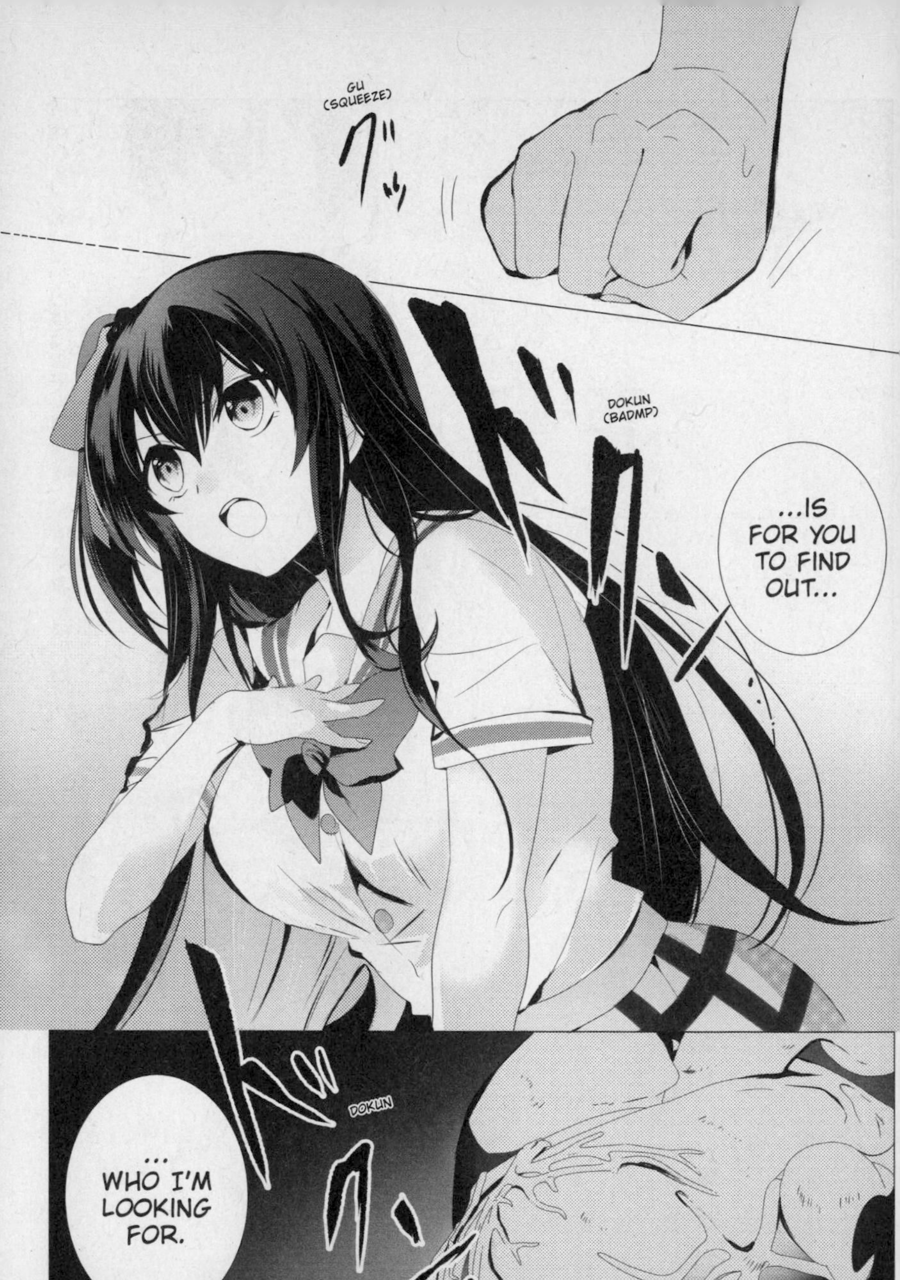
GU
(SQUEEZE)
DOKUN
(BADMP)
...IS FOR YOU TO FIND OUT...
DOKUN
... WHO I'M LOOKING FOR.

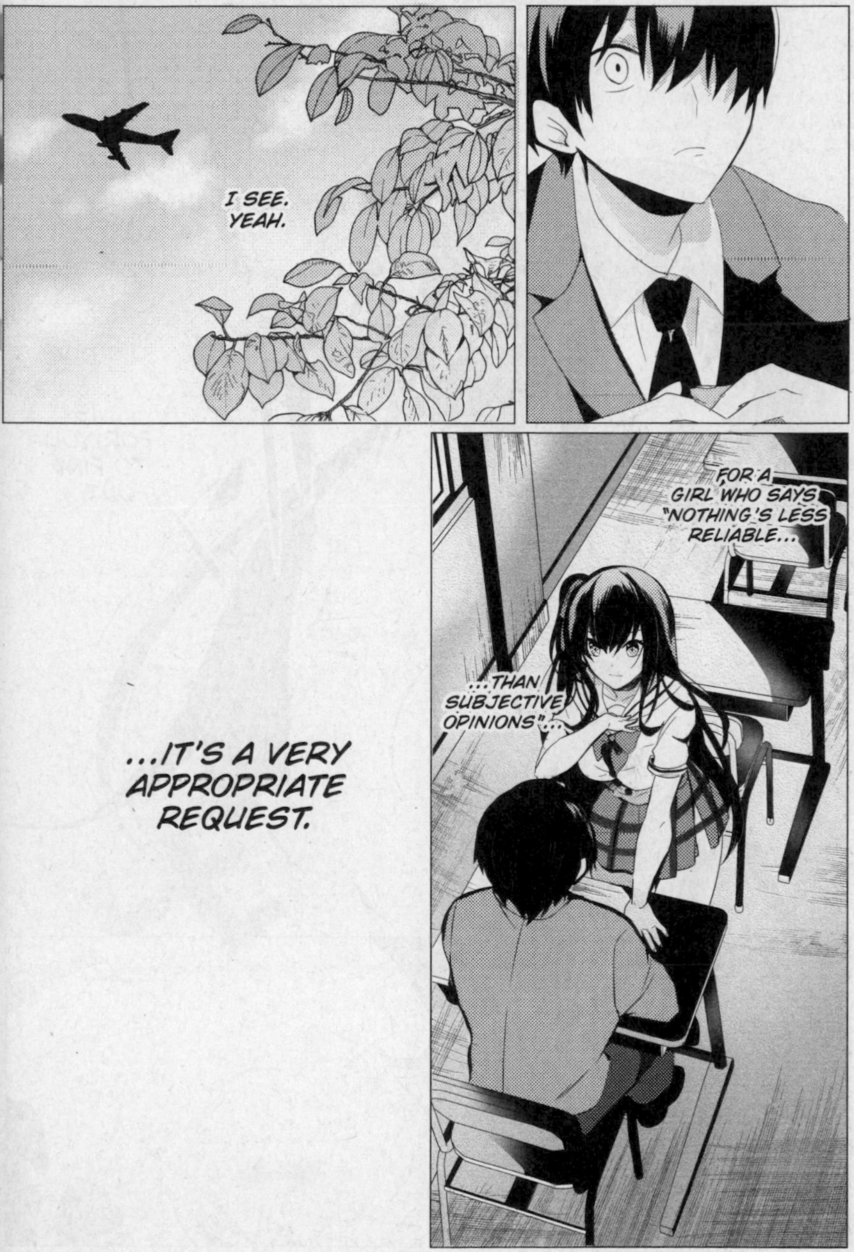
I SEE. YEAH.
FOR A GIRL WHO SAYS "NOTHING'S LESS RELIABLE...
...THAN SUBJECTIVE OPINIONS"...
...IT'S A VERY APPROPRIATE REQUEST.

The Detective Is Already Dead

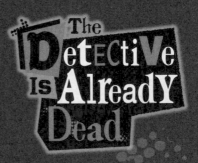

The Detective Is Already Dead

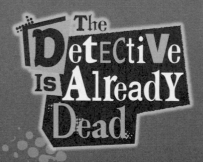

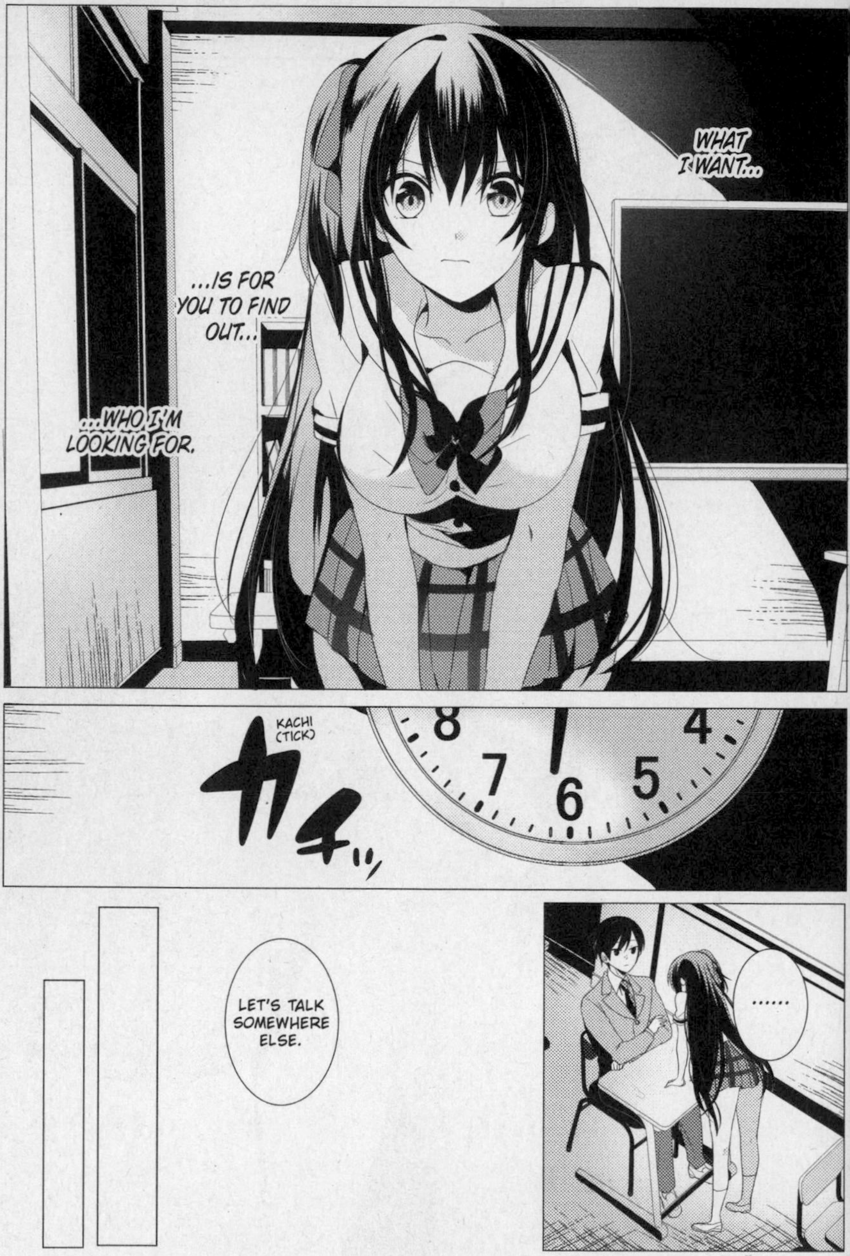
WHAT I WANT...
...IS FOR YOU TO FIND OUT...
...WHO I'M LOOKING FOR.
KACHI (TICK)
......
LET'S TALK SOMEWHERE ELSE.

Episode. 2

Whose Heart Is This?

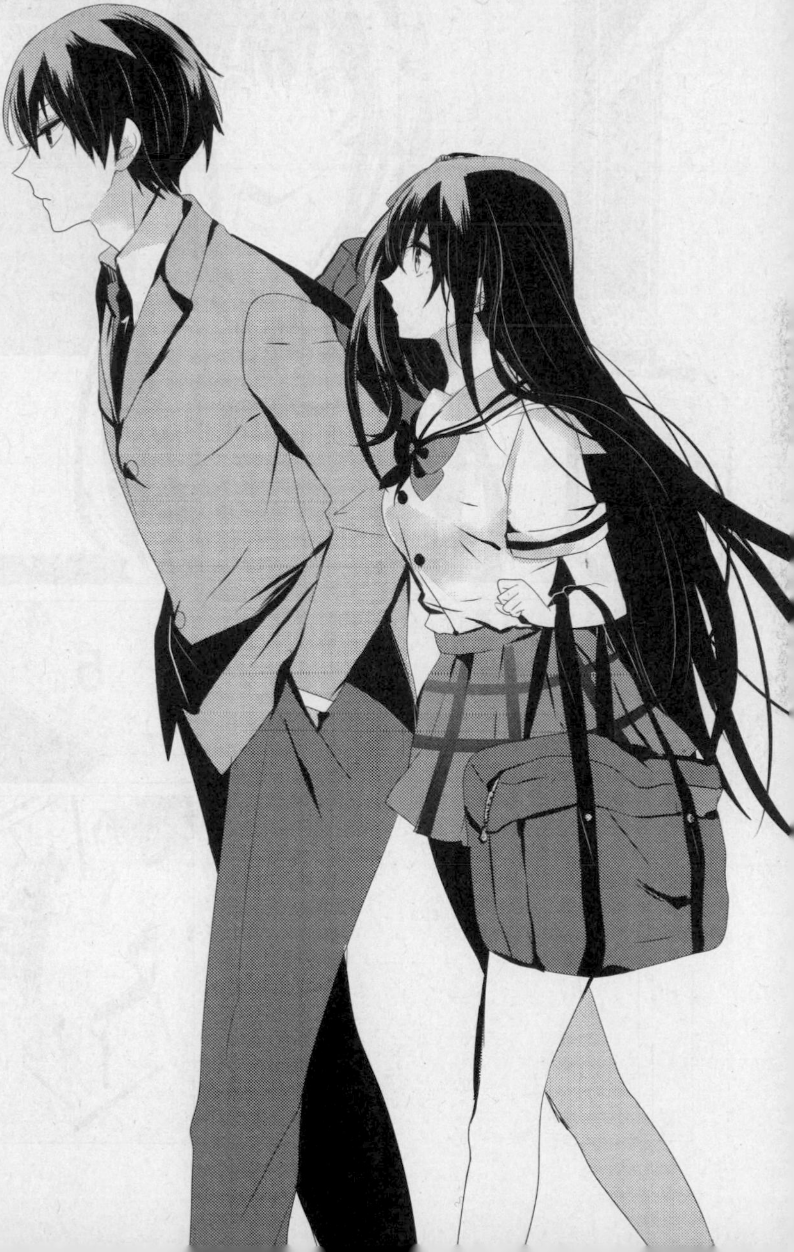

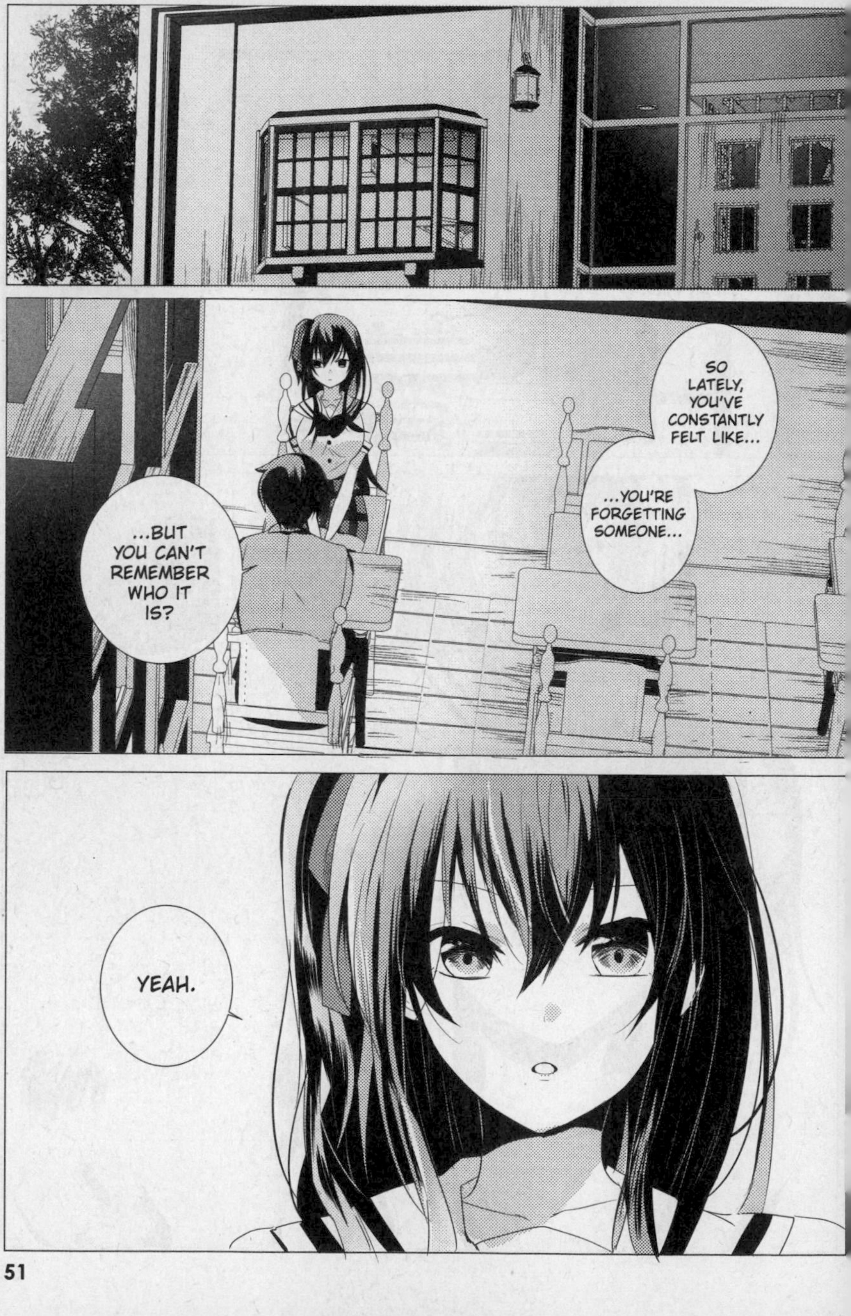
SO LATELY, YOU'VE CONSTANTLY FELT LIKE...
...YOU'RE FORGETTING SOMEONE...
...BUT YOU CAN'T REMEMBER WHO IT IS?
YEAH.

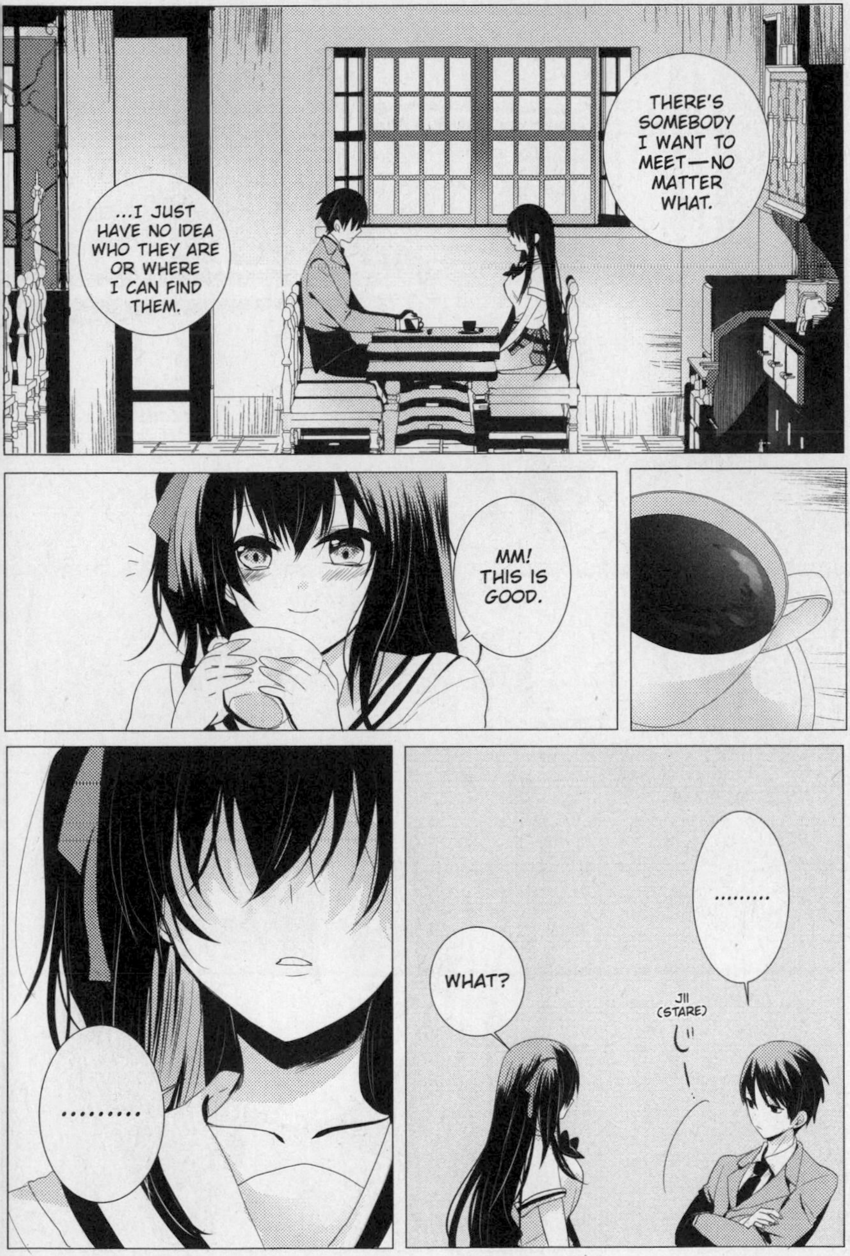
THERE'S SOMEBODY I WANT TO MEET—NO MATTER WHAT.
...I JUST HAVE NO IDEA WHO THEY ARE OR WHERE I CAN FIND THEM.
MM! THIS IS GOOD.
....
JII (STARE)
じー
WHAT?
....

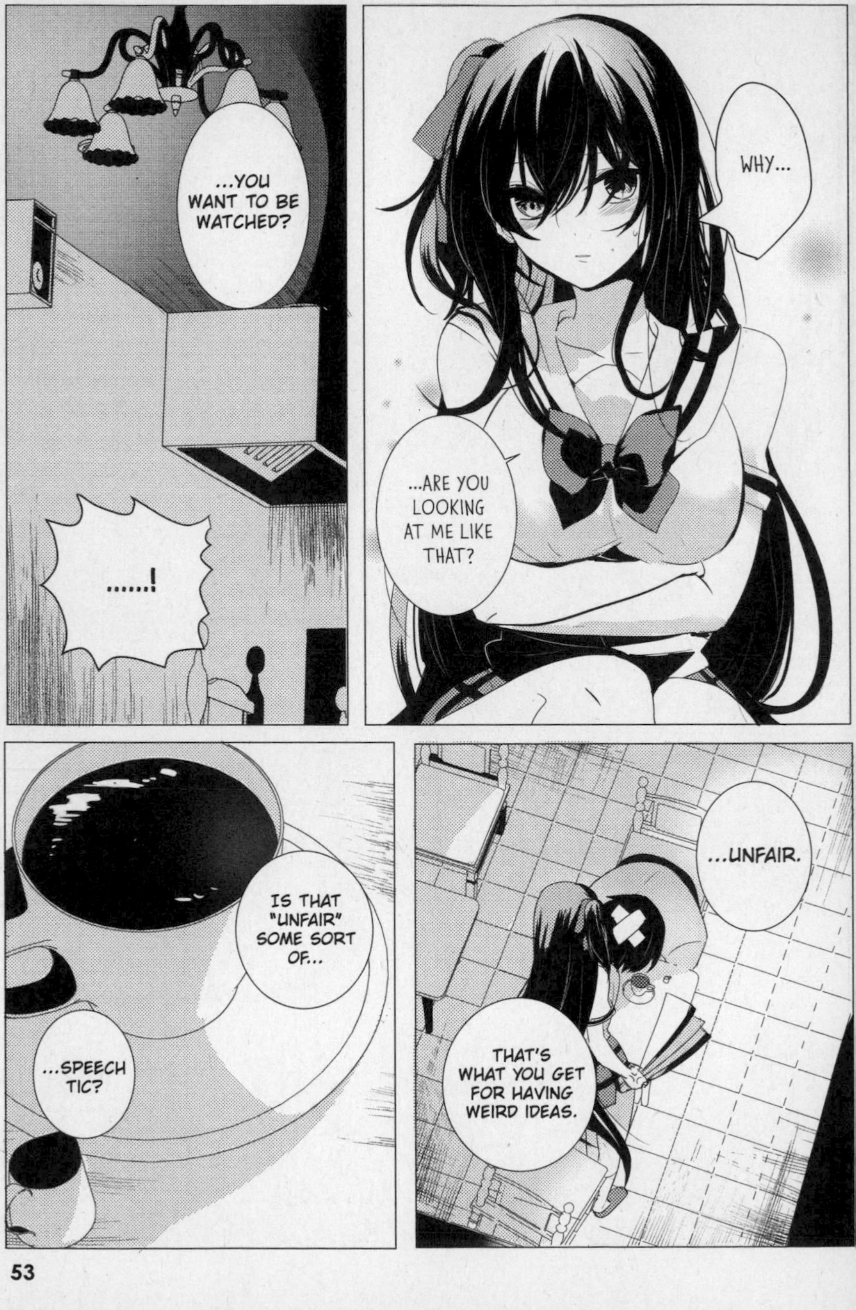
WHY...
...ARE YOU LOOKING AT ME LIKE THAT?
...YOU WANT TO BE WATCHED?
......!
...UNFAIR.
THAT'S WHAT YOU GET FOR HAVING WEIRD IDEAS.
IS THAT "UNFAIR" SOME SORT OF...
...SPEECH TIC?

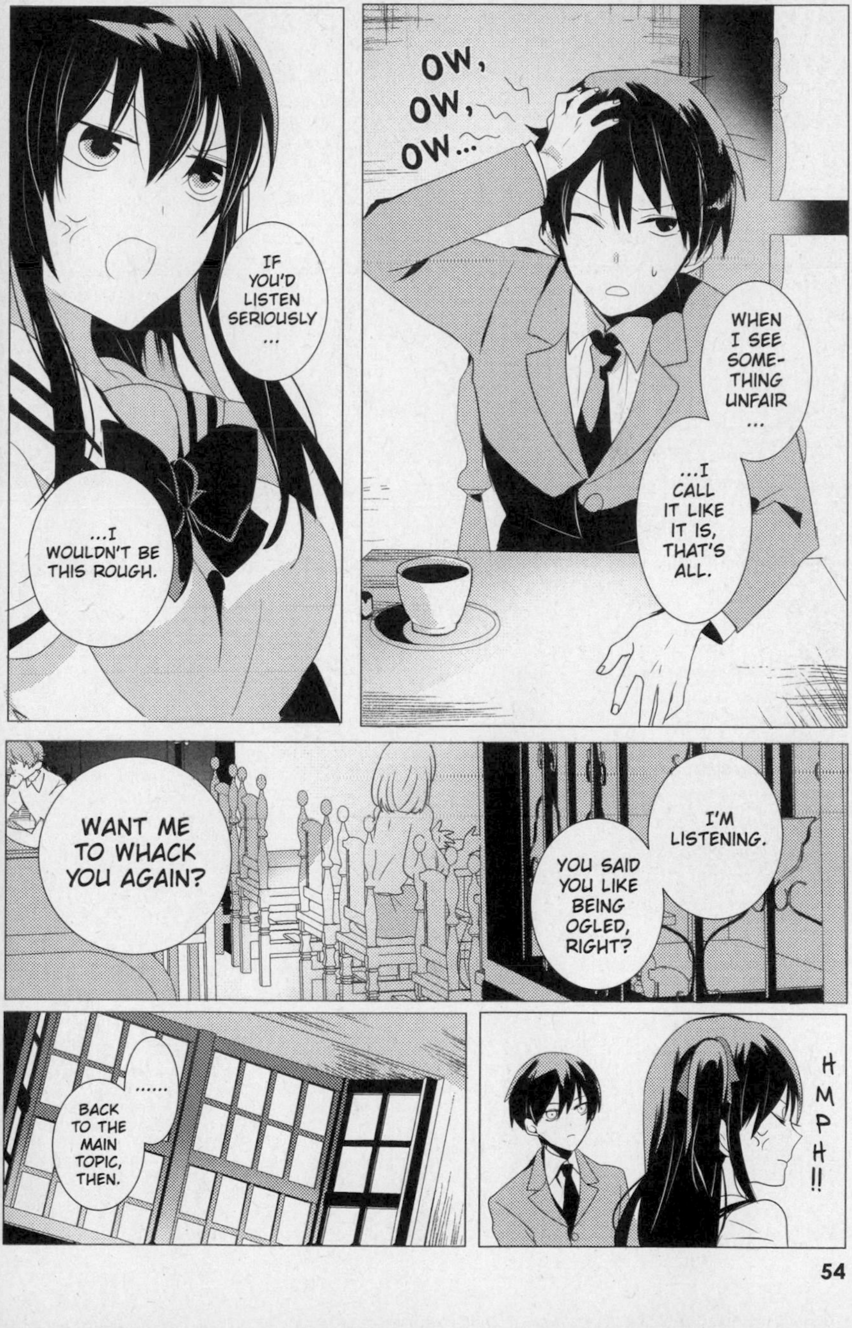
OW, OW, OW...
WHEN I SEE SOME-THING UNFAIR...
...I CALL IT LIKE IT IS, THAT'S ALL.
IF YOU'D LISTEN SERIOUSLY...
...I WOULDN'T BE THIS ROUGH.
I'M LISTENING.
YOU SAID YOU LIKE BEING OGLED, RIGHT?
WANT ME TO WHACK YOU AGAIN?
HMPH!!
......
BACK TO THE MAIN TOPIC, THEN.

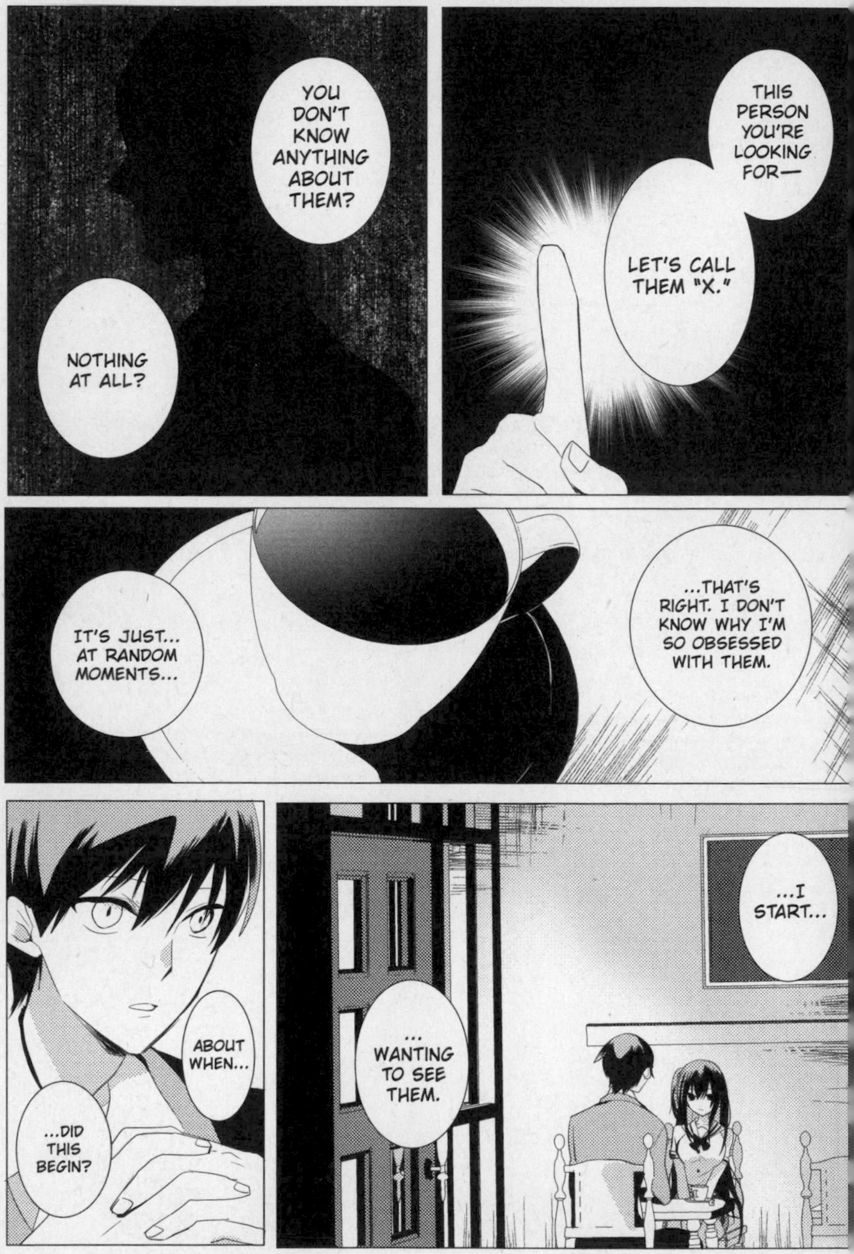
THIS PERSON YOU'RE LOOKING FOR—
LET'S CALL THEM "X."
YOU DON'T KNOW ANYTHING ABOUT THEM?
NOTHING AT ALL?
...THAT'S RIGHT. I DON'T KNOW WHY I'M SO OBSESSED WITH THEM.
IT'S JUST... AT RANDOM MOMENTS...
...I START...
... WANTING TO SEE THEM.
ABOUT WHEN...
...DID THIS BEGIN?

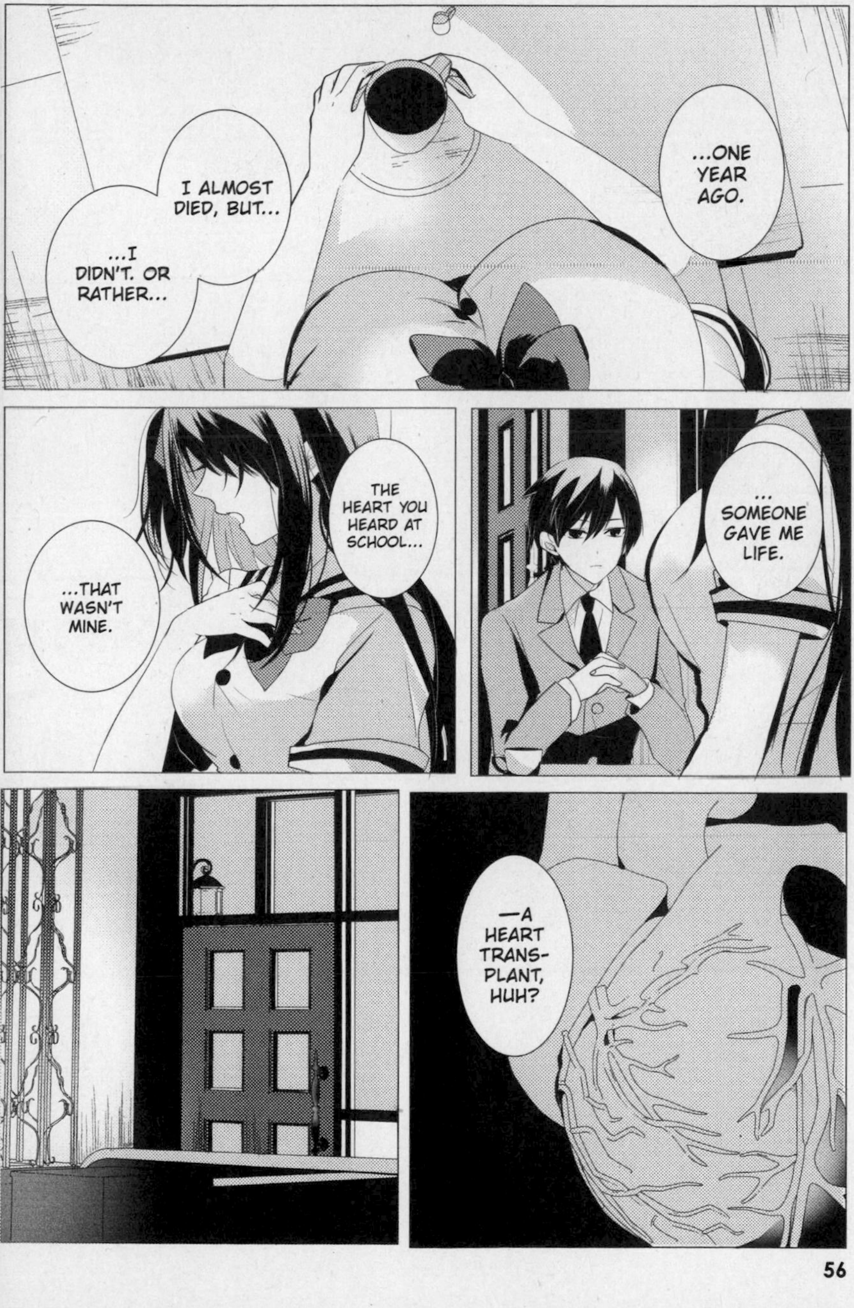
...ONE YEAR AGO.
I ALMOST DIED, BUT...
...I DIDN'T. OR RATHER...
... SOMEONE GAVE ME LIFE.
THE HEART YOU HEARD AT SCHOOL...
...THAT WASN'T MINE.
—A HEART TRANS-PLANT, HUH?

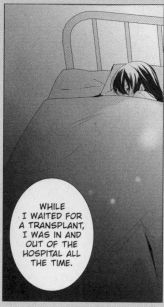

I'VE HAD A HEART DISORDER EVER SINCE I WAS SMALL.

WHILE I WAITED FOR A TRANSPLANT, I WAS IN AND OUT OF THE HOSPITAL ALL THE TIME.

I COULDN'T EVEN GO TO SCHOOL.

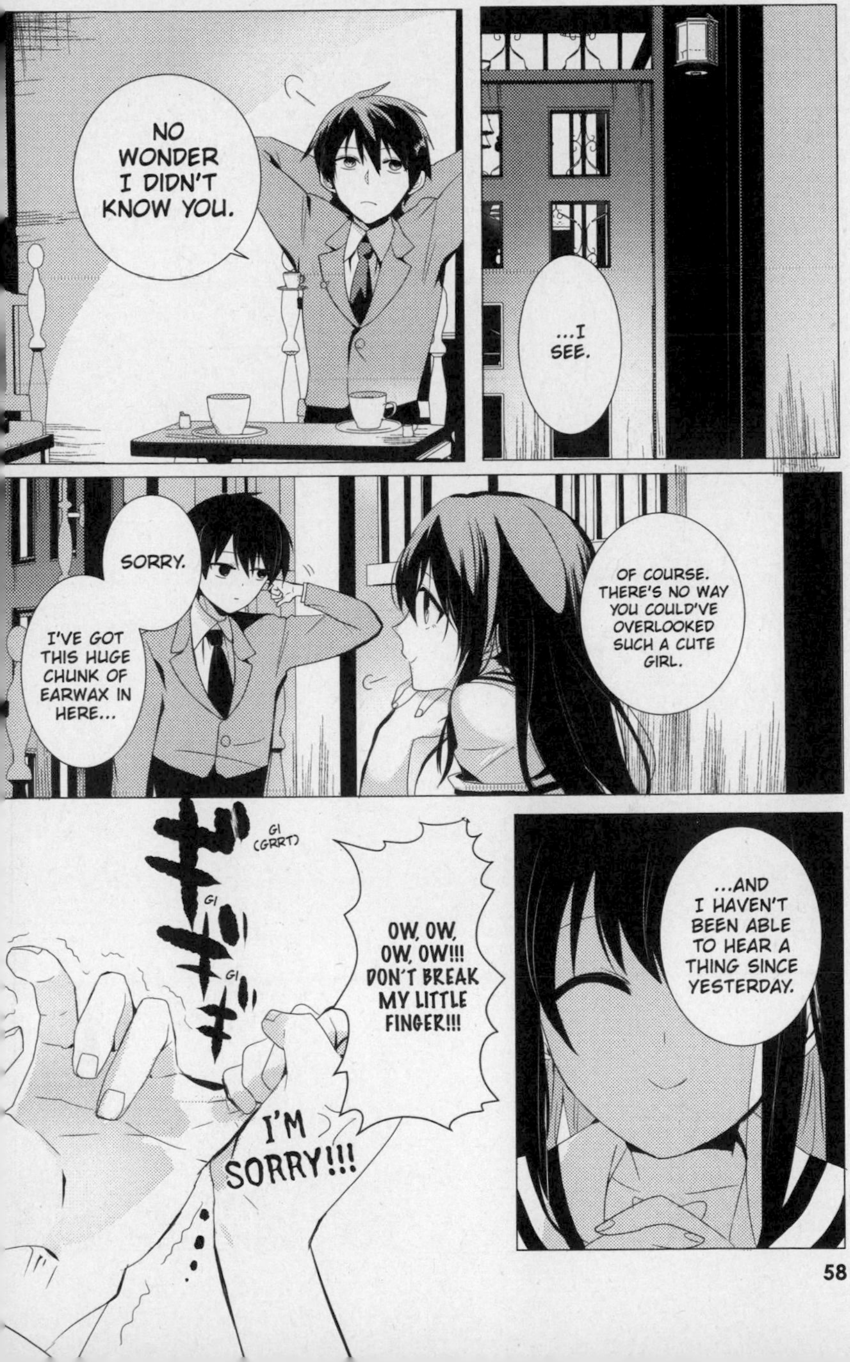
...I SEE.
NO WONDER I DIDN'T KNOW YOU.
OF COURSE. THERE'S NO WAY YOU COULD'VE OVERLOOKED SUCH A CUTE GIRL.
SORRY.
I'VE GOT THIS HUGE CHUNK OF EARWAX IN HERE...
...AND I HAVEN'T BEEN ABLE TO HEAR A THING SINCE YESTERDAY.
GI (GRRT)
GI
GI
OW, OW, OW, OW!!! DON'T BREAK MY LITTLE FINGER!!!
I'M SORRY!!!

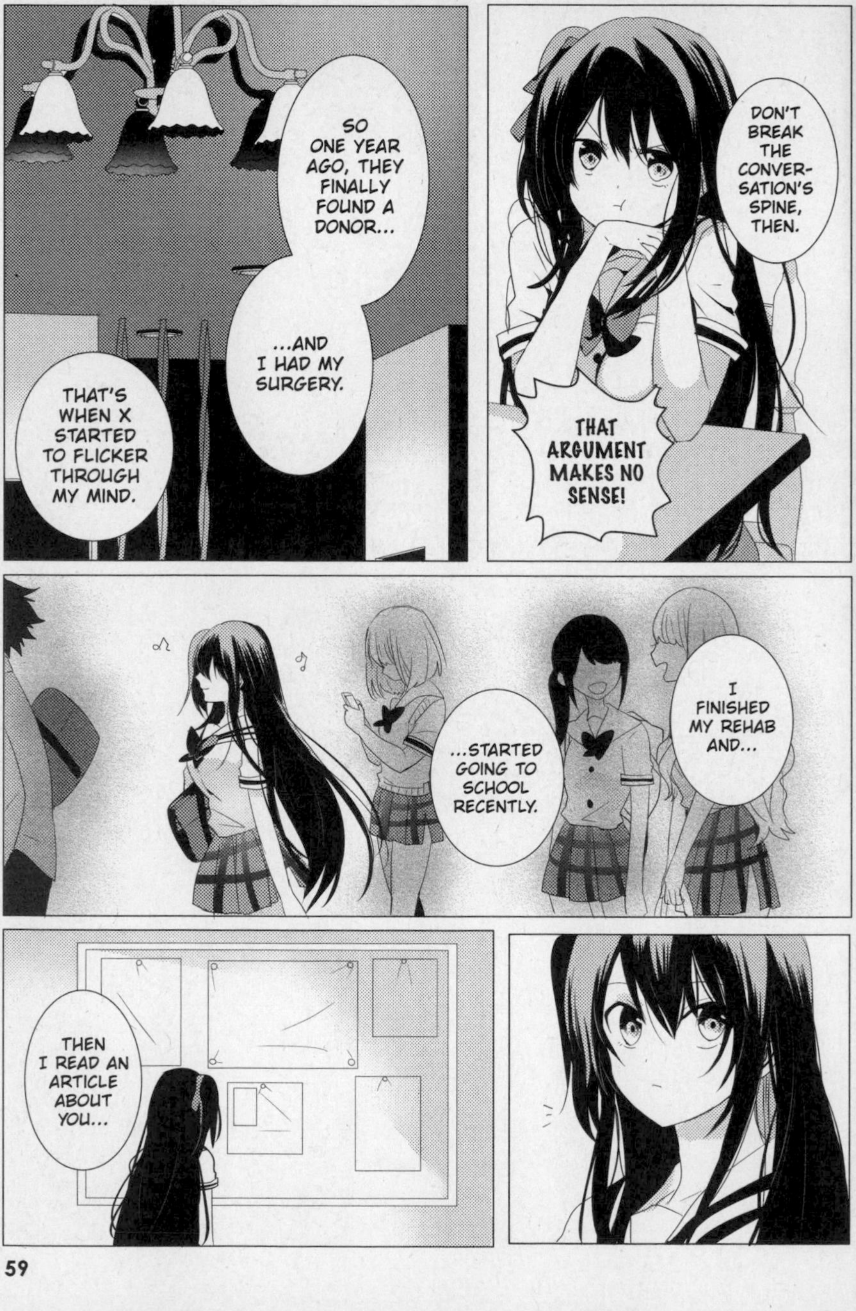
DON'T BREAK THE CONVER-SATION'S SPINE, THEN.
THAT ARGUMENT MAKES NO SENSE!
SO ONE YEAR AGO, THEY FINALLY FOUND A DONOR...
...AND I HAD MY SURGERY.
THAT'S WHEN X STARTED TO FLICKER THROUGH MY MIND.
I FINISHED MY REHAB AND...
...STARTED GOING TO SCHOOL RECENTLY.
THEN I READ AN ARTICLE ABOUT YOU...

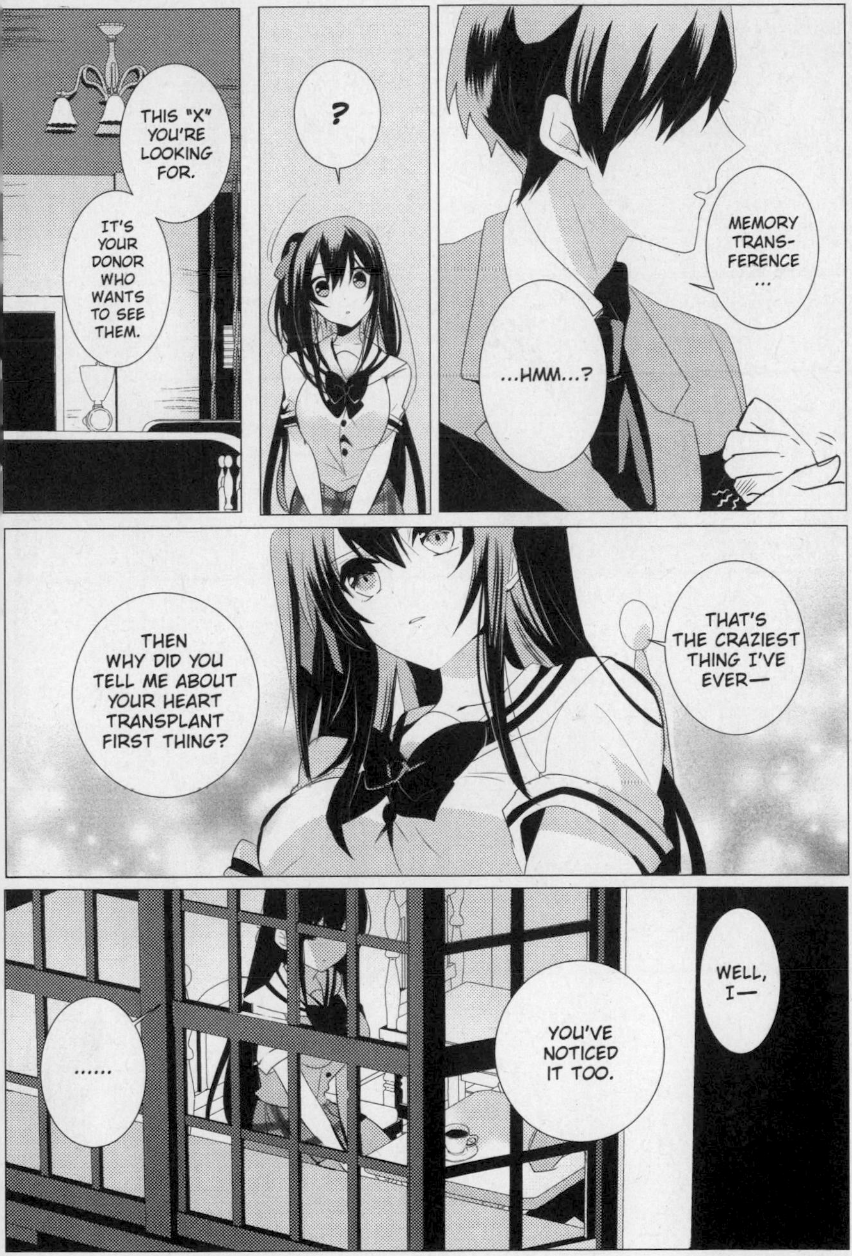
MEMORY TRANSFERENCE ...
...HMM...?
?
THIS "X" YOU'RE LOOKING FOR.
IT'S YOUR DONOR WHO WANTS TO SEE THEM.
THAT'S THE CRAZIEST THING I'VE EVER—
THEN WHY DID YOU TELL ME ABOUT YOUR HEART TRANSPLANT FIRST THING?
WELL, I—
YOU'VE NOTICED IT TOO.
......

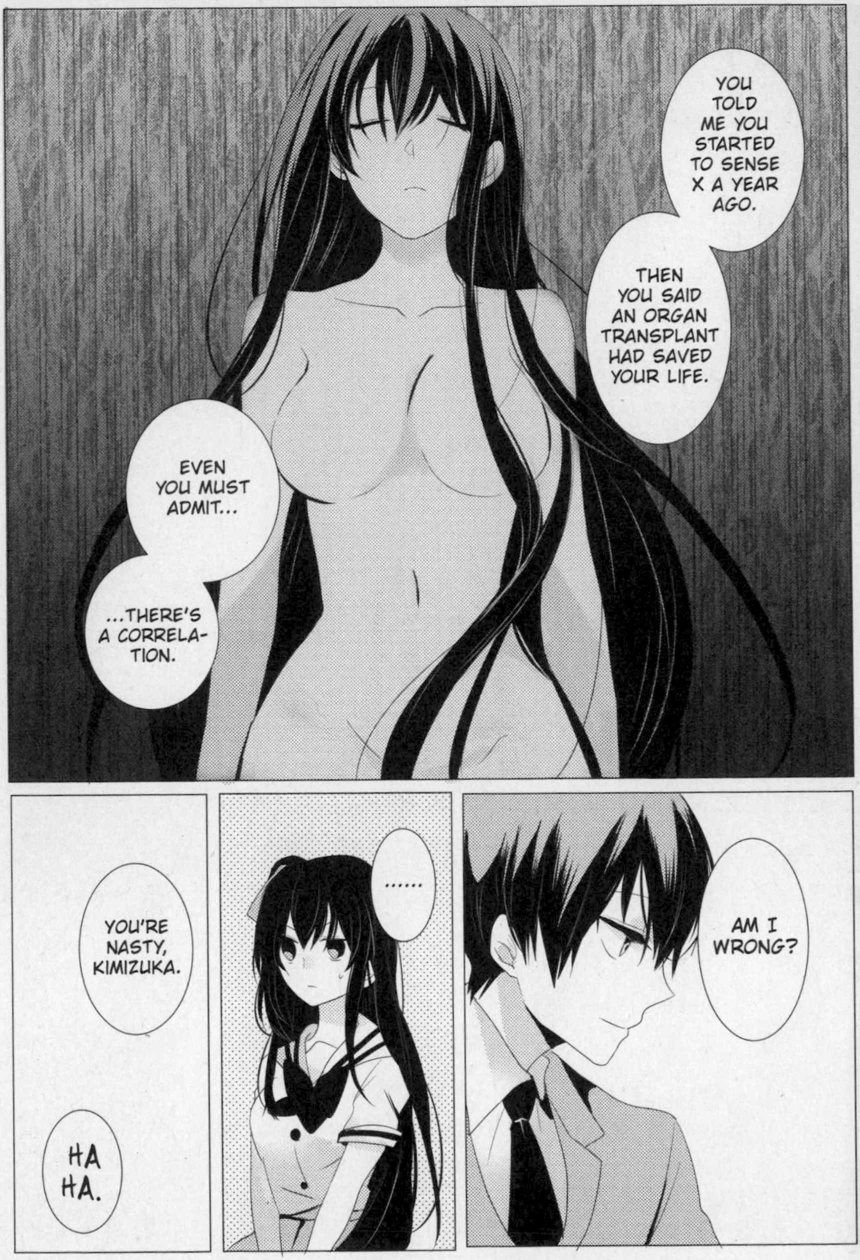
YOU TOLD ME YOU STARTED TO SENSE X A YEAR AGO.
THEN YOU SAID AN ORGAN TRANSPLANT HAD SAVED YOUR LIFE.
EVEN YOU MUST ADMIT...
...THERE'S A CORRELA-TION.
AM I WRONG?
......
YOU'RE NASTY, KIMIZUKA.
HA HA.

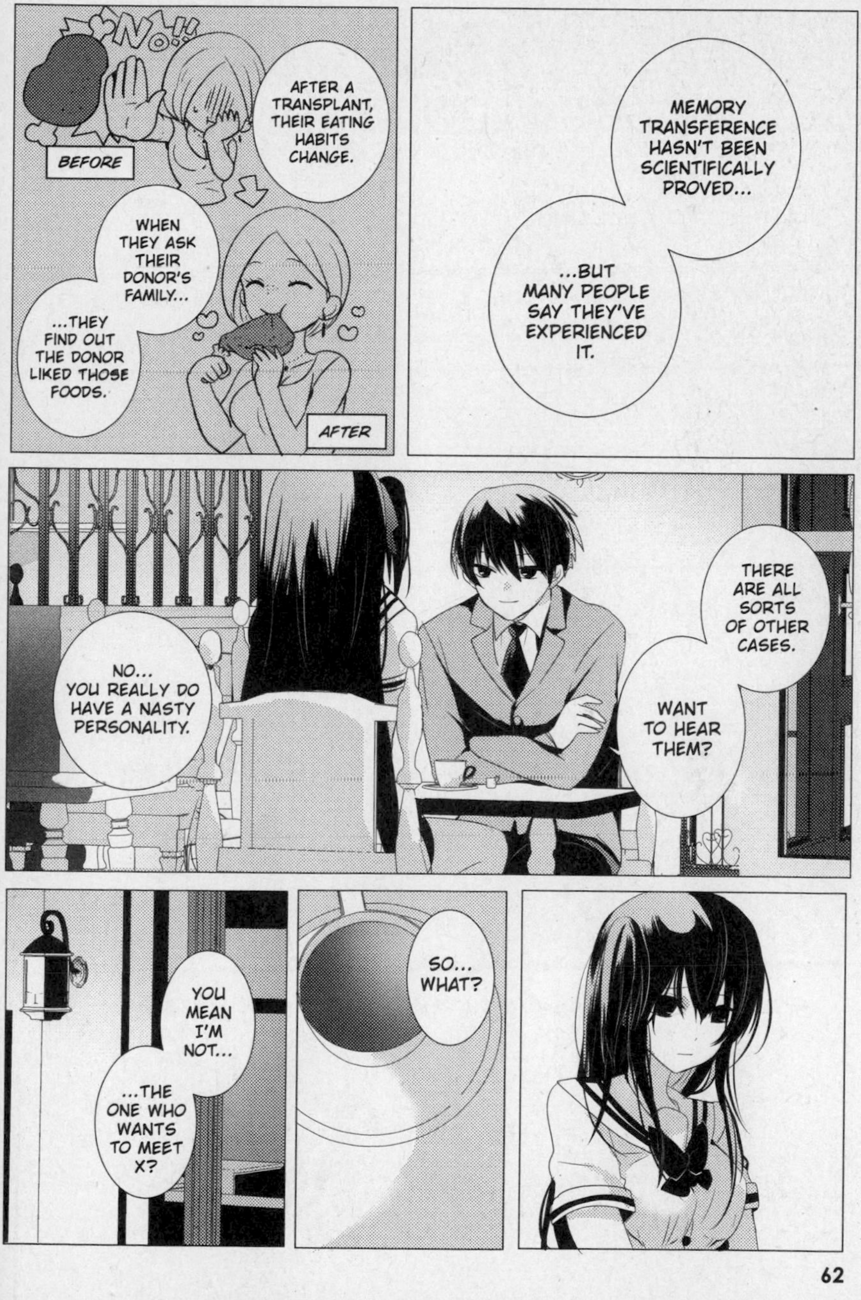
MEMORY TRANSFERENCE HASN'T BEEN SCIENTIFICALLY PROVED...
...BUT MANY PEOPLE SAY THEY'VE EXPERIENCED IT.
NO!!
AFTER A TRANSPLANT, THEIR EATING HABITS CHANGE.
BEFORE
WHEN THEY ASK THEIR DONOR'S FAMILY...
...THEY FIND OUT THE DONOR LIKED THOSE FOODS.
AFTER
THERE ARE ALL SORTS OF OTHER CASES.
WANT TO HEAR THEM?
NO... YOU REALLY DO HAVE A NASTY PERSONALITY.
SO... WHAT?
YOU MEAN I'M NOT...
...THE ONE WHO WANTS TO MEET X?

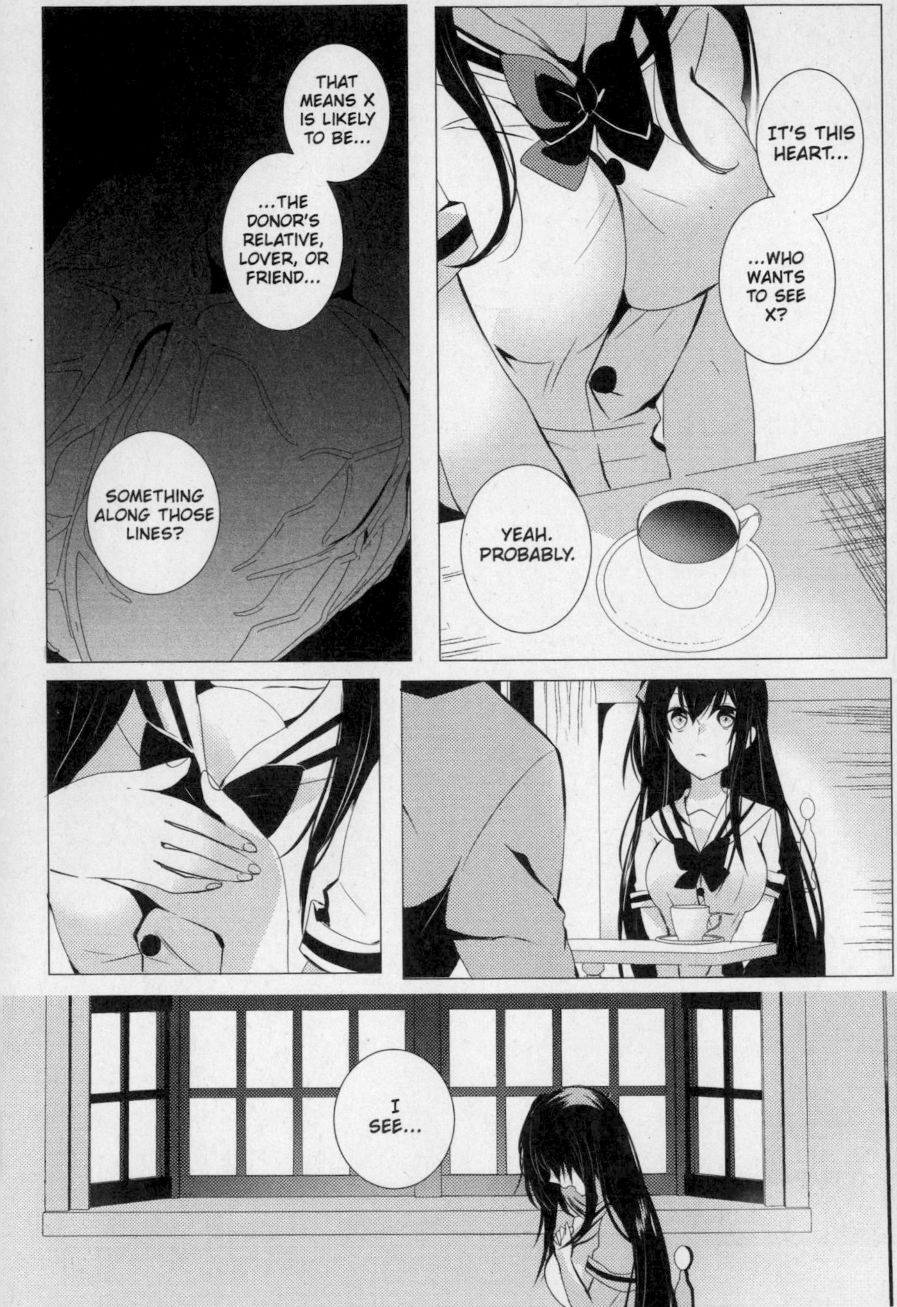
IT'S THIS HEART...
...WHO WANTS TO SEE X?
YEAH. PROBABLY.
THAT MEANS X IS LIKELY TO BE...
...THE DONOR'S RELATIVE, LOVER, OR FRIEND...
SOMETHING ALONG THOSE LINES?
I SEE...

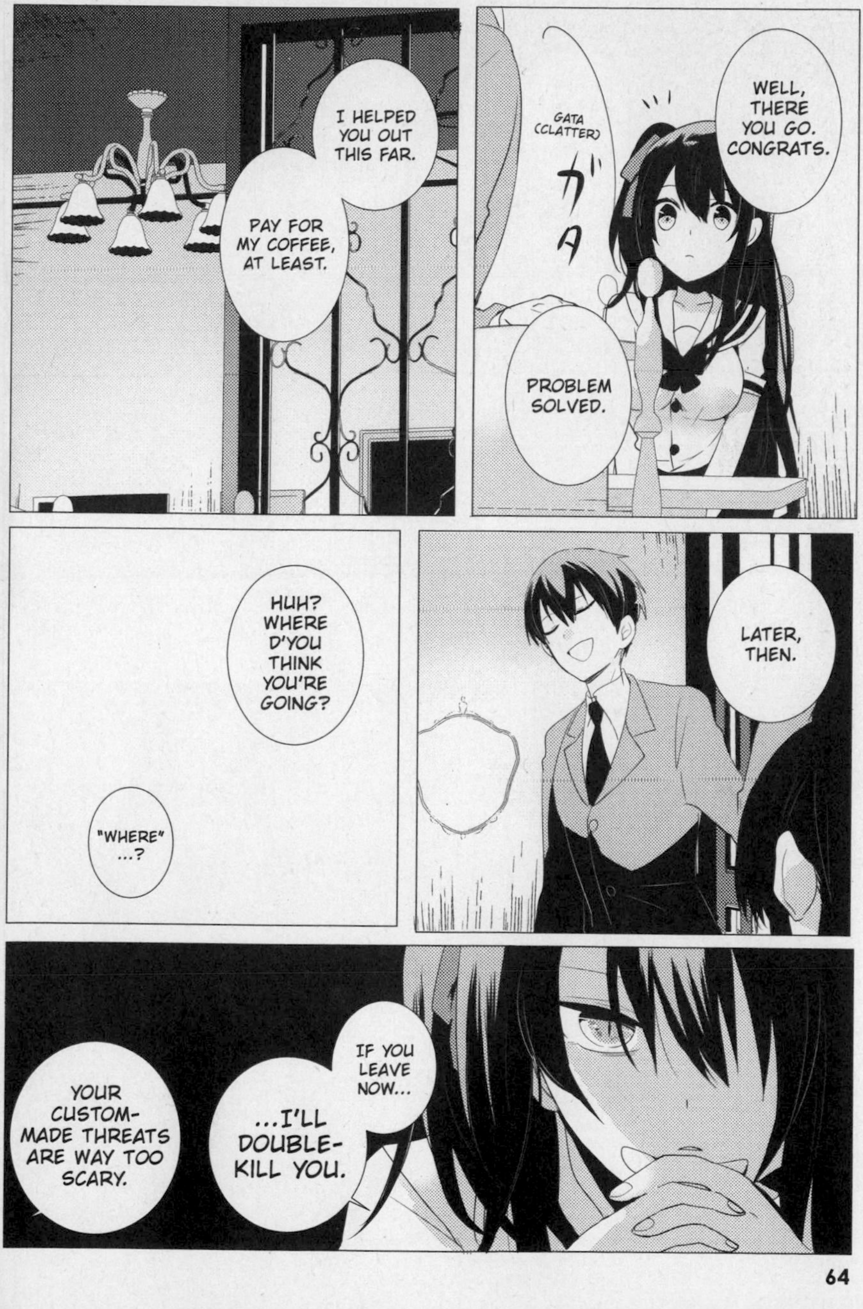

WELL, THERE YOU GO. CONGRATS.
GATA (CLATTER)
ガタ
PROBLEM SOLVED.
I HELPED YOU OUT THIS FAR.
PAY FOR MY COFFEE, AT LEAST.
LATER, THEN.
HUH? WHERE D'YOU THINK YOU'RE GOING?
"WHERE" ...?
IF YOU LEAVE NOW...
...I'LL DOUBLE-KILL YOU.
YOUR CUSTOM-MADE THREATS ARE WAY TOO SCARY.

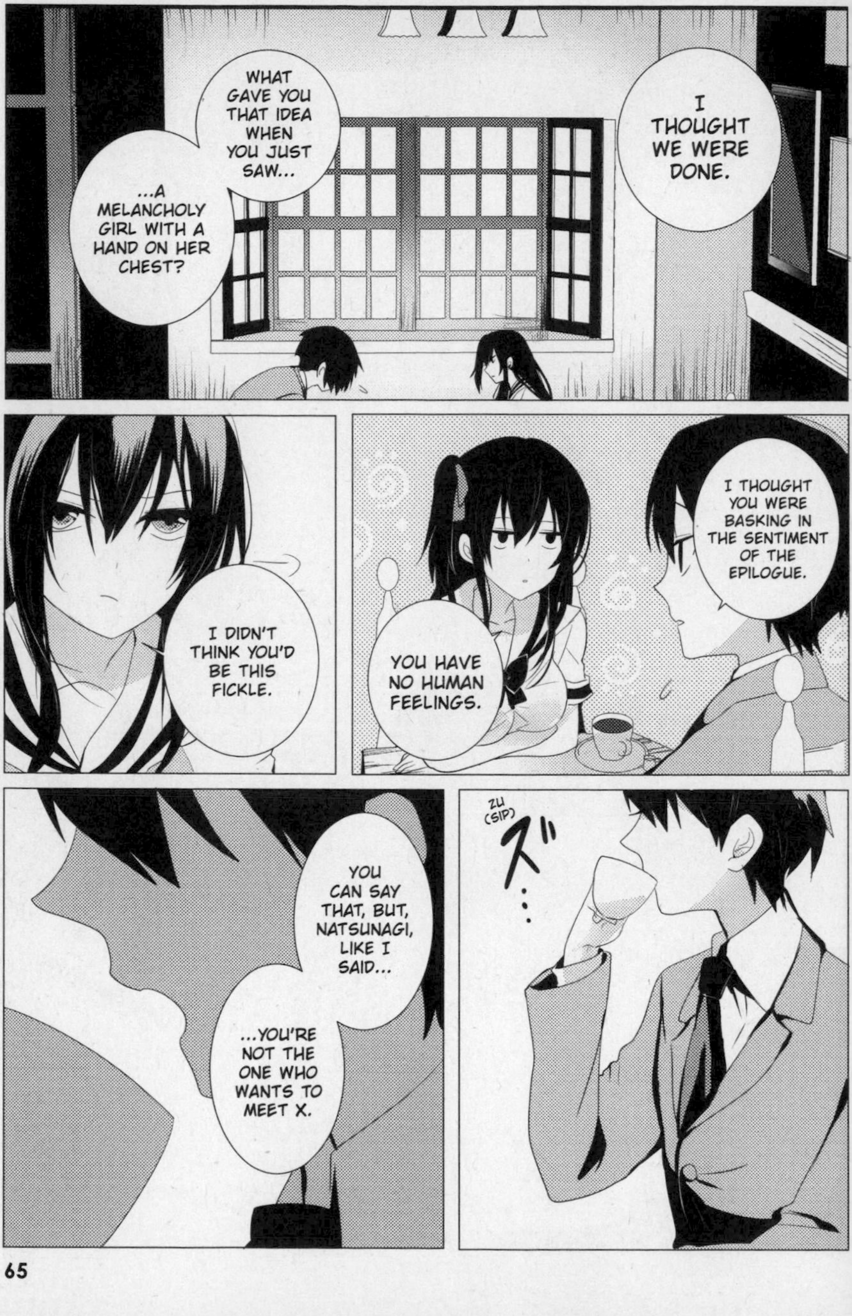
I THOUGHT WE WERE DONE.
WHAT GAVE YOU THAT IDEA WHEN YOU JUST SAW...
...A MELANCHOLY GIRL WITH A HAND ON HER CHEST?
I THOUGHT YOU WERE BASKING IN THE SENTIMENT OF THE EPILOGUE.
YOU HAVE NO HUMAN FEELINGS.
I DIDN'T THINK YOU'D BE THIS FICKLE.
ZU (SIP)
ズ...
YOU CAN SAY THAT, BUT, NATSUNAGI, LIKE I SAID...
...YOU'RE NOT THE ONE WHO WANTS TO MEET X.

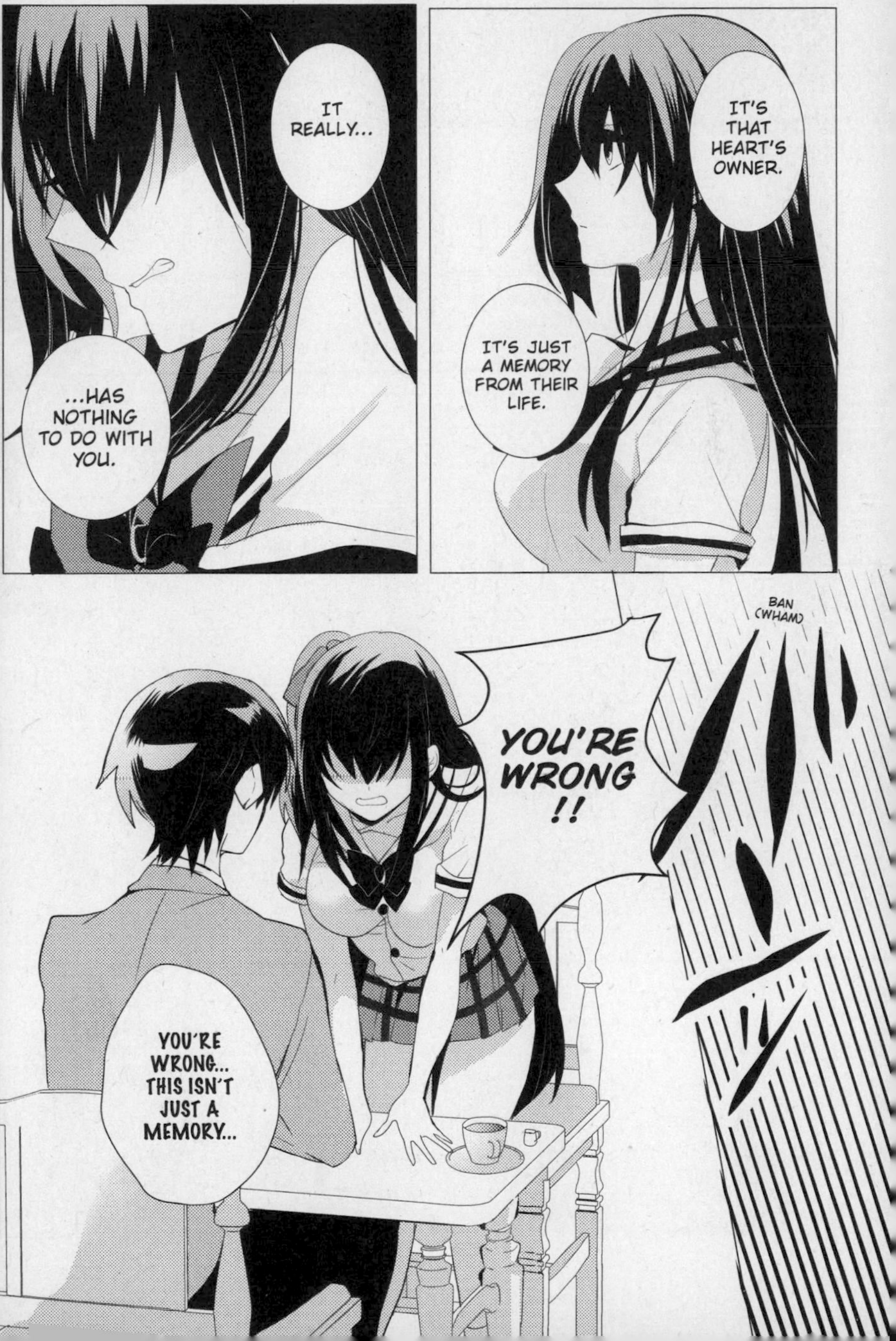
IT'S THAT HEART'S OWNER.
IT'S JUST A MEMORY FROM THEIR LIFE.
IT REALLY...
...HAS NOTHING TO DO WITH YOU.
BAN (WHAM)
YOU'RE WRONG !!
YOU'RE WRONG... THIS ISN'T JUST A MEMORY...

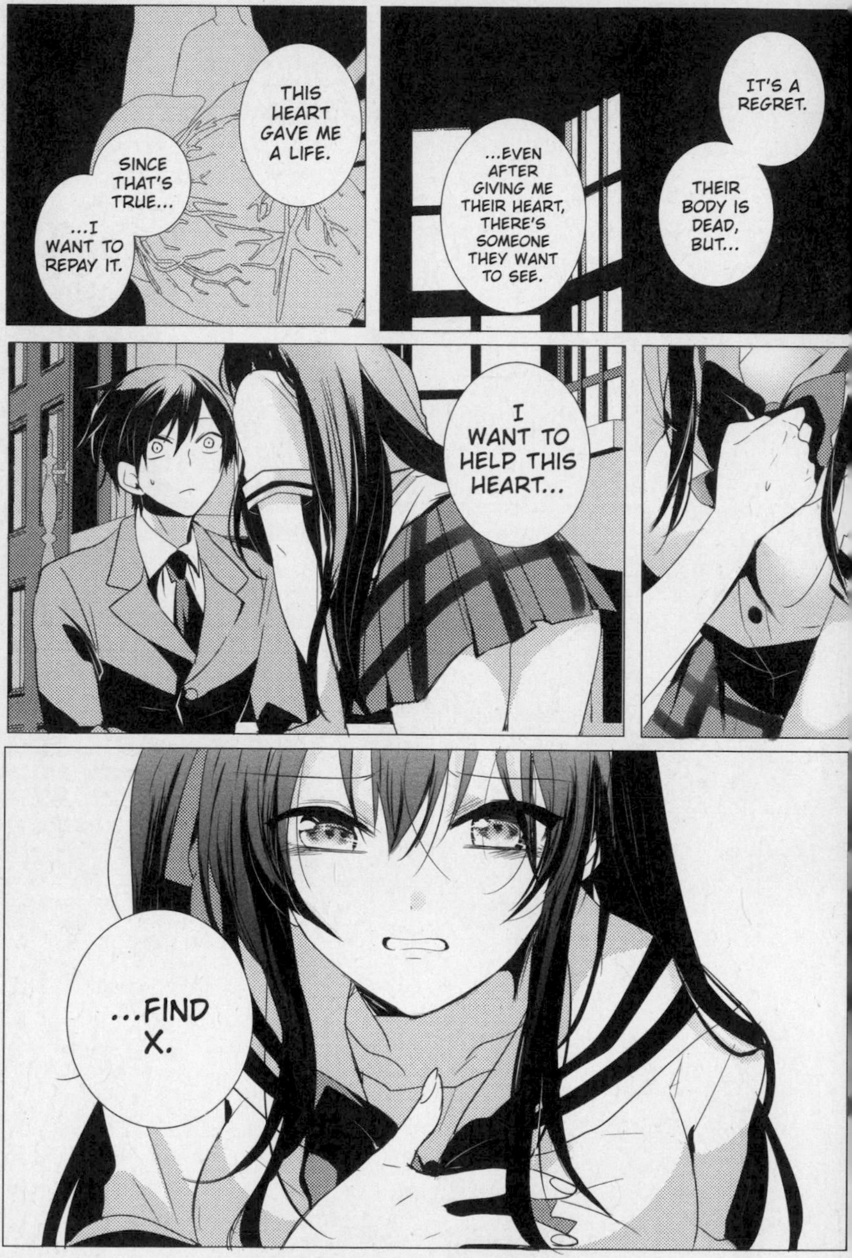
IT'S A REGRET.
THEIR BODY IS DEAD, BUT...
...EVEN AFTER GIVING ME THEIR HEART, THERE'S SOMEONE THEY WANT TO SEE.
THIS HEART GAVE ME A LIFE.
SINCE THAT'S TRUE...
...I WANT TO REPAY IT.
I WANT TO HELP THIS HEART...
...FIND X.

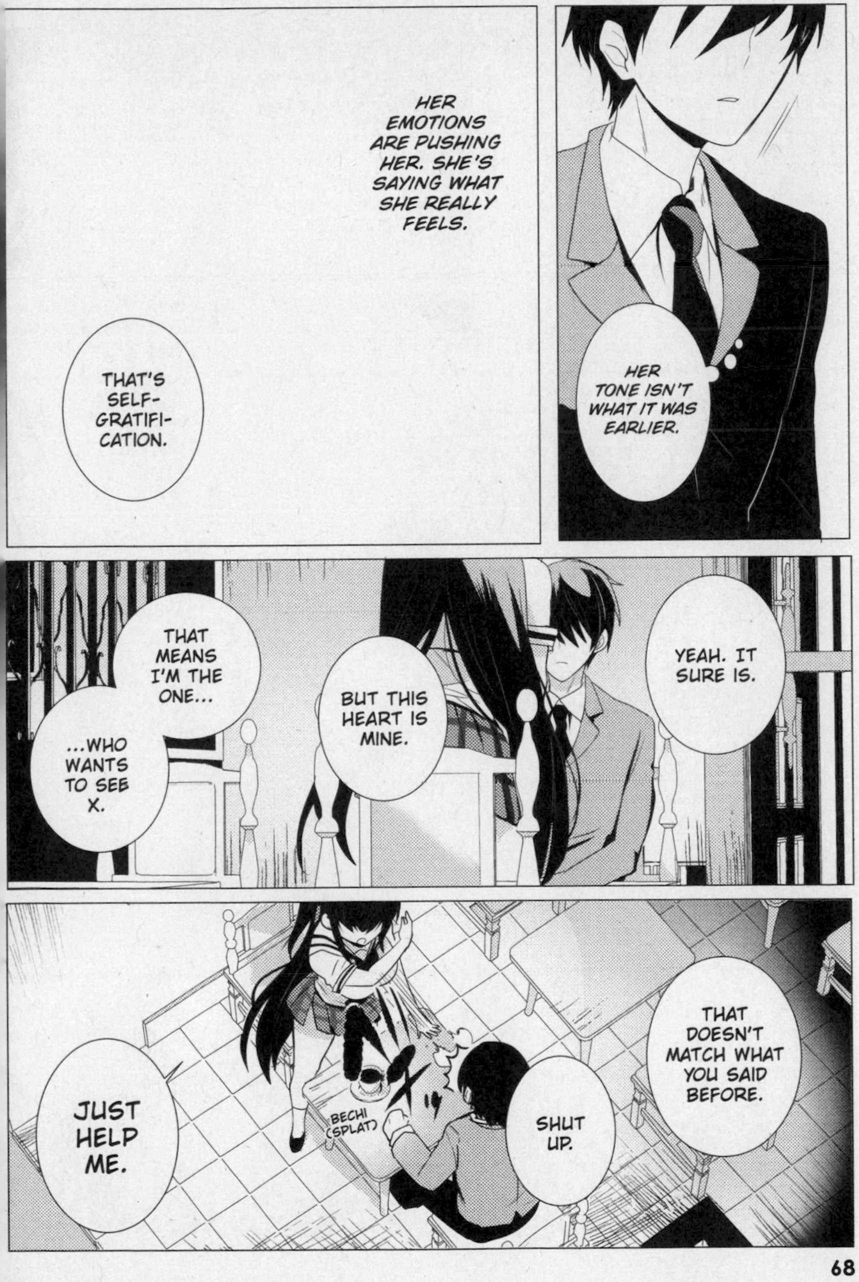
HER TONE ISN'T WHAT IT WAS EARLIER.
HER EMOTIONS ARE PUSHING HER. SHE'S SAYING WHAT SHE REALLY FEELS.
THAT'S SELF-GRATIFI-CATION.
YEAH. IT SURE IS.
BUT THIS HEART IS MINE.
THAT MEANS I'M THE ONE...
...WHO WANTS TO SEE X.
THAT DOESN'T MATCH WHAT YOU SAID BEFORE.
SHUT UP.
BECHI (SPLAT)
JUST HELP ME.

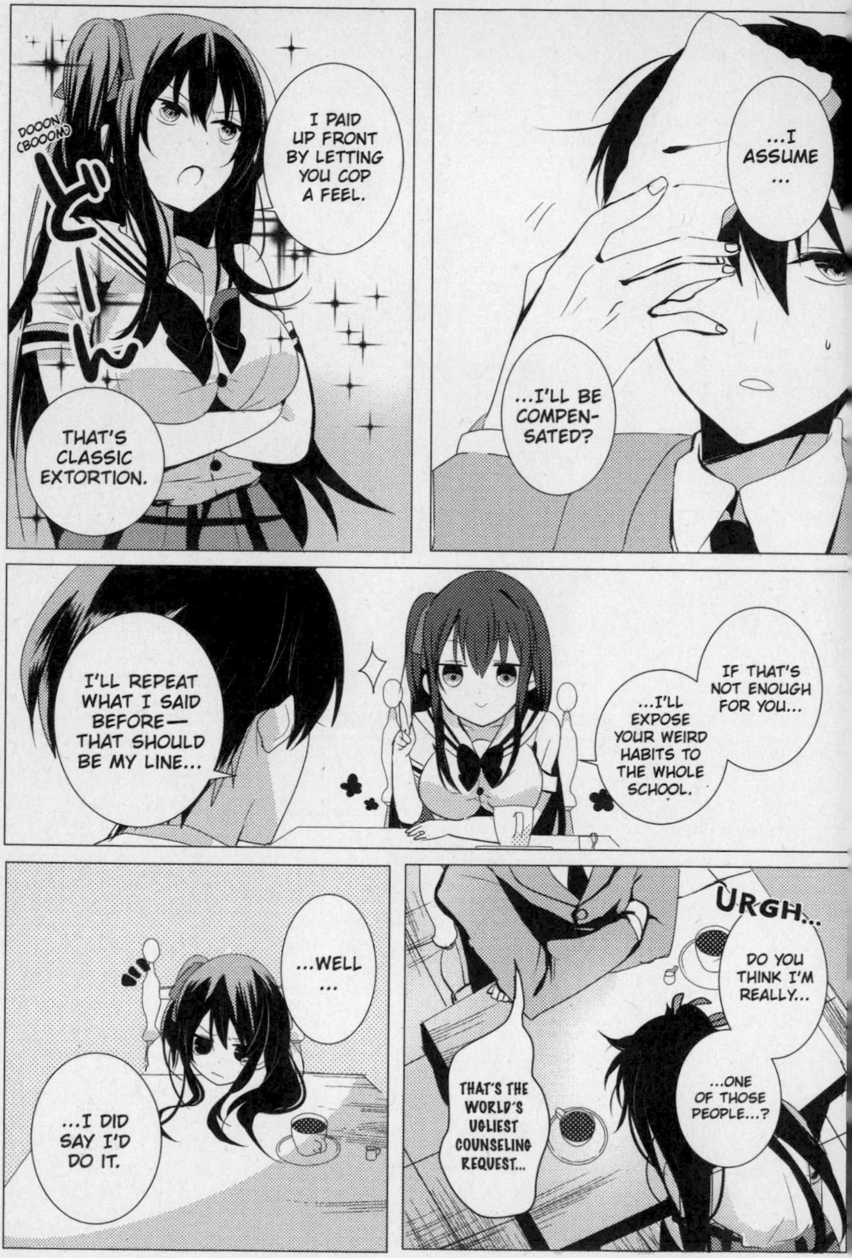
...I ASSUME ...
...I'LL BE COMPENSATED?
I PAID UP FRONT BY LETTING YOU COP A FEEL.
DOOON (BOOOON)
THAT'S CLASSIC EXTORTION.
IF THAT'S NOT ENOUGH FOR YOU...
...I'LL EXPOSE YOUR WEIRD HABITS TO THE WHOLE SCHOOL.
I'LL REPEAT WHAT I SAID BEFORE—THAT SHOULD BE MY LINE...
URGH...
DO YOU THINK I'M REALLY...
...ONE OF THOSE PEOPLE...?
THAT'S THE WORLD'S UGLIEST COUNSELING REQUEST...
...WELL ...
...I DID SAY I'D DO IT.

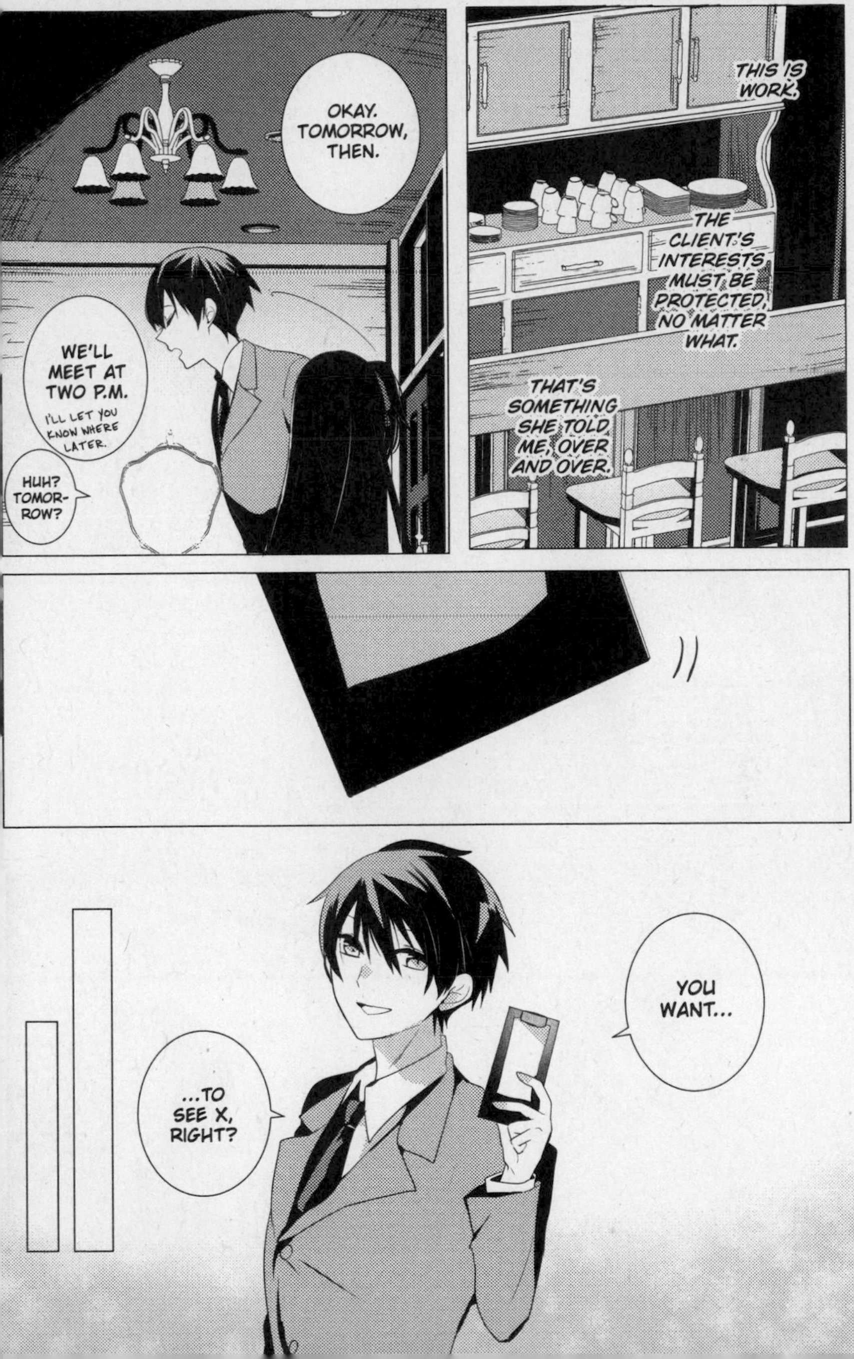
THIS IS WORK.
THE CLIENT'S INTERESTS MUST BE PROTECTED, NO MATTER WHAT.
THAT'S SOMETHING SHE TOLD ME, OVER AND OVER.
OKAY. TOMORROW, THEN.
WE'LL MEET AT TWO P.M.
I'LL LET YOU KNOW WHERE LATER.
HUH? TOMORROW?
YOU WANT...
...TO SEE X, RIGHT?

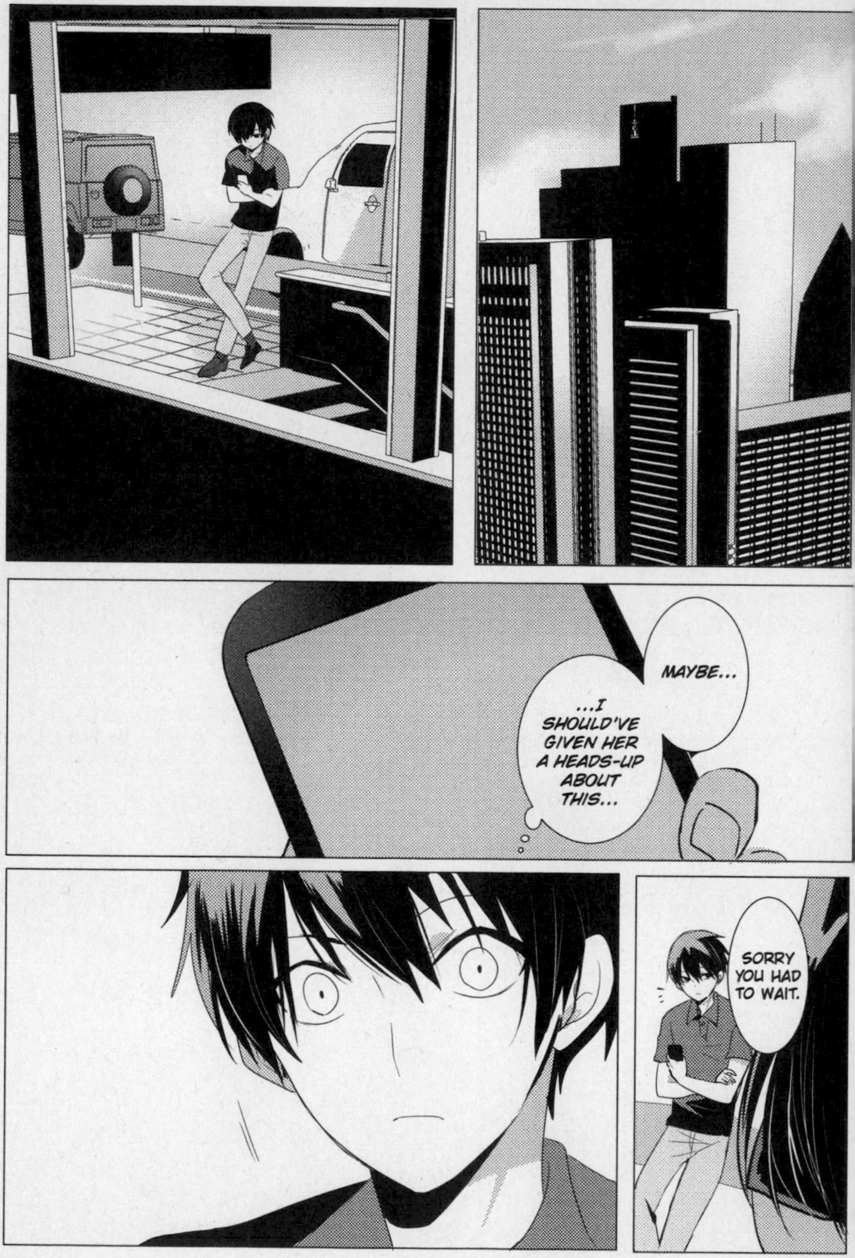
MAYBE...
...I SHOULD'VE GIVEN HER A HEADS-UP ABOUT THIS...
SORRY YOU HAD TO WAIT.

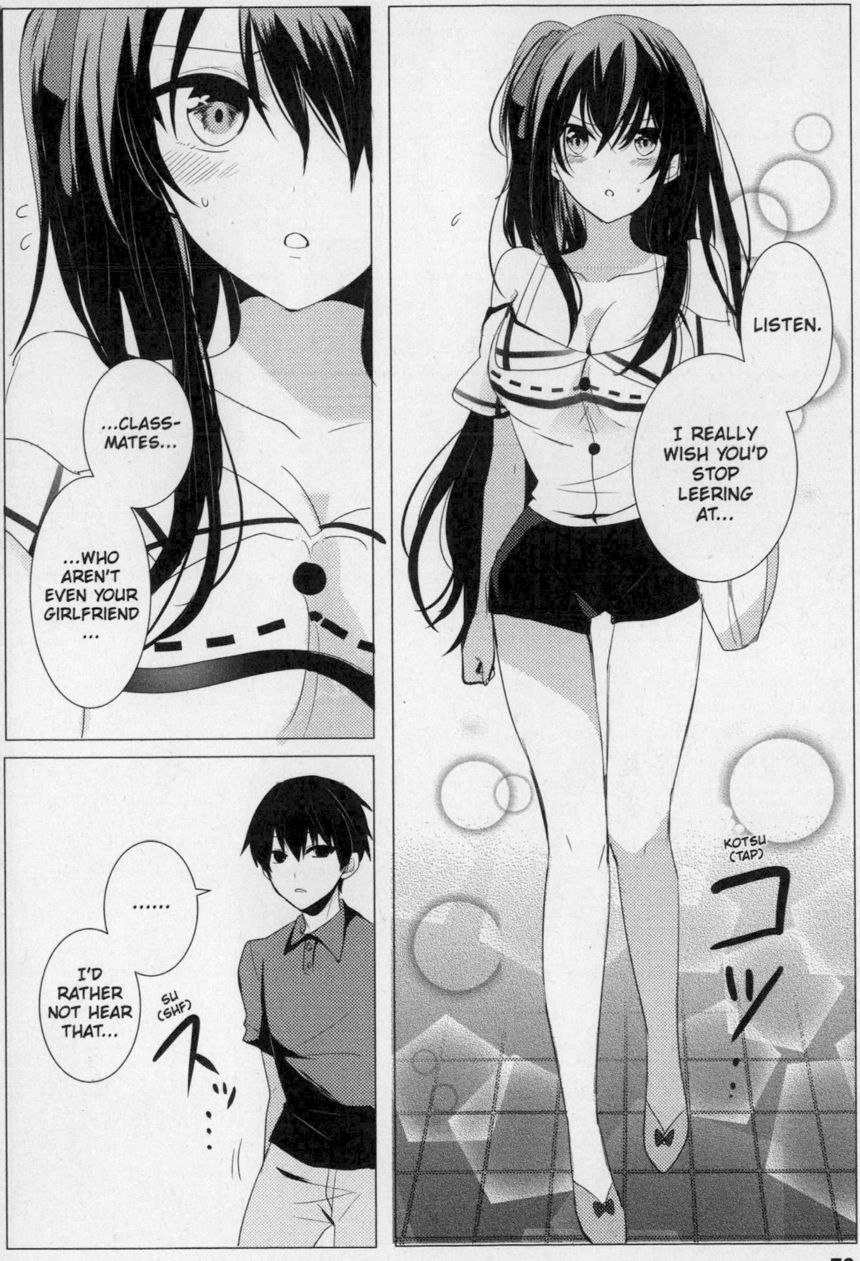
LISTEN.
I REALLY WISH YOU'D STOP LEERING AT...
KOTSU (TAP)
コッ...
...CLASS-MATES...
...WHO AREN'T EVEN YOUR GIRLFRIEND...
......
I'D RATHER NOT HEAR THAT...
SU (SHF)
スッ...

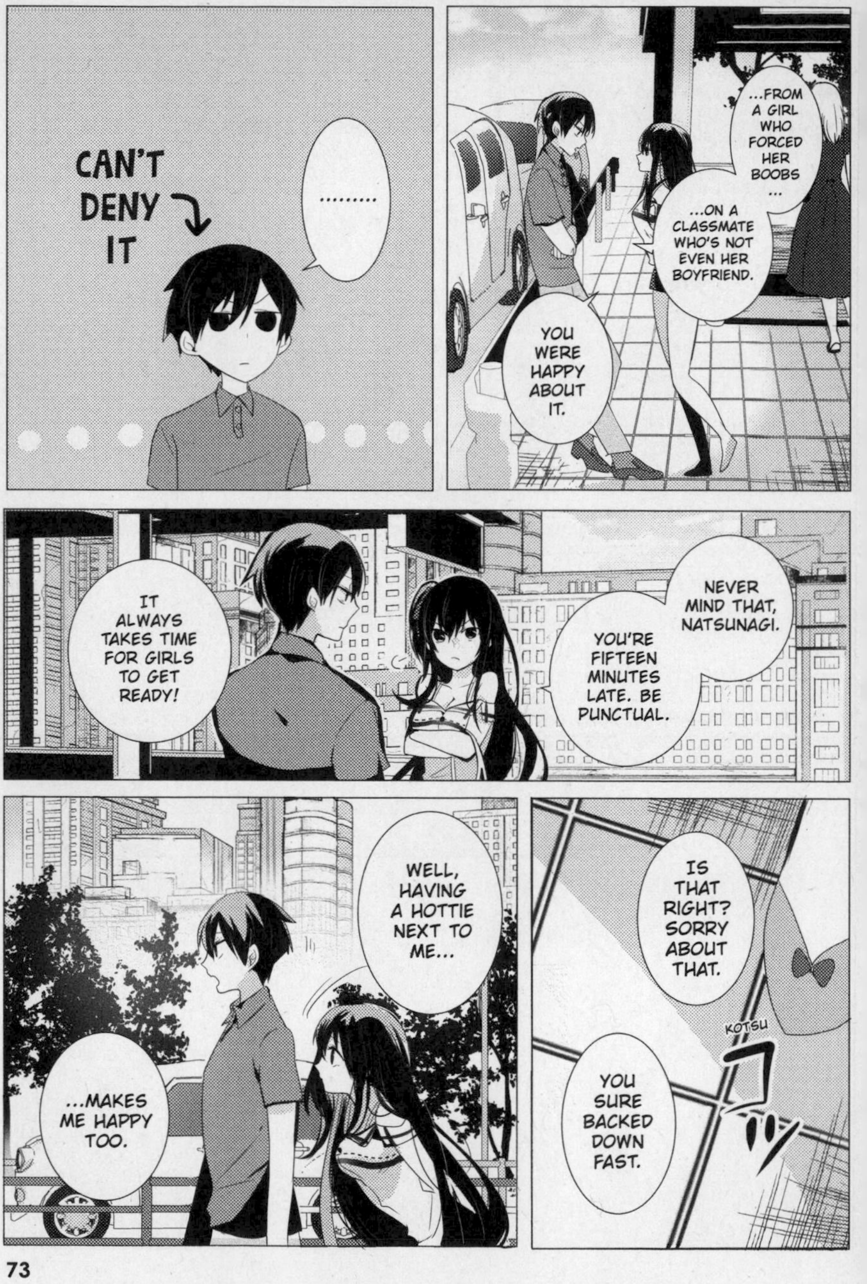
...FROM A GIRL WHO FORCED HER BOOBS...
...ON A CLASSMATE WHO'S NOT EVEN HER BOYFRIEND.
YOU WERE HAPPY ABOUT IT.
....
CAN'T DENY IT
NEVER MIND THAT, NATSUNAGI.
YOU'RE FIFTEEN MINUTES LATE. BE PUNCTUAL.
IT ALWAYS TAKES TIME FOR GIRLS TO GET READY!
IS THAT RIGHT? SORRY ABOUT THAT.
KOTSU
YOU SURE BACKED DOWN FAST.
WELL, HAVING A HOTTIE NEXT TO ME...
...MAKES ME HAPPY TOO.

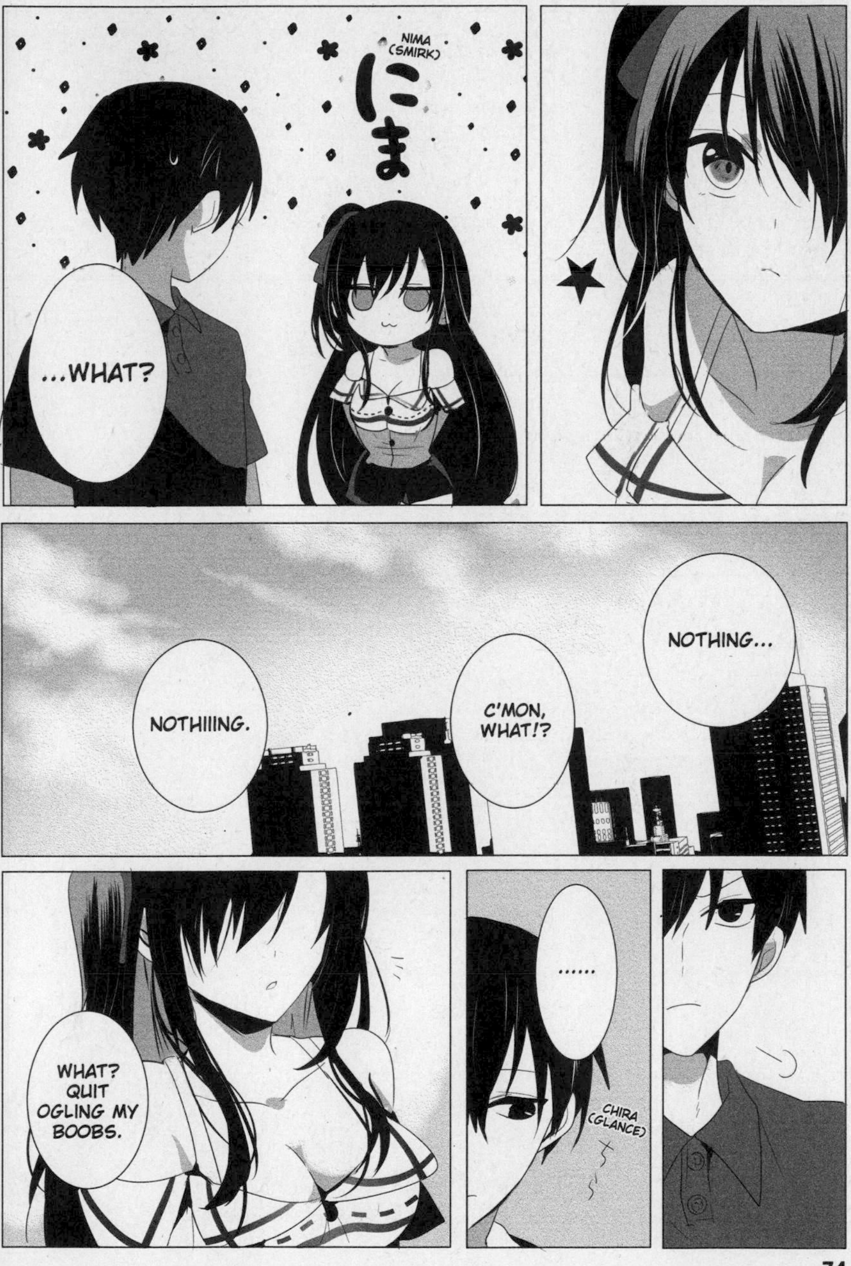
にま
NIMA (SMIRK)
...WHAT?
NOTHING...
C'MON, WHAT!?
NOTHIIING.
......
CHIRA (GLANCE)
WHAT? QUIT OGLING MY BOOBS.

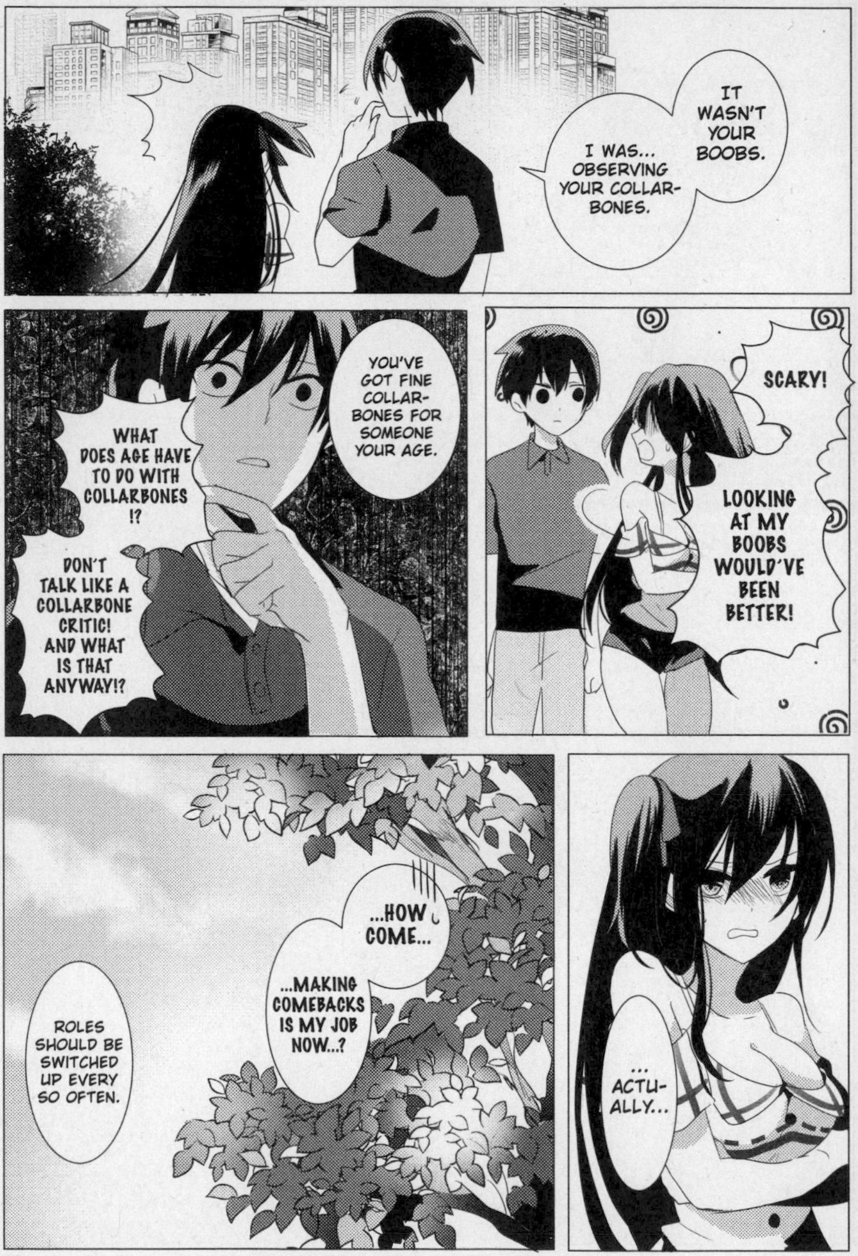
IT WASN'T YOUR BOOBS.
I WAS... OBSERVING YOUR COLLAR-BONES.
SCARY!
LOOKING AT MY BOOBS WOULD'VE BEEN BETTER!
YOU'VE GOT FINE COLLAR-BONES FOR SOMEONE YOUR AGE.
WHAT DOES AGE HAVE TO DO WITH COLLARBONES !?
DON'T TALK LIKE A COLLARBONE CRITIC! AND WHAT IS THAT ANYWAY!?
... ACTU-ALLY...
...HOW COME...
...MAKING COMEBACKS IS MY JOB NOW...?
ROLES SHOULD BE SWITCHED UP EVERY SO OFTEN.

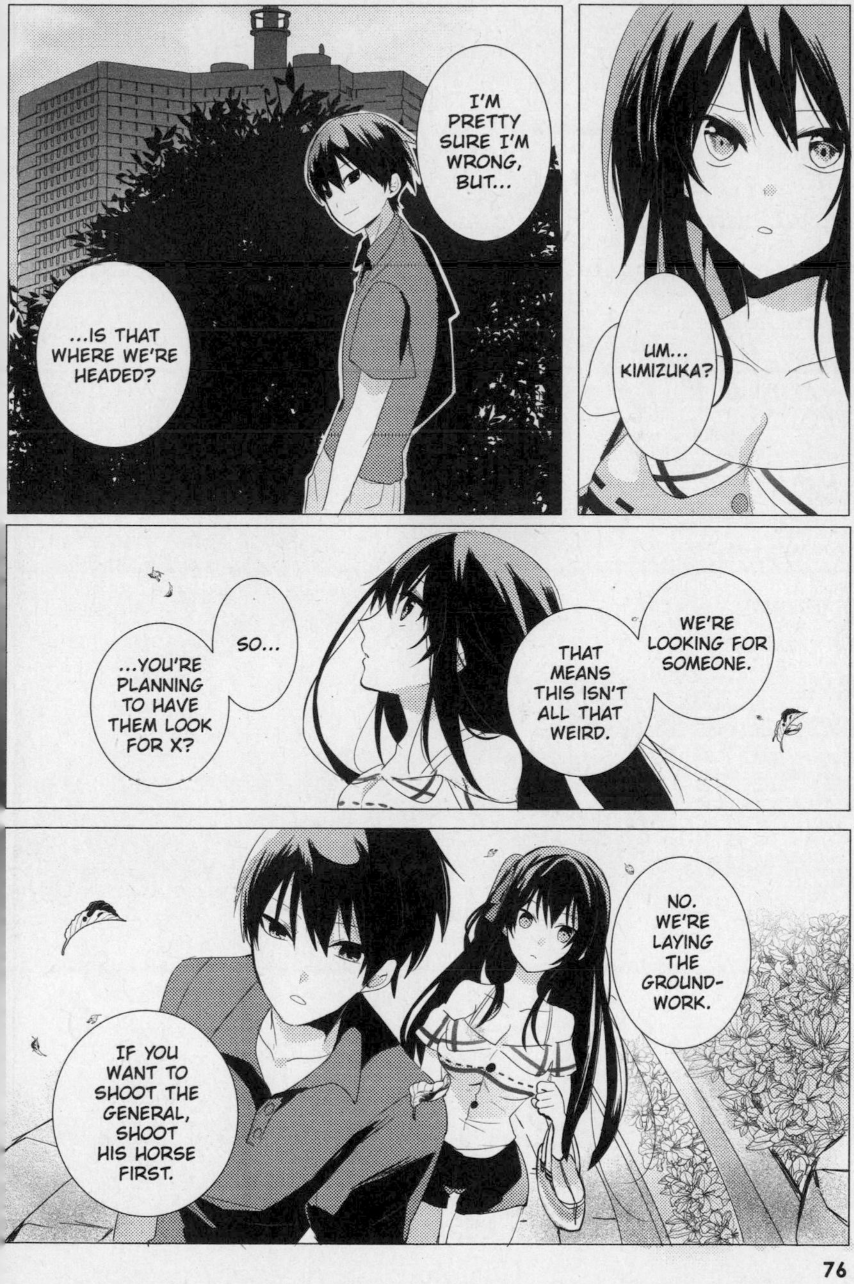
UM... KIMIZUKA?
I'M PRETTY SURE I'M WRONG, BUT...
...IS THAT WHERE WE'RE HEADED?
WE'RE LOOKING FOR SOMEONE.
THAT MEANS THIS ISN'T ALL THAT WEIRD.
SO...
...YOU'RE PLANNING TO HAVE THEM LOOK FOR X?
NO. WE'RE LAYING THE GROUND-WORK.
IF YOU WANT TO SHOOT THE GENERAL, SHOOT HIS HORSE FIRST.

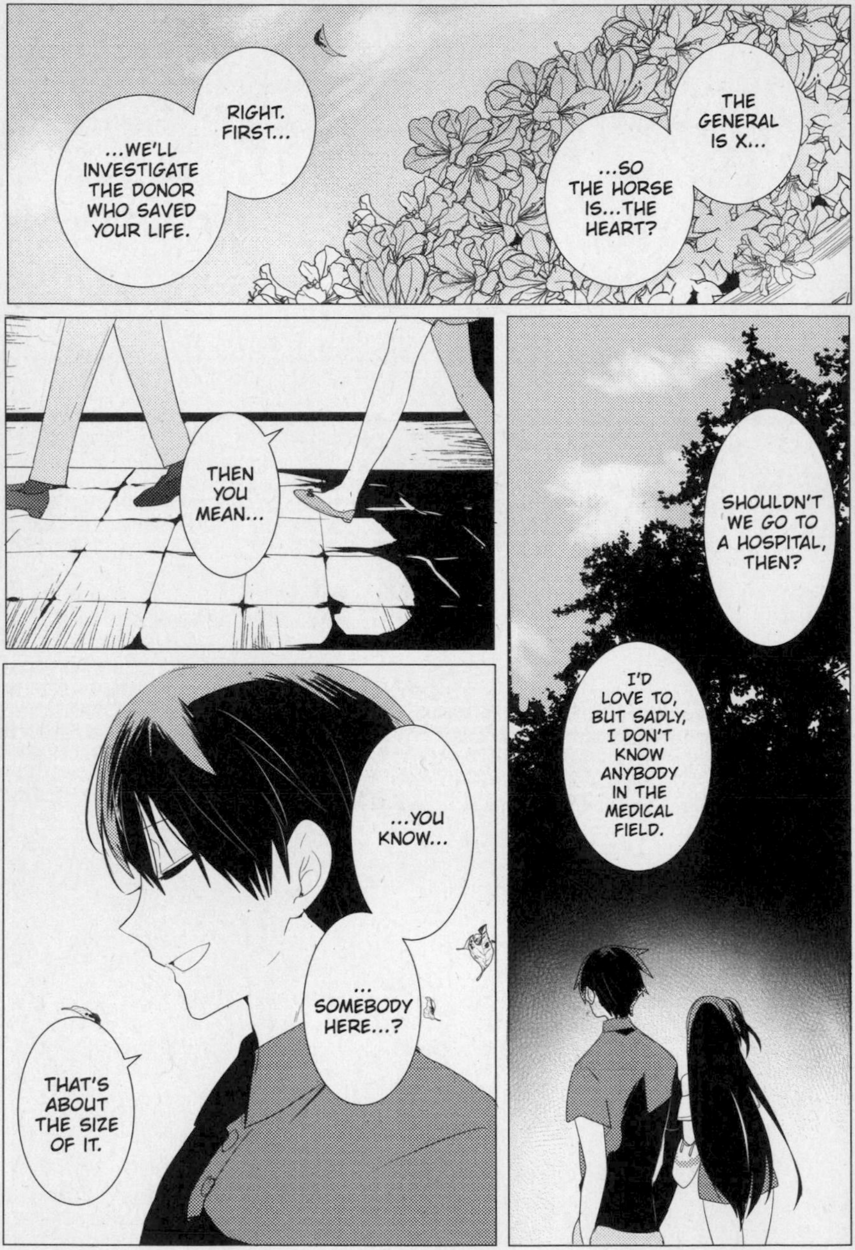
THE GENERAL IS X...
...SO THE HORSE IS...THE HEART?
RIGHT. FIRST...
...WE'LL INVESTIGATE THE DONOR WHO SAVED YOUR LIFE.
SHOULDN'T WE GO TO A HOSPITAL, THEN?
I'D LOVE TO, BUT SADLY, I DON'T KNOW ANYBODY IN THE MEDICAL FIELD.
THEN YOU MEAN...
...YOU KNOW...
...SOMEBODY HERE...?
THAT'S ABOUT THE SIZE OF IT.

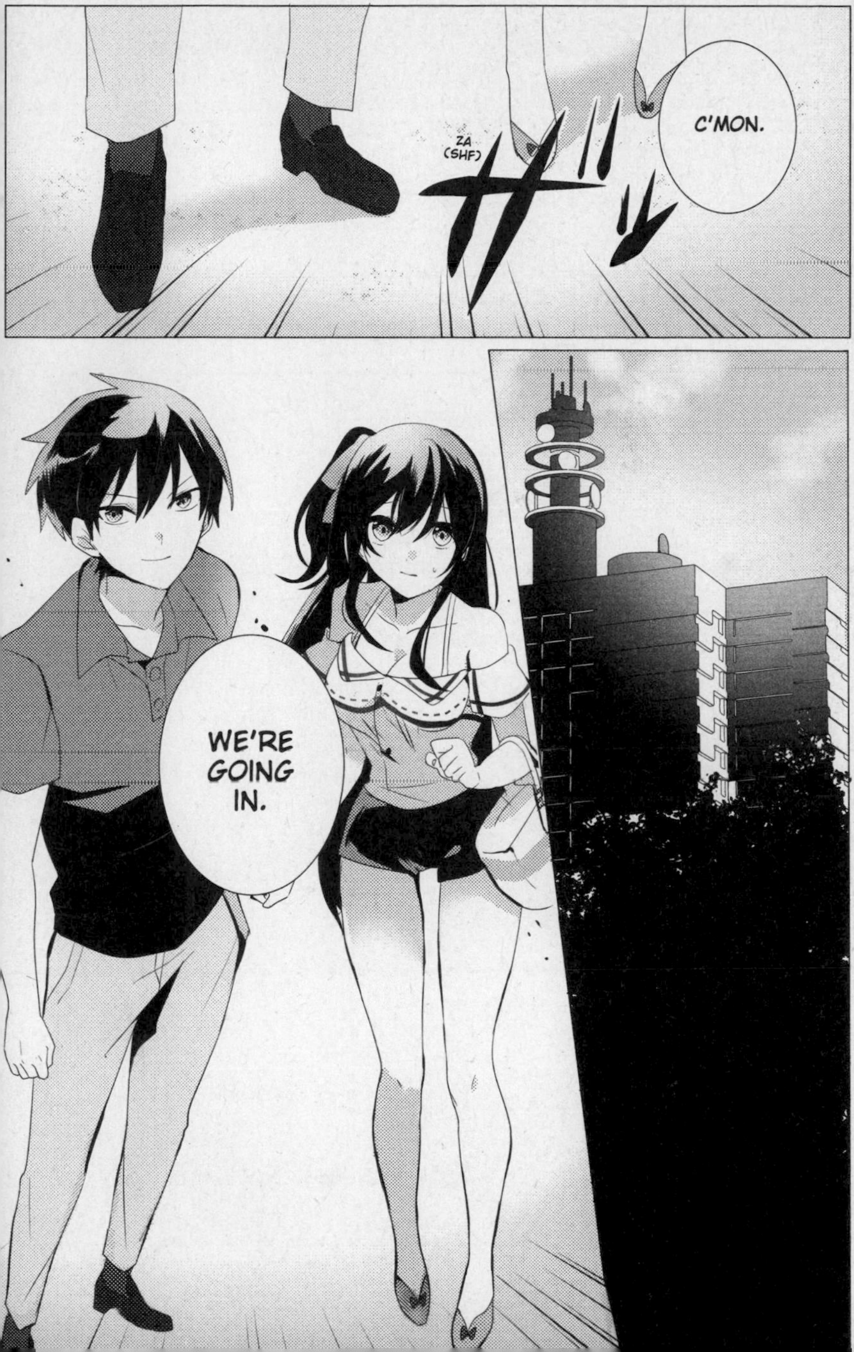
C'MON.
ZA (SHF)
ザッ
WE'RE GOING IN.

The Detective Is Already Dead

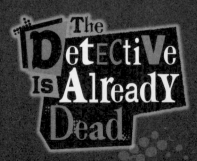

The Detective Is Already Dead

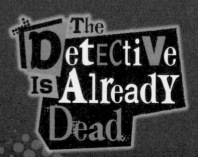

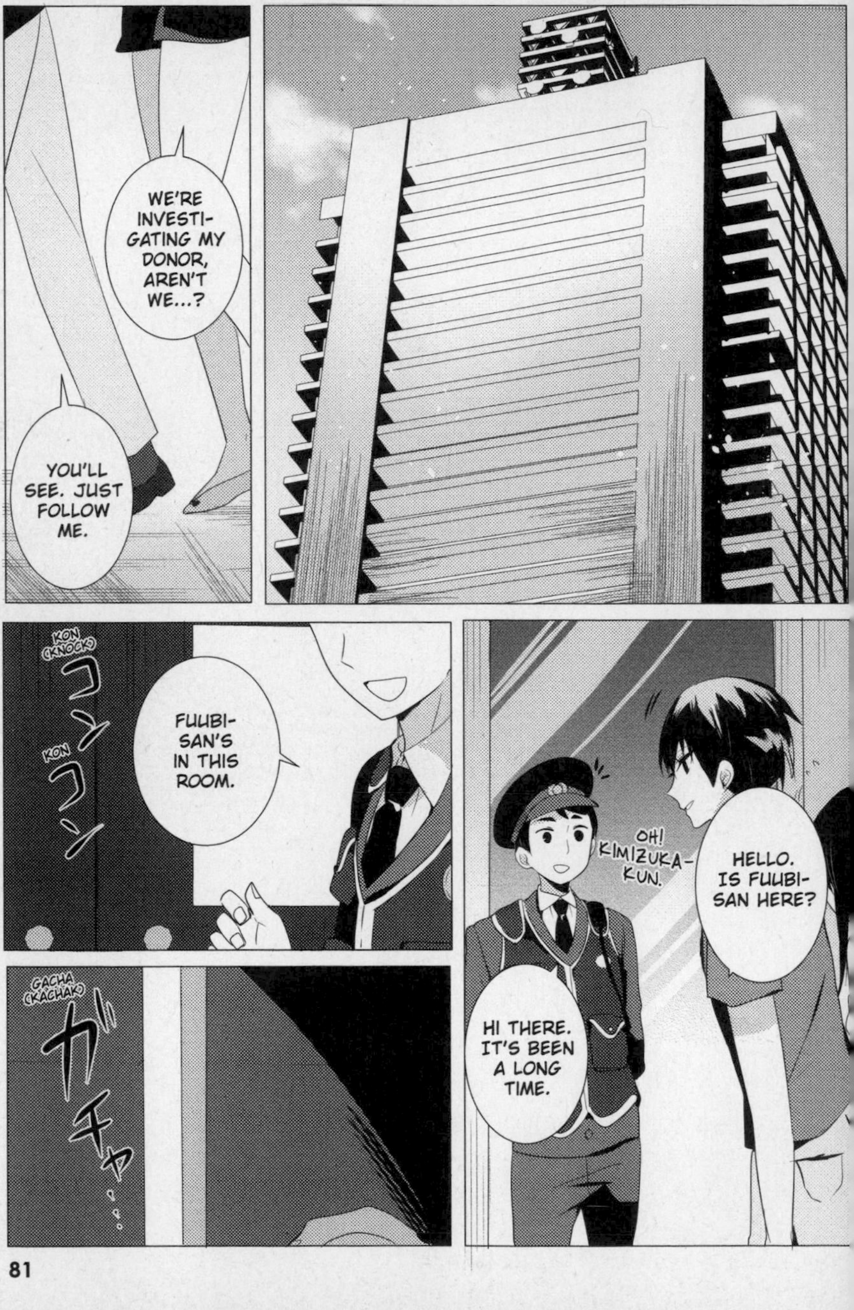
WE'RE INVESTIGATING MY DONOR, AREN'T WE...?
YOU'LL SEE. JUST FOLLOW ME.
HELLO. IS FUUBI-SAN HERE?
OH! KIMIZUKA-KUN.
HI THERE. IT'S BEEN A LONG TIME.
KON (KNOCK)
コン
KON
コン
FUUBI-SAN'S IN THIS ROOM.
GACHA (KACHAK)
ガチャ

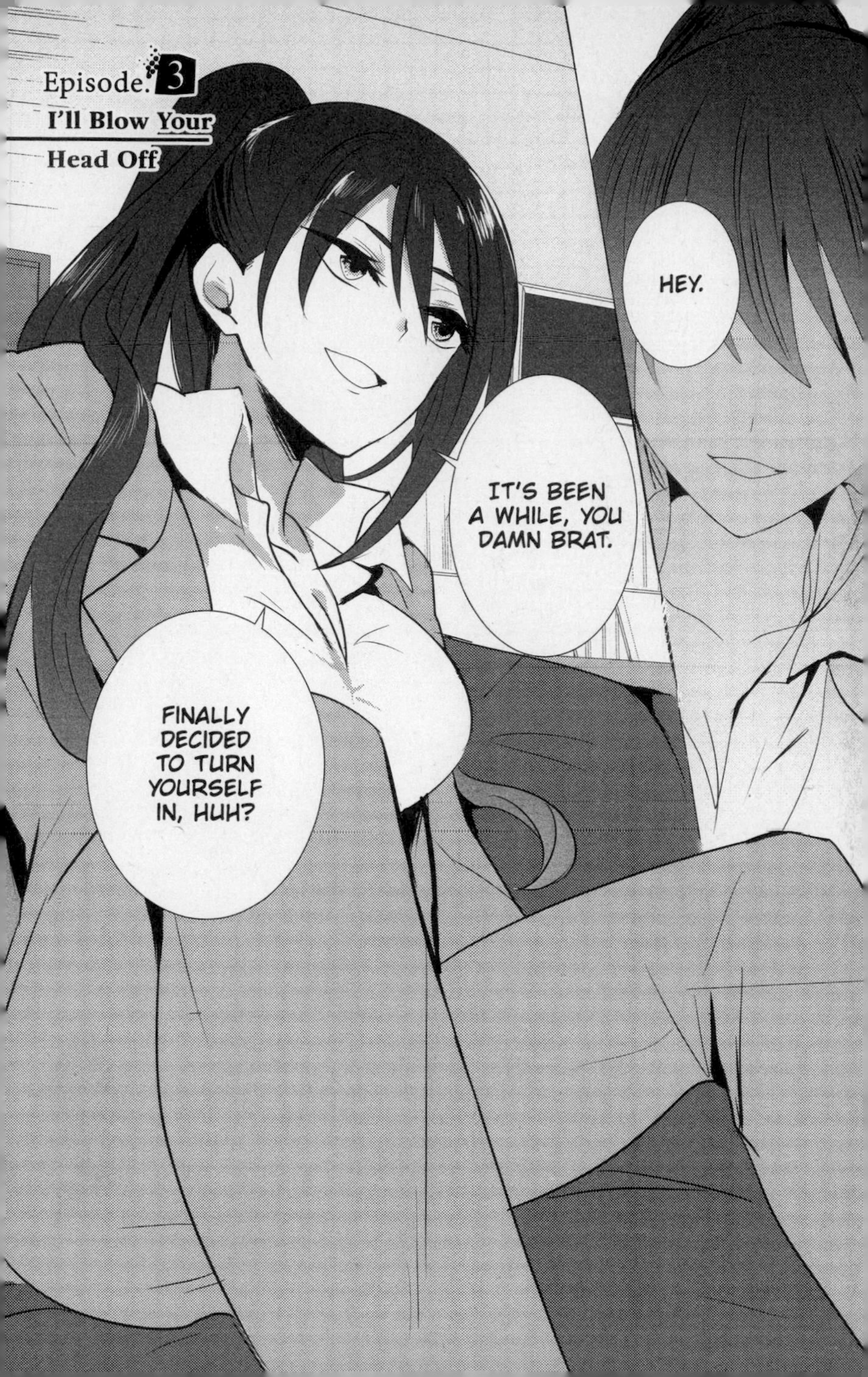
Episode. 3
I'll Blow Your Head Off
HEY.
IT'S BEEN A WHILE, YOU DAMN BRAT.
FINALLY DECIDED TO TURN YOURSELF IN, HUH?

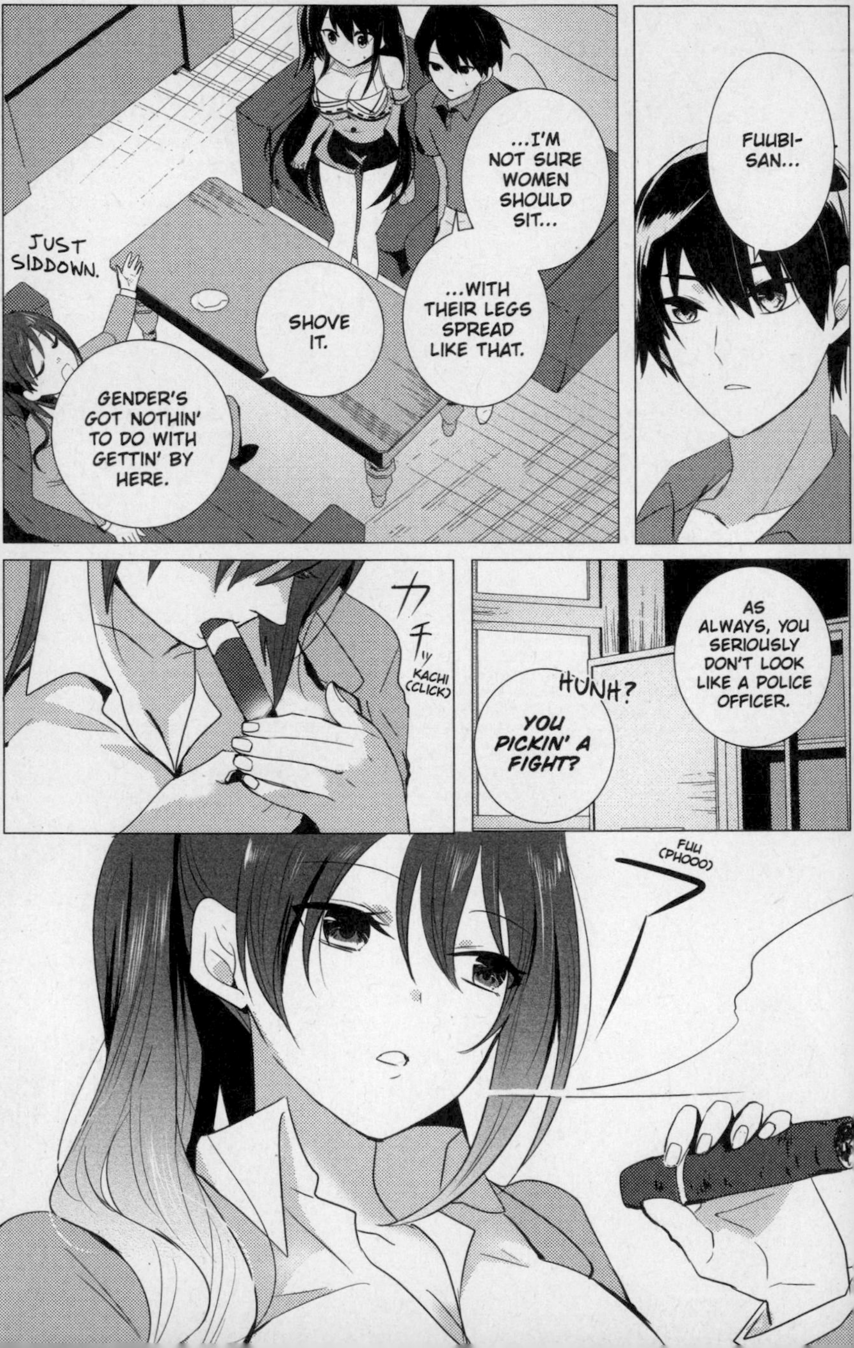
FUUBI-SAN...
...I'M NOT SURE WOMEN SHOULD SIT...
...WITH THEIR LEGS SPREAD LIKE THAT.
SHOVE IT.
GENDER'S GOT NOTHIN' TO DO WITH GETTIN' BY HERE.
JUST SIDDOWN.
AS ALWAYS, YOU SERIOUSLY DON'T LOOK LIKE A POLICE OFFICER.
HUNH?
YOU PICKIN' A FIGHT?
カチッ
KACHI (CLICK)
FUU (PHOOO)

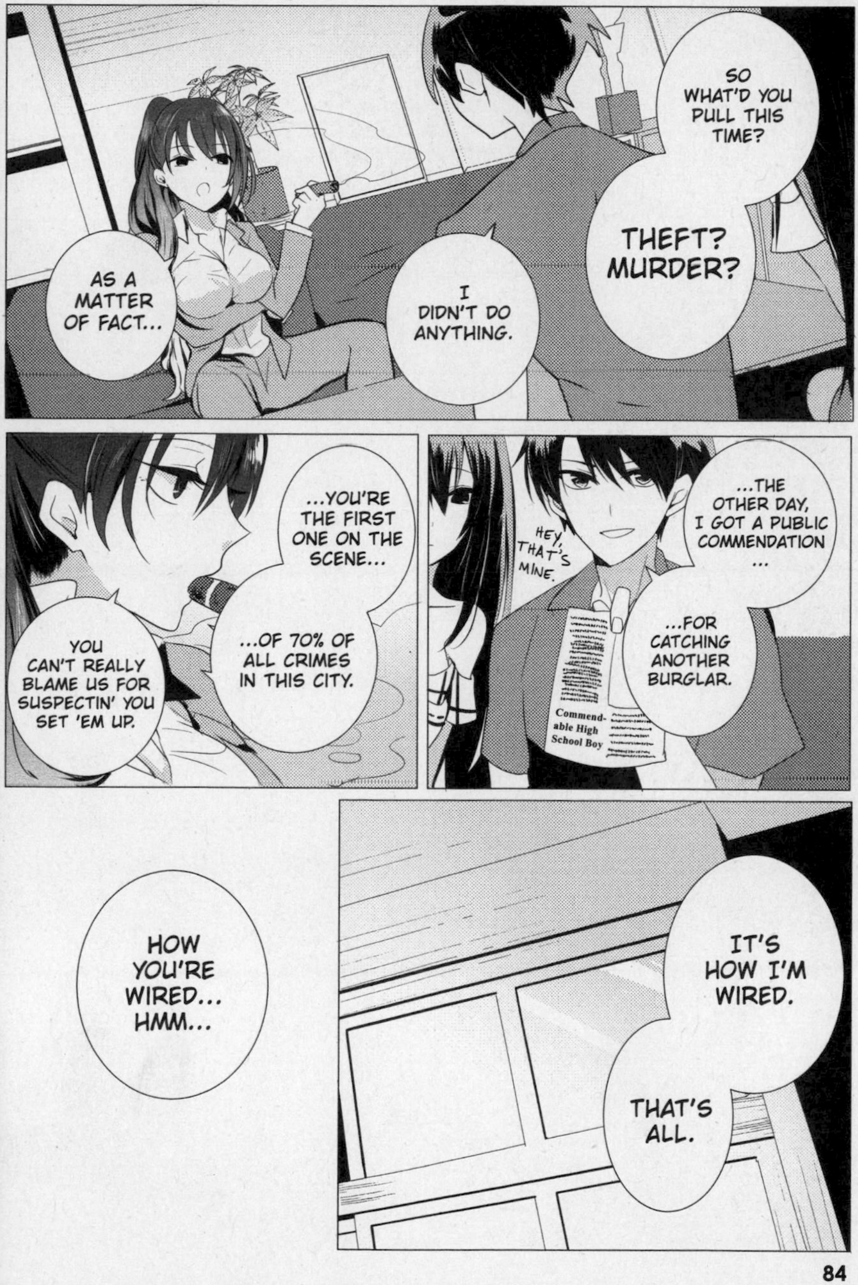
SO WHAT'D YOU PULL THIS TIME?
THEFT? MURDER?
I DIDN'T DO ANYTHING.
AS A MATTER OF FACT...
...THE OTHER DAY, I GOT A PUBLIC COMMENDATION ...
HEY, THAT'S MINE.
...FOR CATCHING ANOTHER BURGLAR.
Commendable High School Boy
...YOU'RE THE FIRST ONE ON THE SCENE...
...OF 70% OF ALL CRIMES IN THIS CITY.
YOU CAN'T REALLY BLAME US FOR SUSPECTIN' YOU SET 'EM UP.
IT'S HOW I'M WIRED.
THAT'S ALL.
HOW YOU'RE WIRED... HMM...

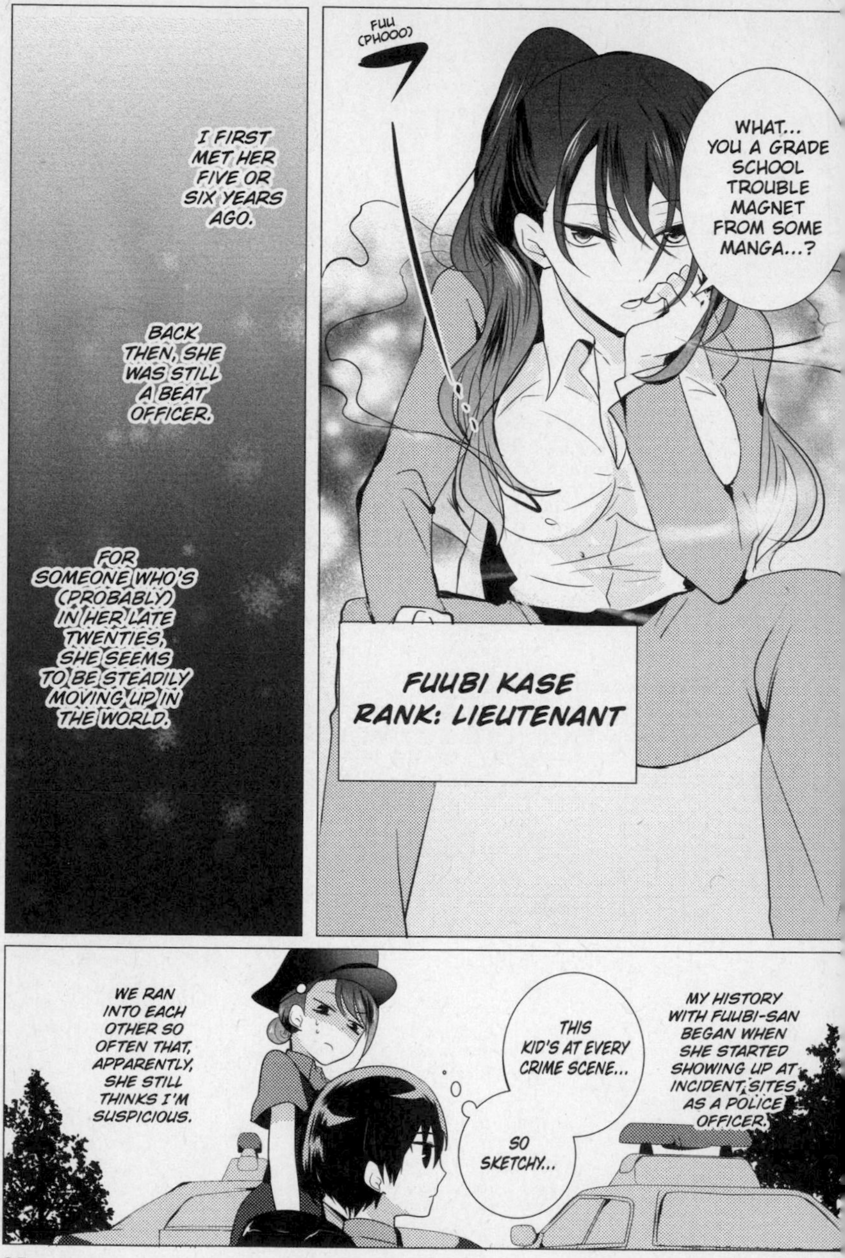
FUU (PHOOO)
WHAT... YOU A GRADE SCHOOL TROUBLE MAGNET FROM SOME MANGA...?
FUUBI KASE RANK: LIEUTENANT
I FIRST MET HER FIVE OR SIX YEARS AGO.
BACK THEN, SHE WAS STILL A BEAT OFFICER.
FOR SOMEONE WHO'S (PROBABLY) IN HER LATE TWENTIES, SHE SEEMS TO BE STEADILY MOVING UP IN THE WORLD.
MY HISTORY WITH FUUBI-SAN BEGAN WHEN SHE STARTED SHOWING UP AT INCIDENT SITES AS A POLICE OFFICER.
THIS KID'S AT EVERY CRIME SCENE...
SO SKETCHY...
WE RAN INTO EACH OTHER SO OFTEN THAT, APPARENTLY, SHE STILL THINKS I'M SUSPICIOUS.

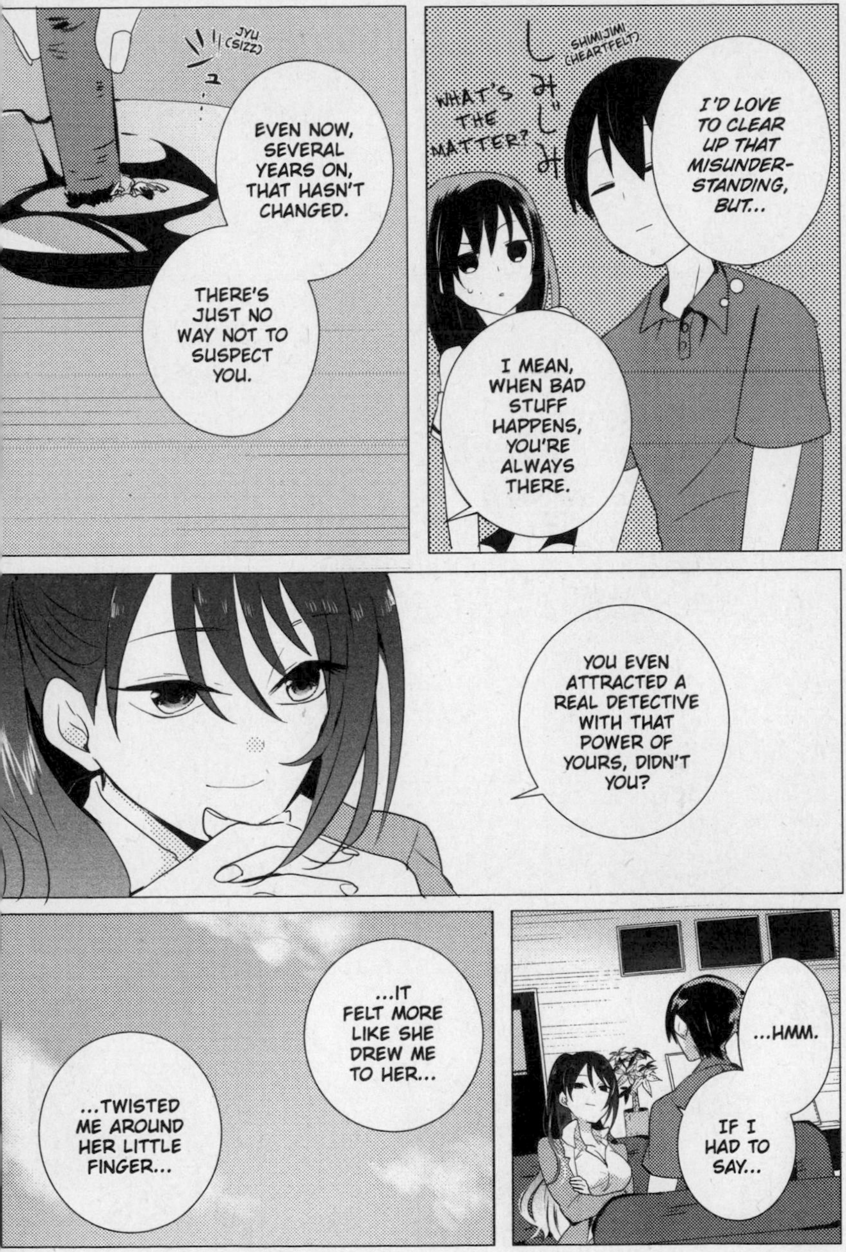
しみじみ
SHIMIJIMI (HEARTFELT)
I'D LOVE TO CLEAR UP THAT MISUNDERSTANDING, BUT...
WHAT'S THE MATTER?
I MEAN, WHEN BAD STUFF HAPPENS, YOU'RE ALWAYS THERE.
JYU (SIZZ)
EVEN NOW, SEVERAL YEARS ON, THAT HASN'T CHANGED.
THERE'S JUST NO WAY NOT TO SUSPECT YOU.
YOU EVEN ATTRACTED A REAL DETECTIVE WITH THAT POWER OF YOURS, DIDN'T YOU?
...HMM.
IF I HAD TO SAY...
...IT FELT MORE LIKE SHE DREW ME TO HER...
...TWISTED ME AROUND HER LITTLE FINGER...

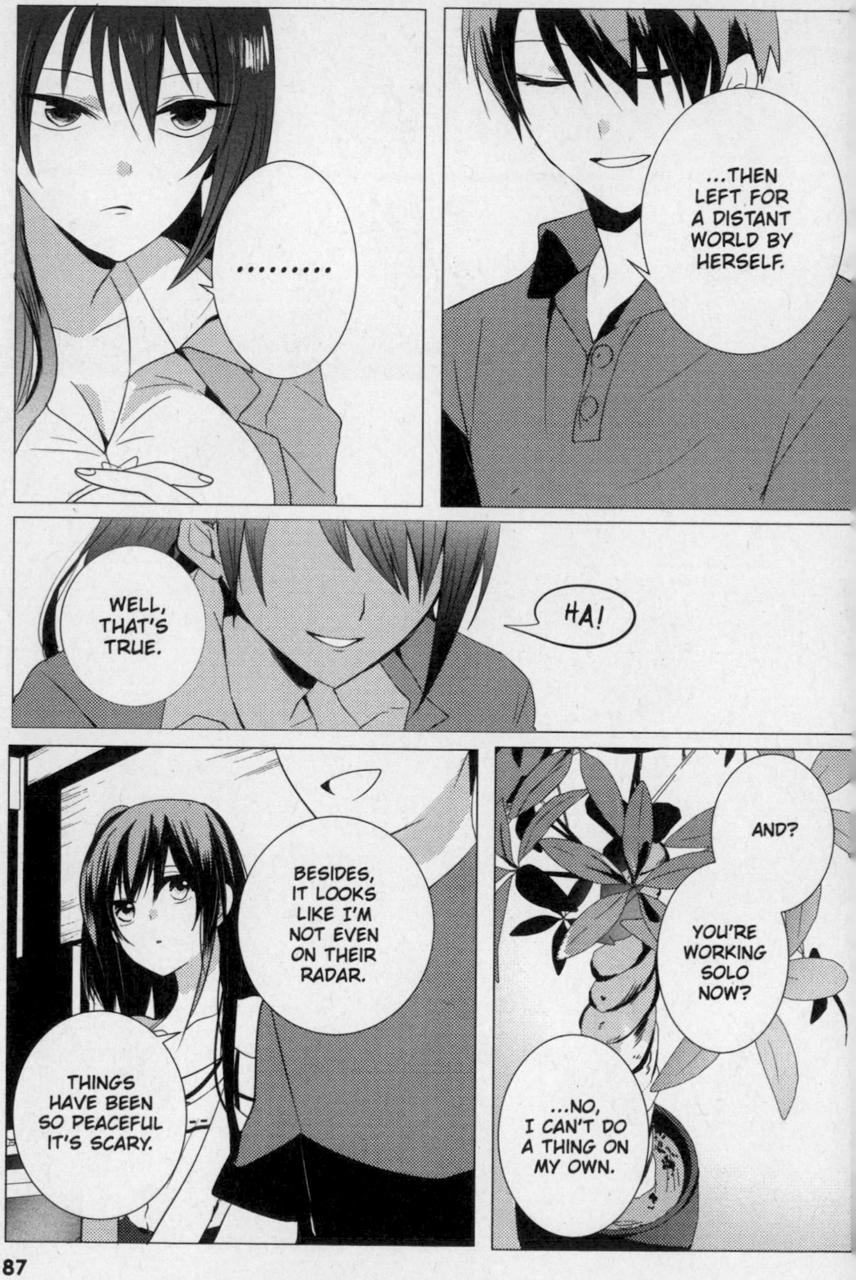
...THEN LEFT FOR A DISTANT WORLD BY HERSELF.
....
HA!
WELL, THAT'S TRUE.
AND?
YOU'RE WORKING SOLO NOW?
...NO, I CAN'T DO A THING ON MY OWN.
BESIDES, IT LOOKS LIKE I'M NOT EVEN ON THEIR RADAR.
THINGS HAVE BEEN SO PEACEFUL IT'S SCARY.

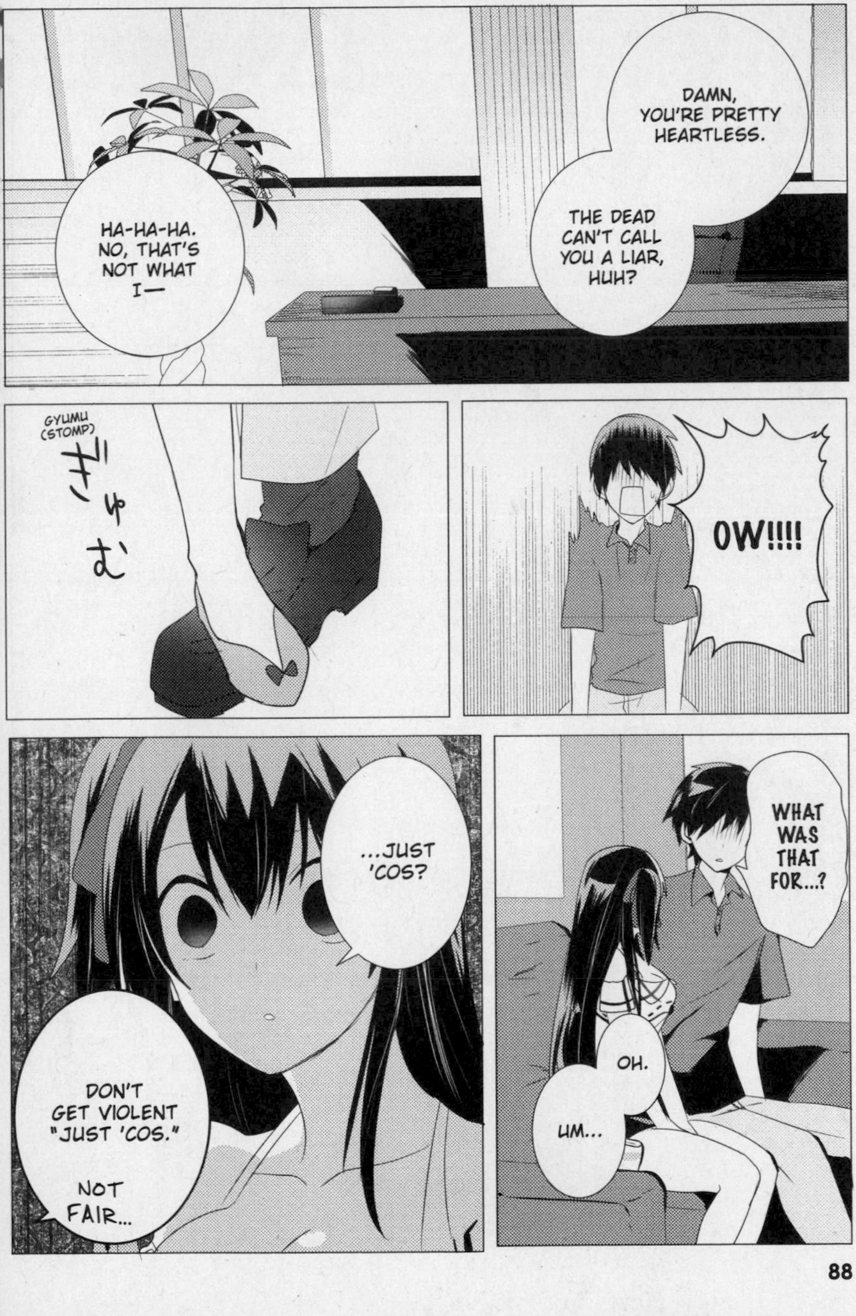
DAMN, YOU'RE PRETTY HEARTLESS.
THE DEAD CAN'T CALL YOU A LIAR, HUH?
HA-HA-HA. NO, THAT'S NOT WHAT I—
OW!!!!
GYUMU (STOMP)
ぎゅむ
WHAT WAS THAT FOR...?
OH.
UM...
...JUST 'COS?
DON'T GET VIOLENT "JUST 'COS."
NOT FAIR...

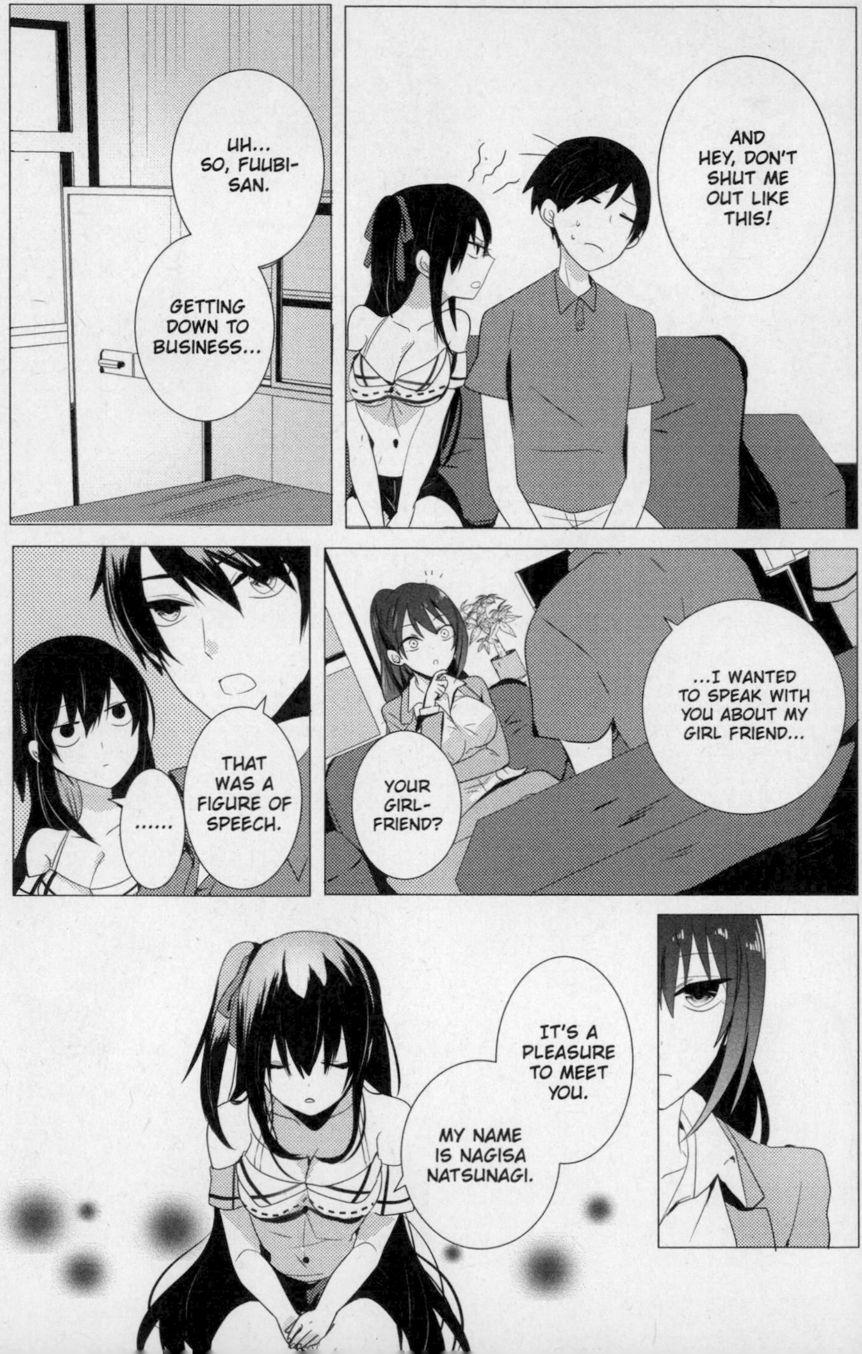
AND HEY, DON'T SHUT ME OUT LIKE THIS!
UH... SO, FUUBI-SAN.
GETTING DOWN TO BUSINESS...
...I WANTED TO SPEAK WITH YOU ABOUT MY GIRL FRIEND...
YOUR GIRL-FRIEND?
THAT WAS A FIGURE OF SPEECH.
......
IT'S A PLEASURE TO MEET YOU.
MY NAME IS NAGISA NATSUNAGI.

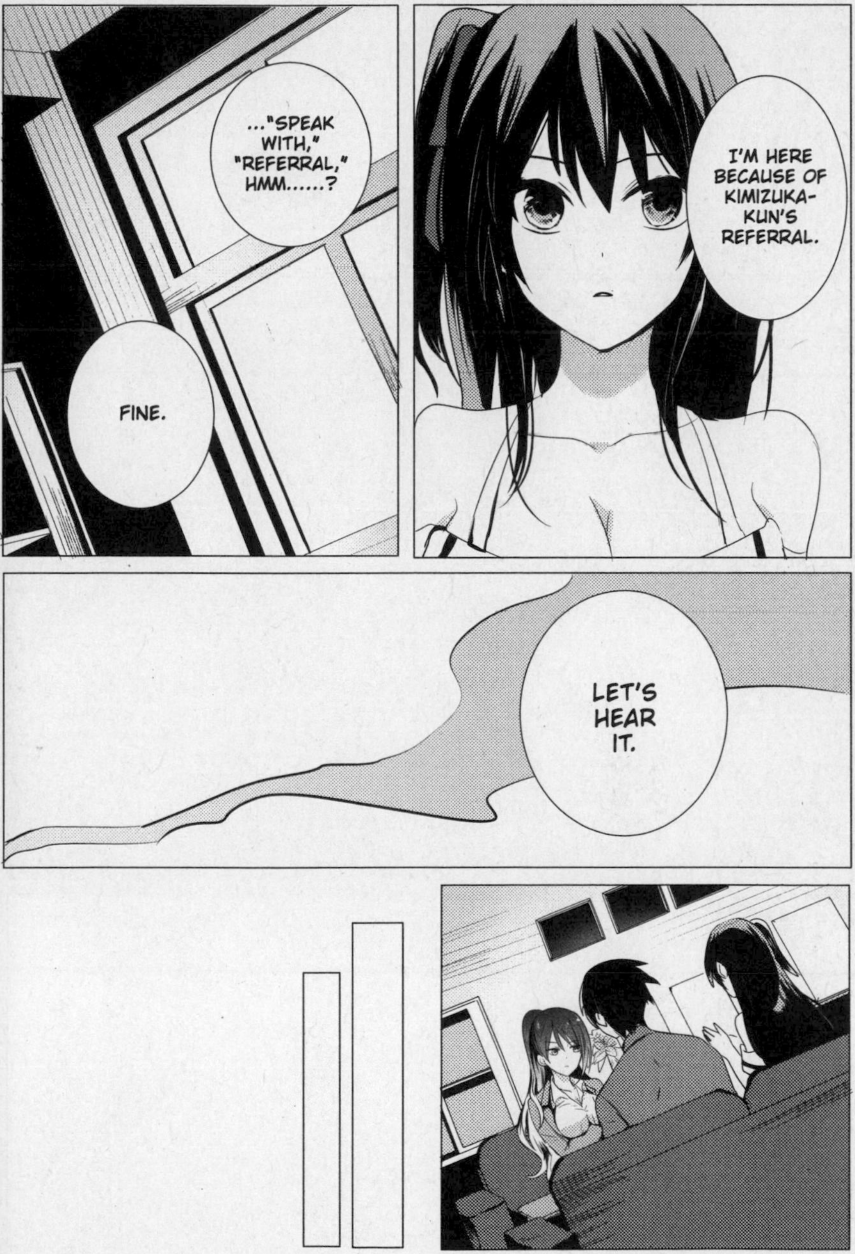
I'M HERE BECAUSE OF KIMIZUKA-KUN'S REFERRAL.
..."SPEAK WITH," "REFERRAL," HMM......?
FINE.
LET'S HEAR IT.

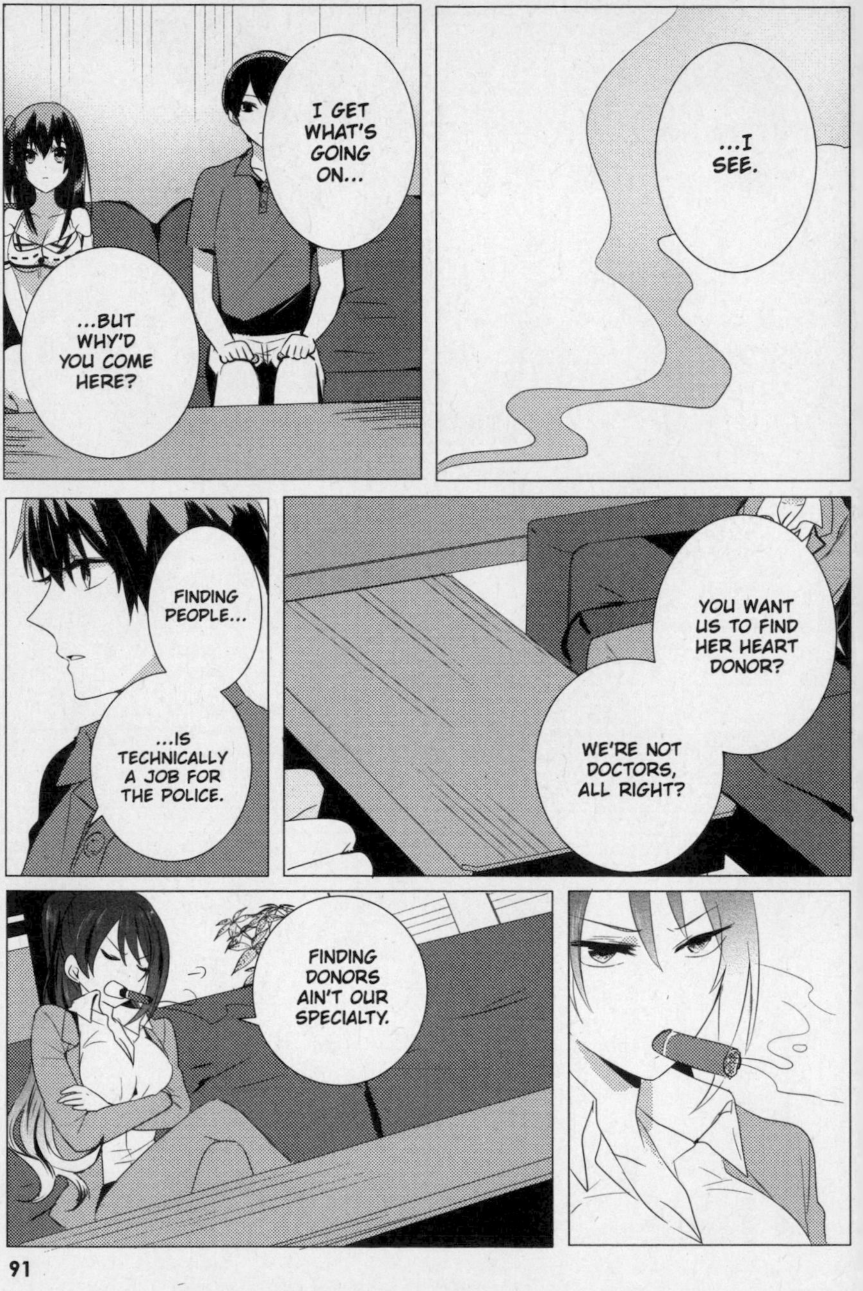
...I SEE.
I GET WHAT'S GOING ON...
...BUT WHY'D YOU COME HERE?
YOU WANT US TO FIND HER HEART DONOR?
WE'RE NOT DOCTORS, ALL RIGHT?
FINDING PEOPLE...
...IS TECHNICALLY A JOB FOR THE POLICE.
FINDING DONORS AIN'T OUR SPECIALTY.

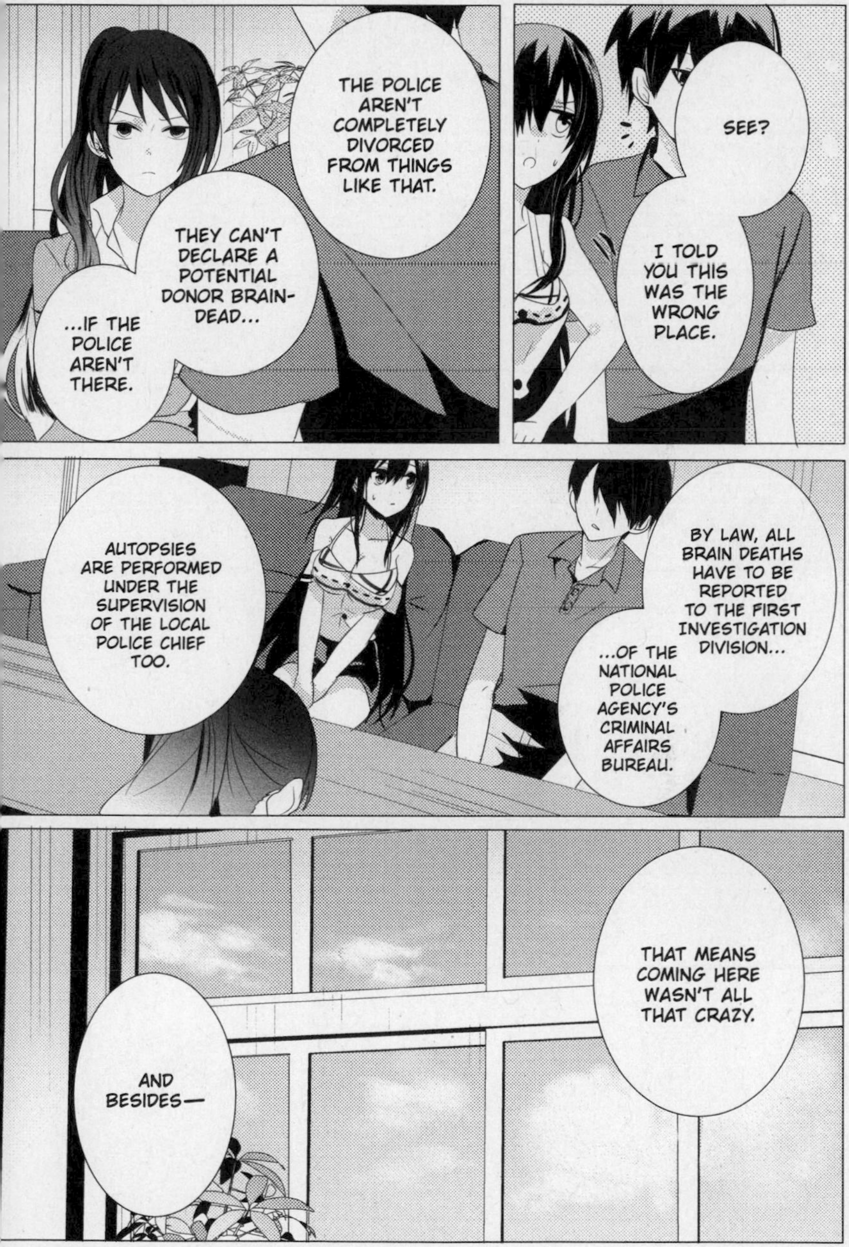
SEE?
I TOLD YOU THIS WAS THE WRONG PLACE.
THE POLICE AREN'T COMPLETELY DIVORCED FROM THINGS LIKE THAT.
THEY CAN'T DECLARE A POTENTIAL DONOR BRAIN-DEAD...
...IF THE POLICE AREN'T THERE.
BY LAW, ALL BRAIN DEATHS HAVE TO BE REPORTED TO THE FIRST INVESTIGATION DIVISION...
...OF THE NATIONAL POLICE AGENCY'S CRIMINAL AFFAIRS BUREAU.
AUTOPSIES ARE PERFORMED UNDER THE SUPERVISION OF THE LOCAL POLICE CHIEF TOO.
THAT MEANS COMING HERE WASN'T ALL THAT CRAZY.
AND BESIDES—

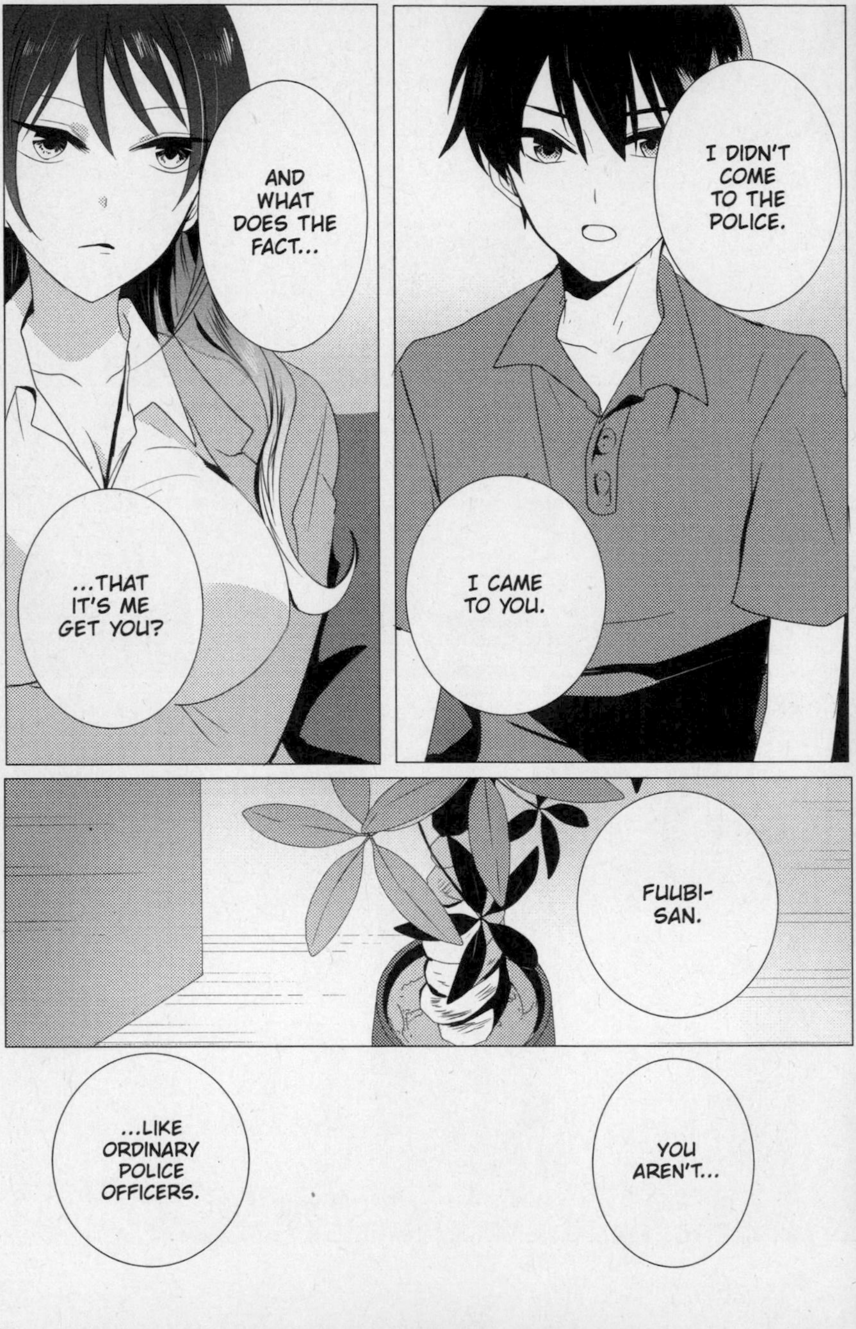
I DIDN'T COME TO THE POLICE.
I CAME TO YOU.
AND WHAT DOES THE FACT...
...THAT IT'S ME GET YOU?
FUUBI-SAN.
YOU AREN'T...
...LIKE ORDINARY POLICE OFFICERS.

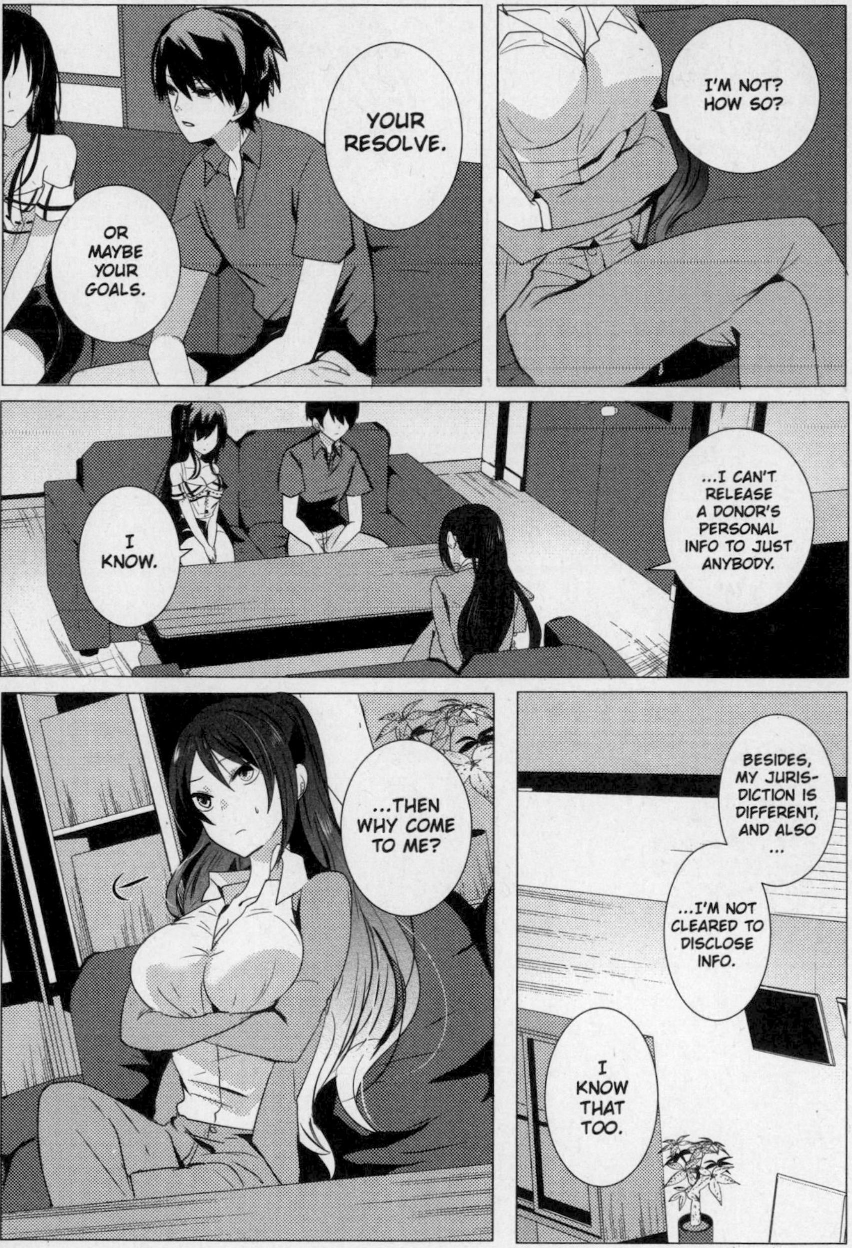
I'M NOT? HOW SO?
YOUR RESOLVE.
OR MAYBE YOUR GOALS.
...I CAN'T RELEASE A DONOR'S PERSONAL INFO TO JUST ANYBODY.
I KNOW.
BESIDES, MY JURIS-DICTION IS DIFFERENT, AND ALSO ...
...I'M NOT CLEARED TO DISCLOSE INFO.
I KNOW THAT TOO.
...THEN WHY COME TO ME?

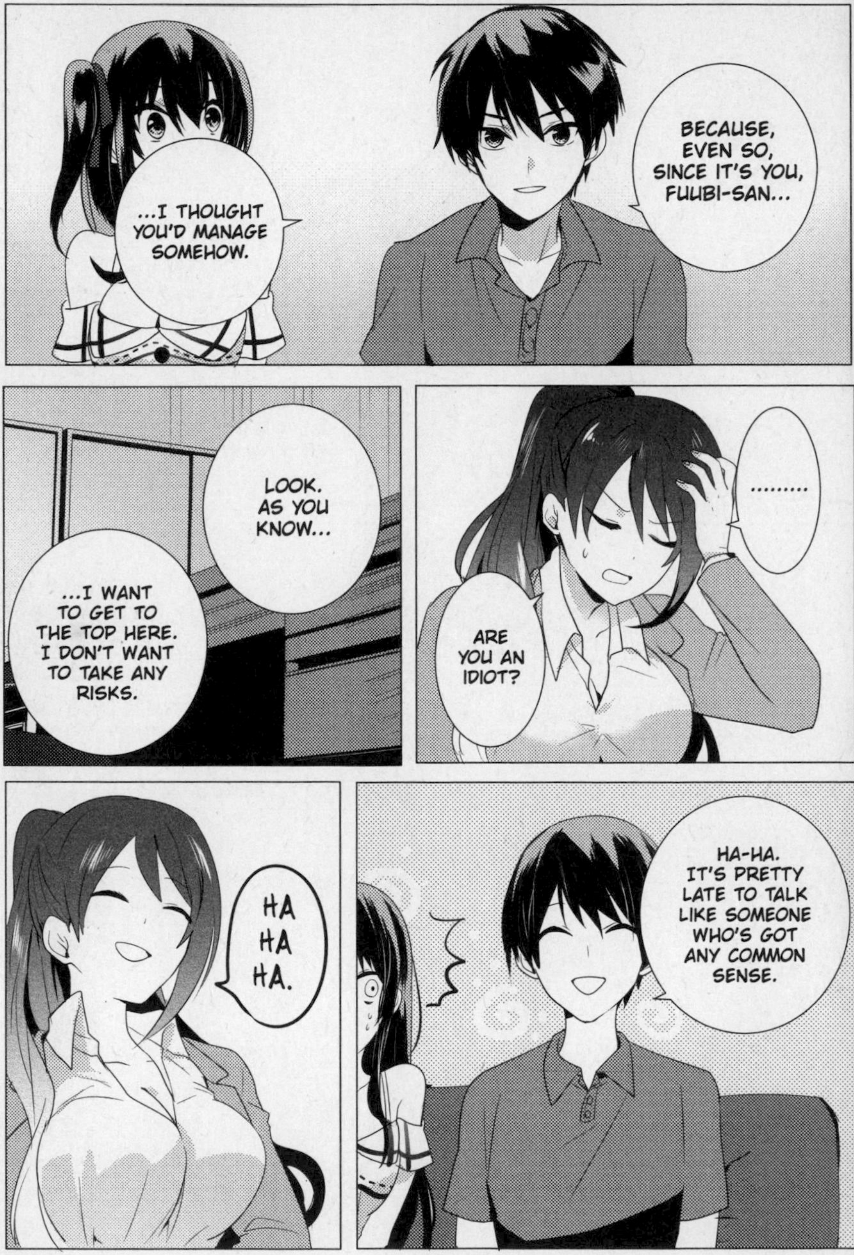
BECAUSE, EVEN SO, SINCE IT'S YOU, FUUBI-SAN...
...I THOUGHT YOU'D MANAGE SOMEHOW.
....
ARE YOU AN IDIOT?
LOOK. AS YOU KNOW...
...I WANT TO GET TO THE TOP HERE. I DON'T WANT TO TAKE ANY RISKS.
HA-HA. IT'S PRETTY LATE TO TALK LIKE SOMEONE WHO'S GOT ANY COMMON SENSE.
HA HA HA.

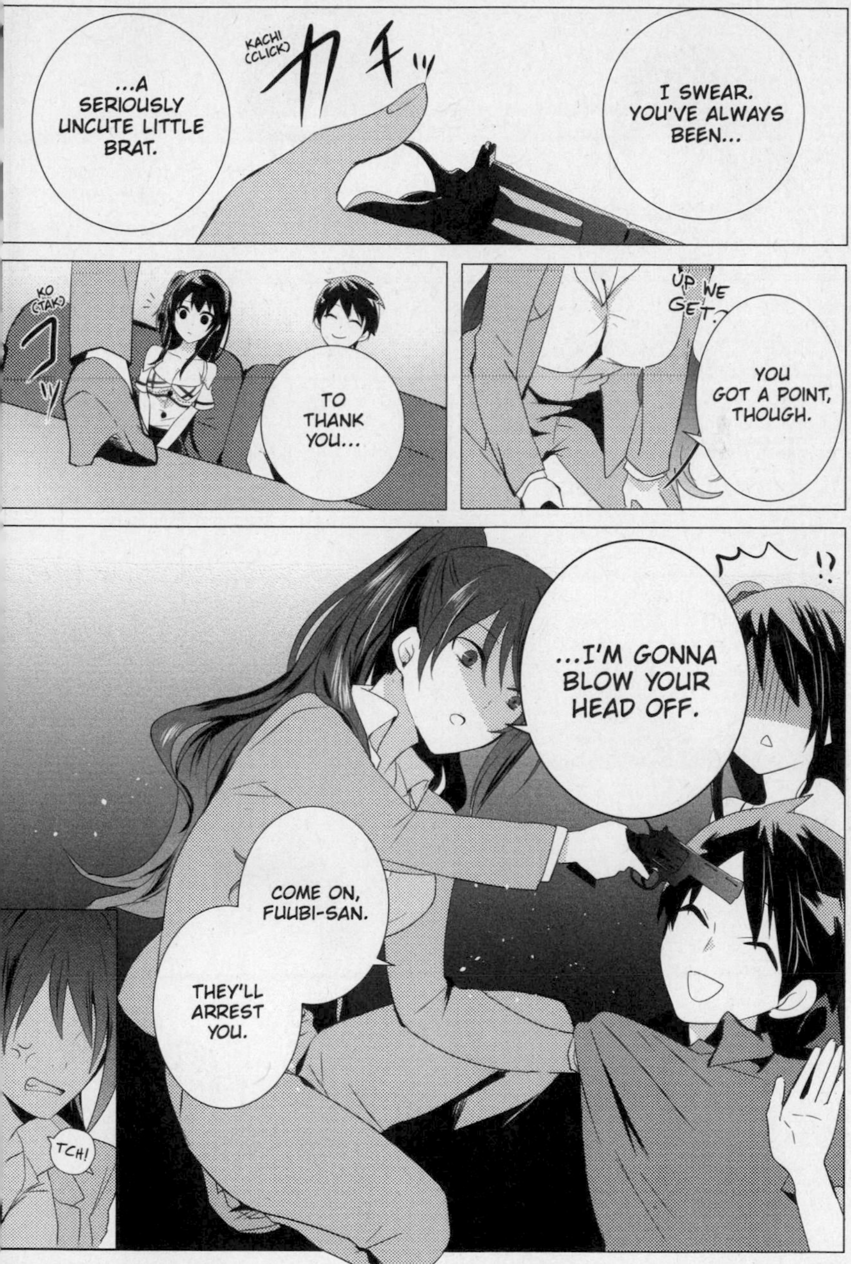
I SWEAR. YOU'VE ALWAYS BEEN...
KACHI (CLICK)
...A SERIOUSLY UNCUTE LITTLE BRAT.
UP WE GET.
YOU GOT A POINT, THOUGH.
KO (TAK)
TO THANK YOU...
!?
...I'M GONNA BLOW YOUR HEAD OFF.
COME ON, FUUBI-SAN.
THEY'LL ARREST YOU.
TCH!

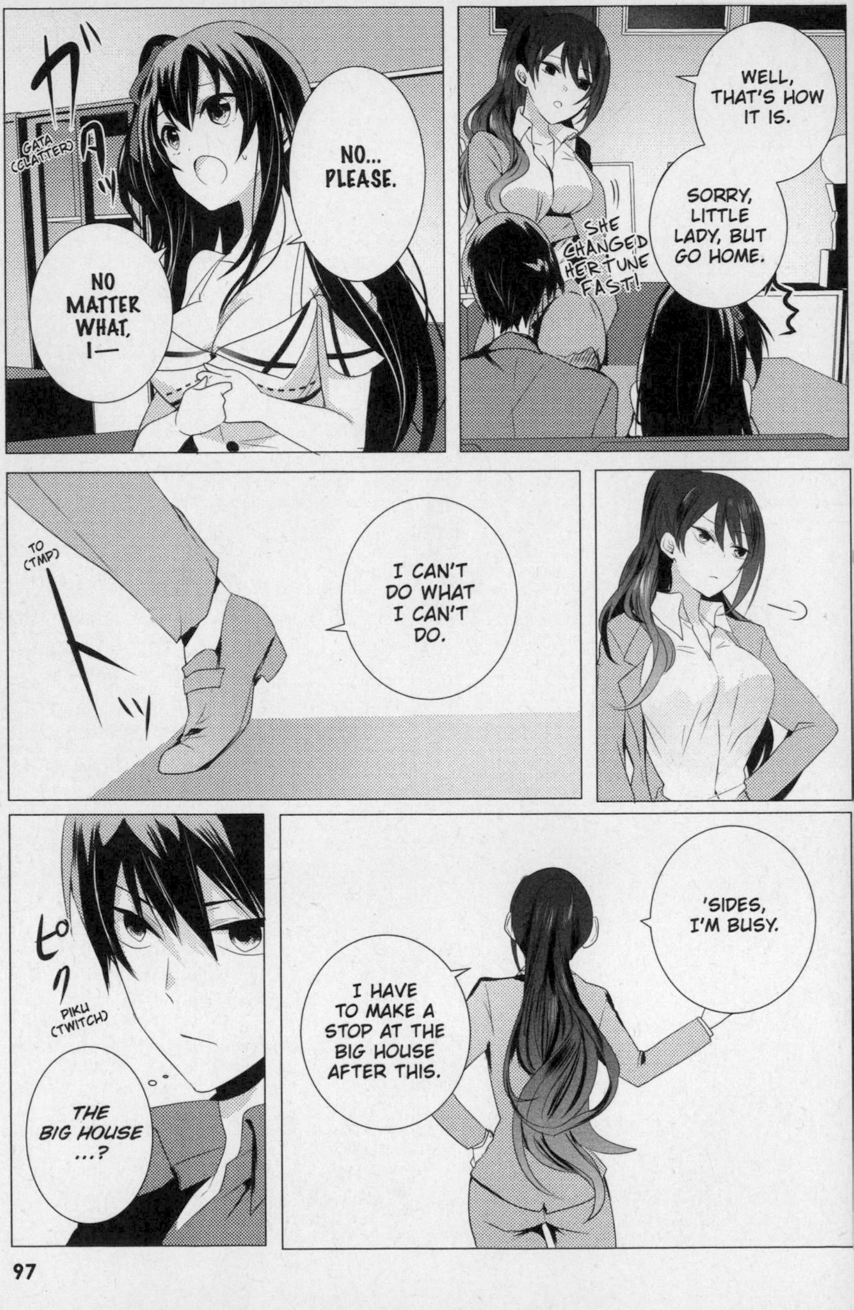
WELL, THAT'S HOW IT IS.
SORRY, LITTLE LADY, BUT GO HOME.
SHE CHANGED HER TUNE FAST!
NO... PLEASE.
GATA (CLATTER)
NO MATTER WHAT, I—
I CAN'T DO WHAT I CAN'T DO.
TO (TMP)
'SIDES, I'M BUSY.
I HAVE TO MAKE A STOP AT THE BIG HOUSE AFTER THIS.
PIKU (TWITCH)
THE BIG HOUSE ...?

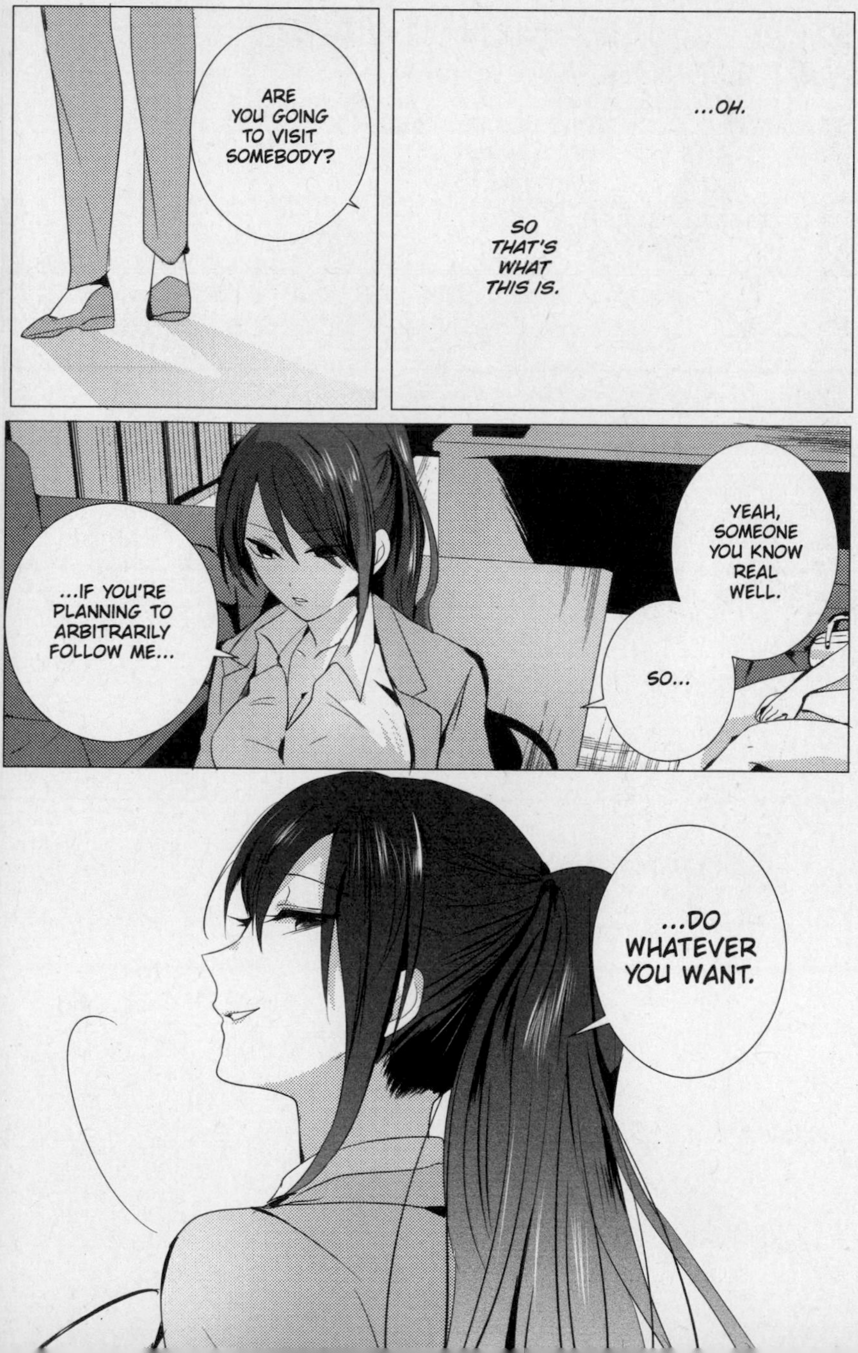
...OH.
SO THAT'S WHAT THIS IS.
ARE YOU GOING TO VISIT SOMEBODY?
YEAH, SOMEONE YOU KNOW REAL WELL.
SO...
...IF YOU'RE PLANNING TO ARBITRARILY FOLLOW ME...
...DO WHATEVER YOU WANT.

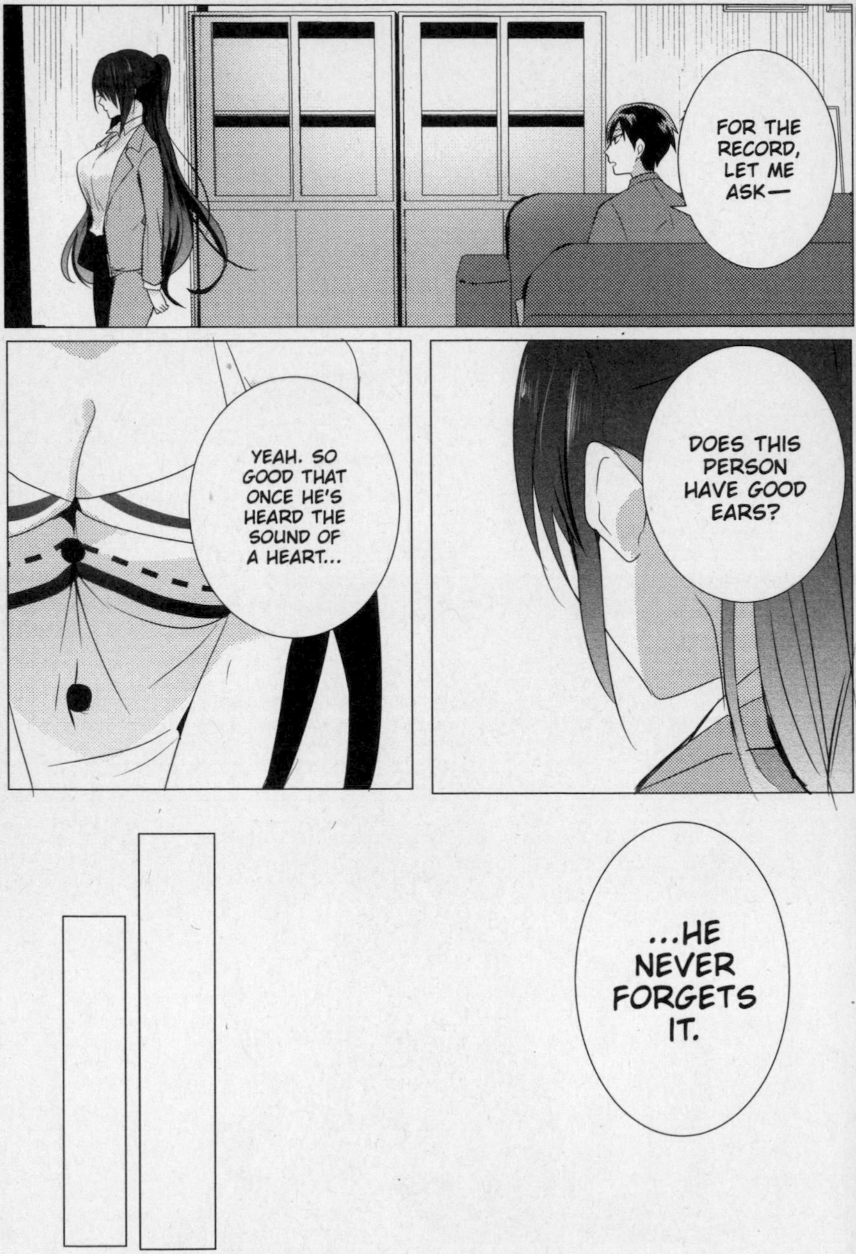
FOR THE RECORD, LET ME ASK—
DOES THIS PERSON HAVE GOOD EARS?
YEAH. SO GOOD THAT ONCE HE'S HEARD THE SOUND OF A HEART...
...HE NEVER FORGETS IT.

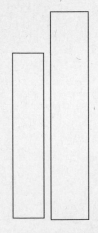

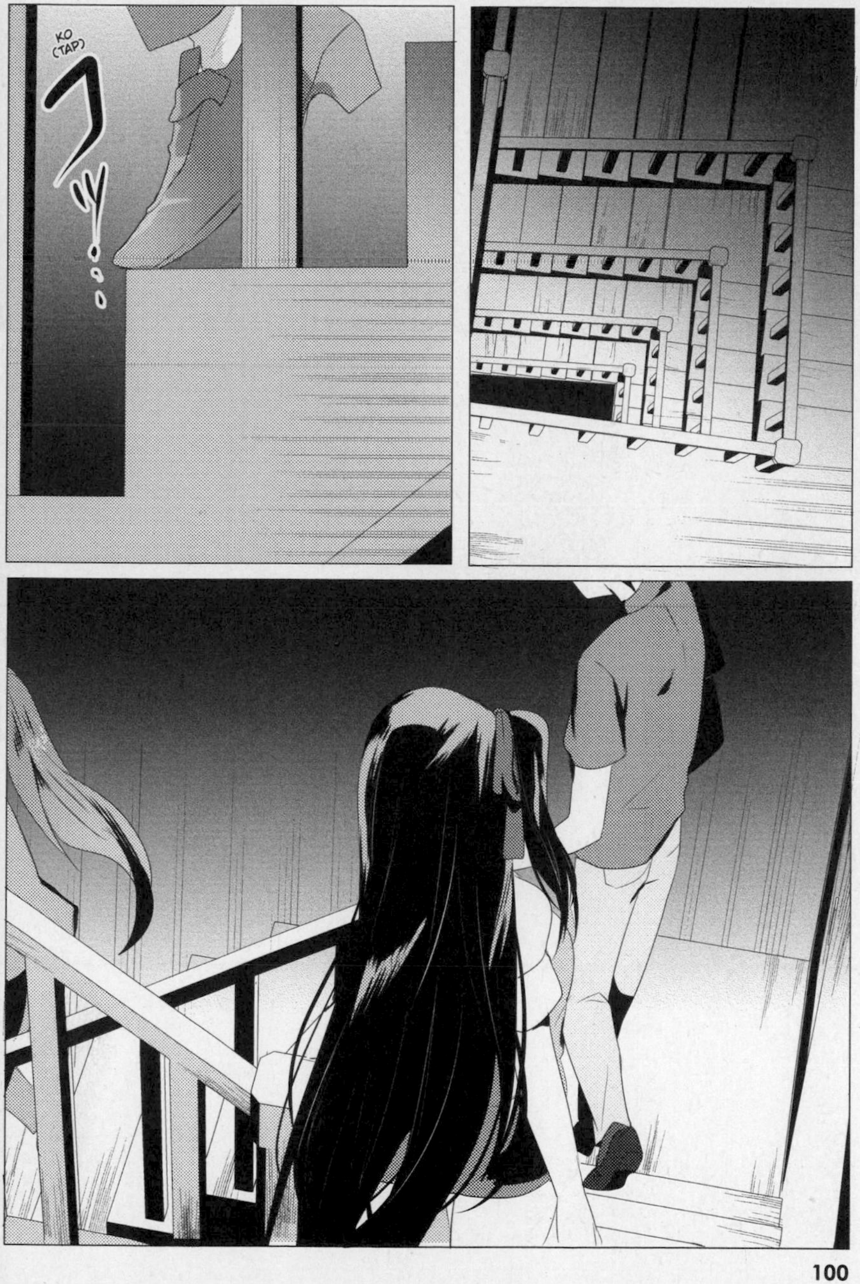
KO (TAP)

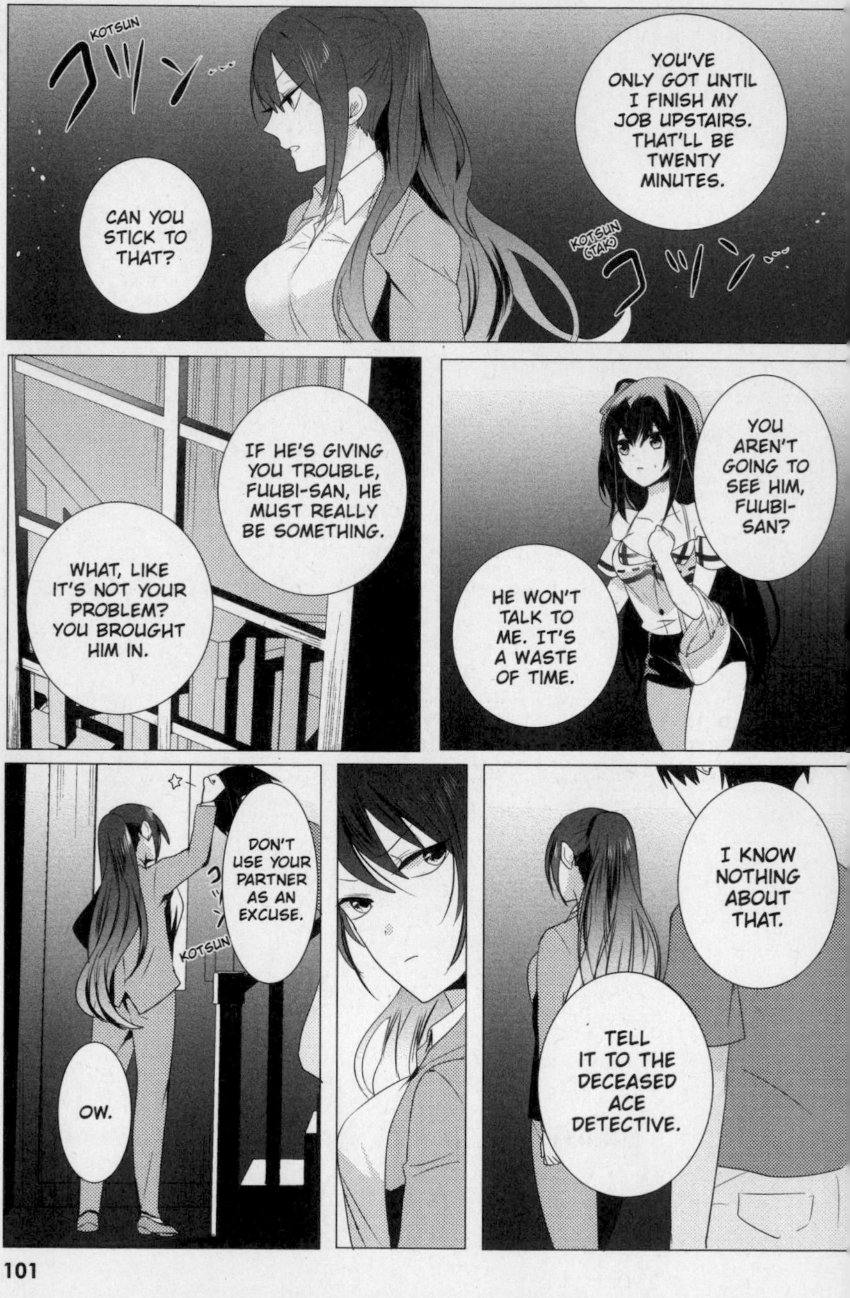
YOU'VE ONLY GOT UNTIL I FINISH MY JOB UPSTAIRS. THAT'LL BE TWENTY MINUTES.
KOTSUN (TAK)
KOTSUN
CAN YOU STICK TO THAT?
YOU AREN'T GOING TO SEE HIM, FUUBI-SAN?
HE WON'T TALK TO ME. IT'S A WASTE OF TIME.
IF HE'S GIVING YOU TROUBLE, FUUBI-SAN, HE MUST REALLY BE SOMETHING.
WHAT, LIKE IT'S NOT YOUR PROBLEM? YOU BROUGHT HIM IN.
I KNOW NOTHING ABOUT THAT.
TELL IT TO THE DECEASED ACE DETECTIVE.
DON'T USE YOUR PARTNER AS AN EXCUSE.
KOTSUN
OW.

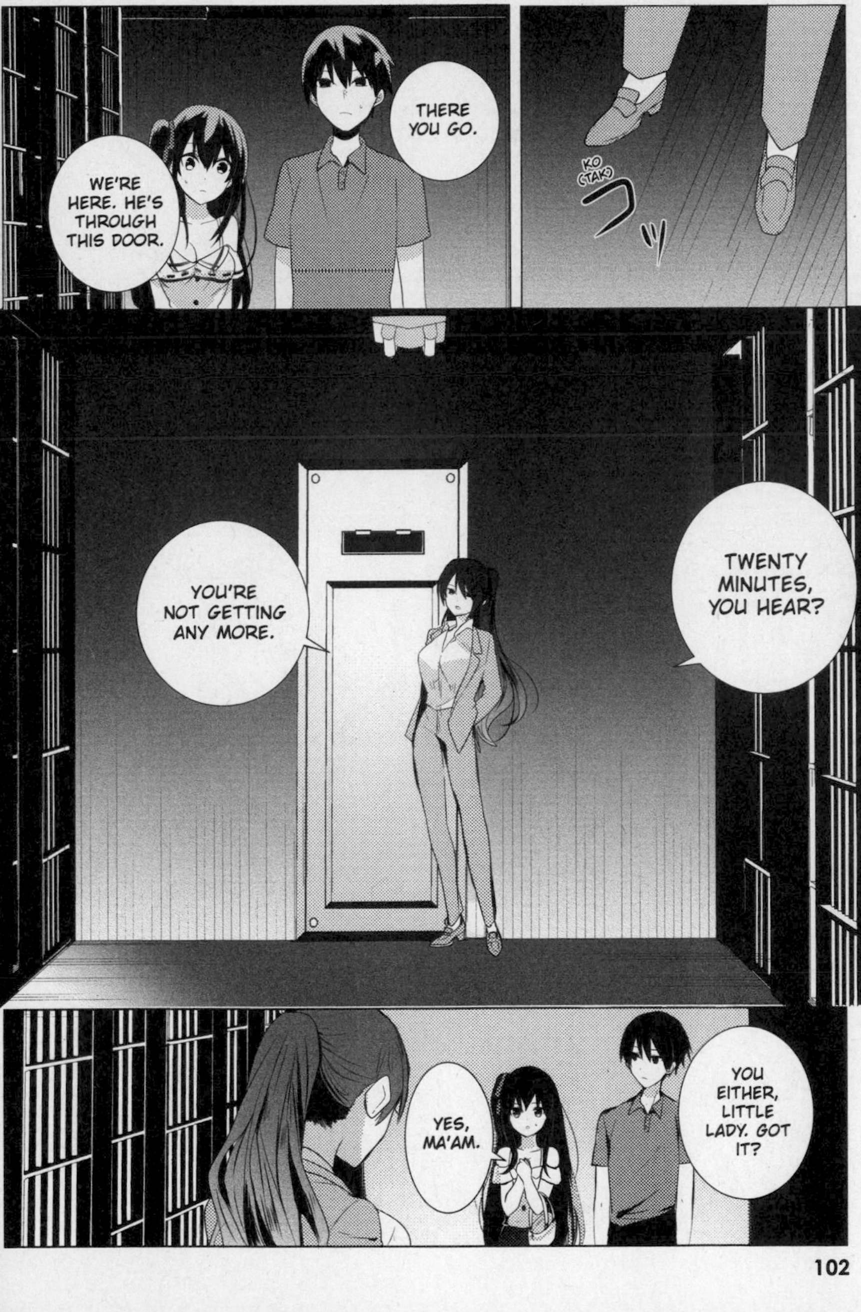
KO (TAK)
コッ
THERE YOU GO.
WE'RE HERE. HE'S THROUGH THIS DOOR.
TWENTY MINUTES, YOU HEAR?
YOU'RE NOT GETTING ANY MORE.
YOU EITHER, LITTLE LADY. GOT IT?
YES, MA'AM.

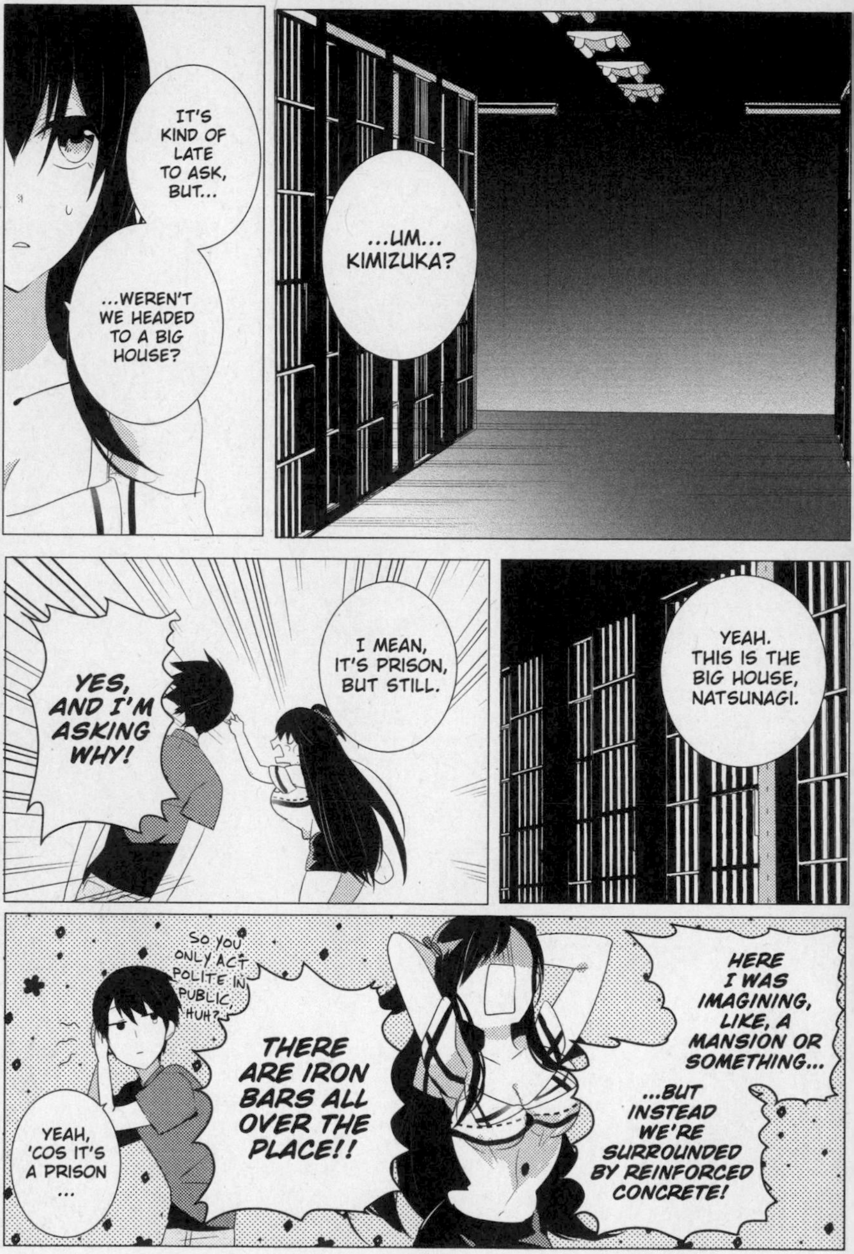
...UM... KIMIZUKA?
IT'S KIND OF LATE TO ASK, BUT...
...WEREN'T WE HEADED TO A BIG HOUSE?
YEAH. THIS IS THE BIG HOUSE, NATSUNAGI.
I MEAN, IT'S PRISON, BUT STILL.
YES, AND I'M ASKING WHY!
HERE I WAS IMAGINING, LIKE, A MANSION OR SOMETHING...
...BUT INSTEAD WE'RE SURROUNDED BY REINFORCED CONCRETE!
THERE ARE IRON BARS ALL OVER THE PLACE!!
SO YOU ONLY ACT POLITE IN PUBLIC, HUH?
YEAH, 'COS IT'S A PRISON ...

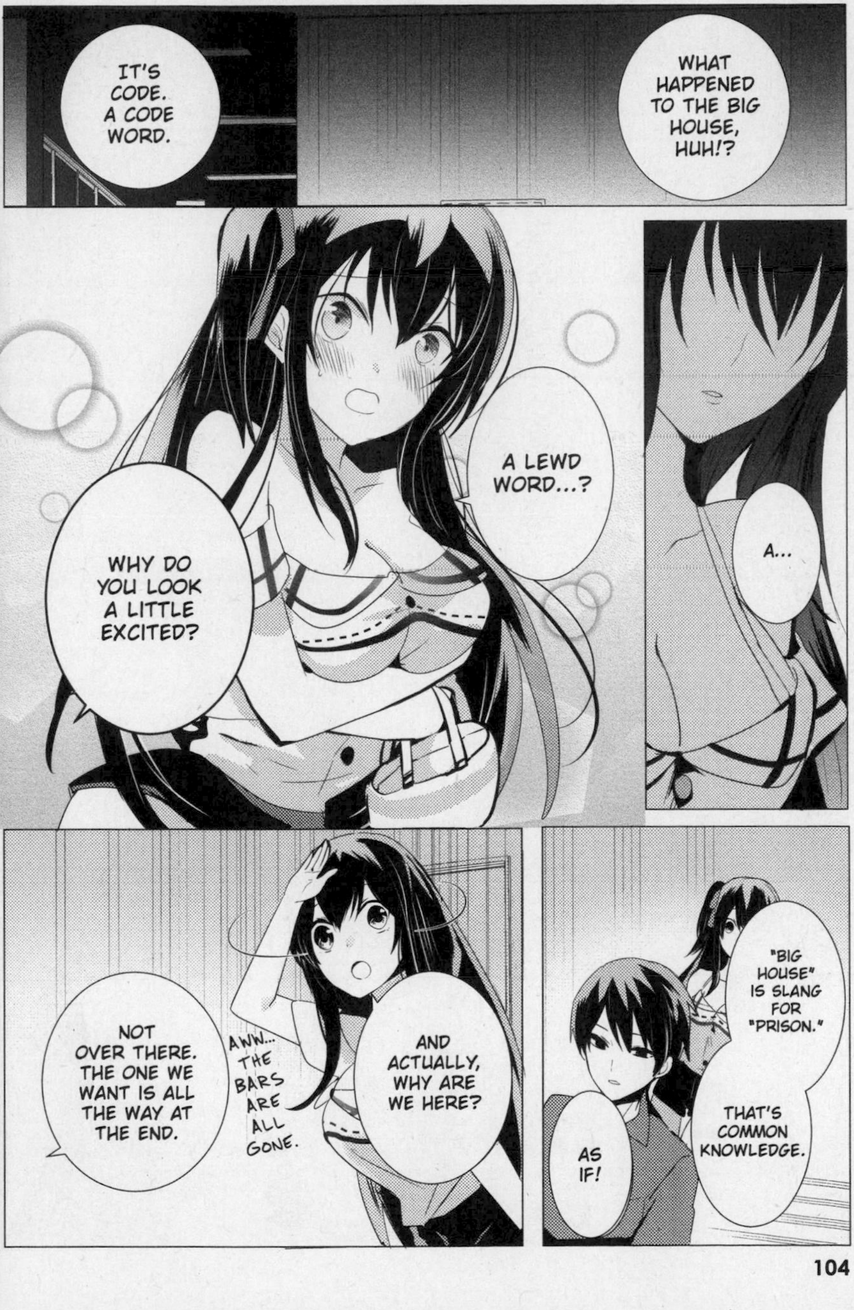
WHAT HAPPENED TO THE BIG HOUSE, HUH!?
IT'S CODE. A CODE WORD.
A...
A LEWD WORD...?
WHY DO YOU LOOK A LITTLE EXCITED?
"BIG HOUSE" IS SLANG FOR "PRISON."
THAT'S COMMON KNOWLEDGE.
AS IF!
AND ACTUALLY, WHY ARE WE HERE?
AWW... THE BARS ARE ALL GONE.
NOT OVER THERE. THE ONE WE WANT IS ALL THE WAY AT THE END.

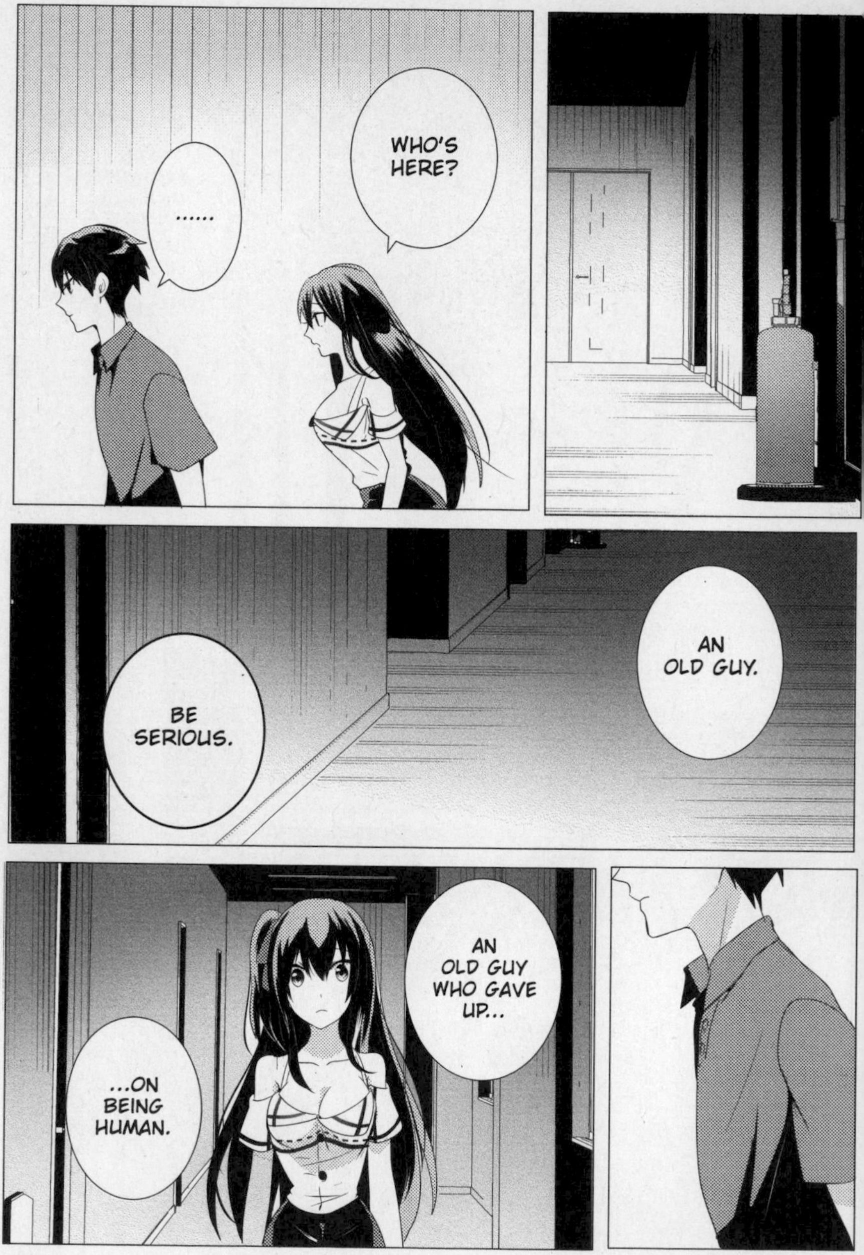
WHO'S HERE?
......
AN OLD GUY.
BE SERIOUS.
AN OLD GUY WHO GAVE UP...
...ON BEING HUMAN.

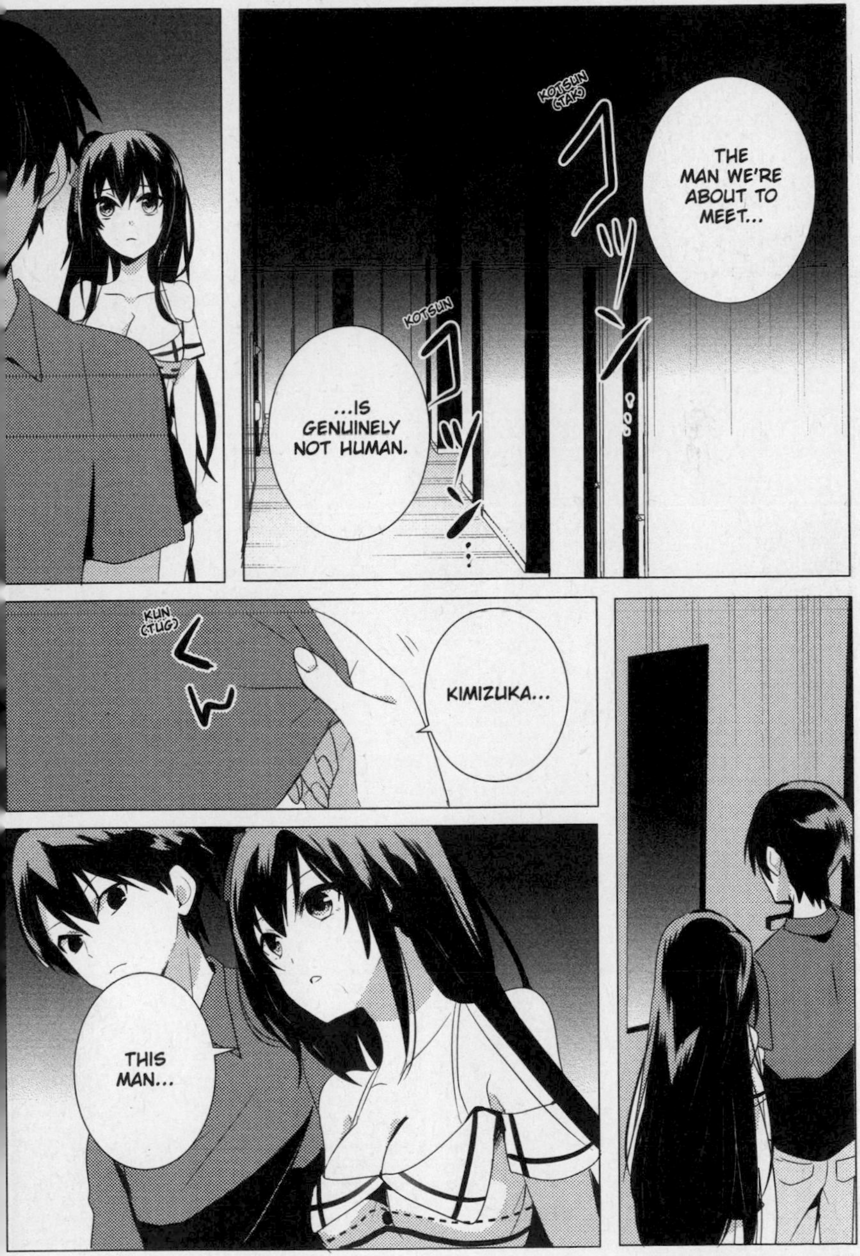
THE MAN WE'RE ABOUT TO MEET...
KOTSUN (TAK)
KOTSUN
...IS GENUINELY NOT HUMAN.
KIMIZUKA...
KUN (TUG)
THIS MAN...

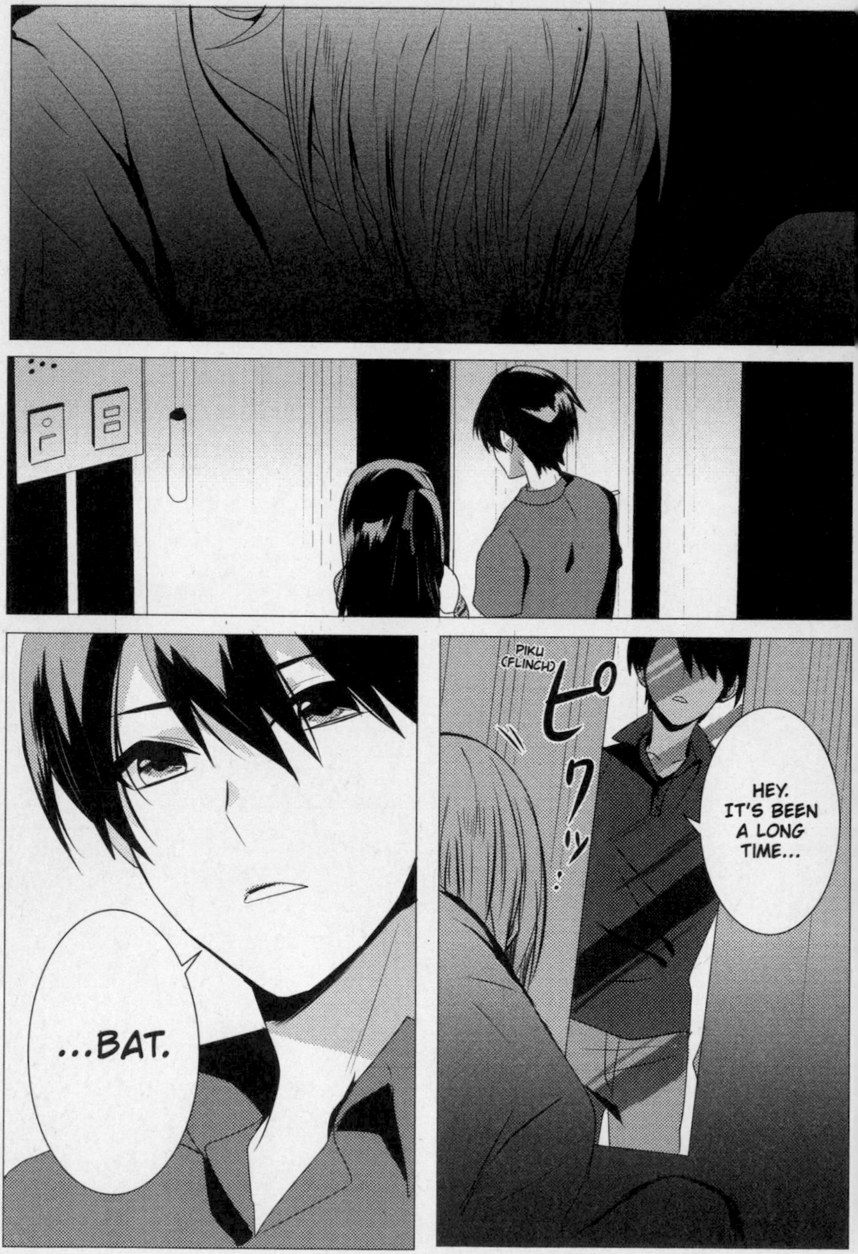
HEY. IT'S BEEN A LONG TIME...
ピクッ
PIKU (FLINCH)
...BAT.

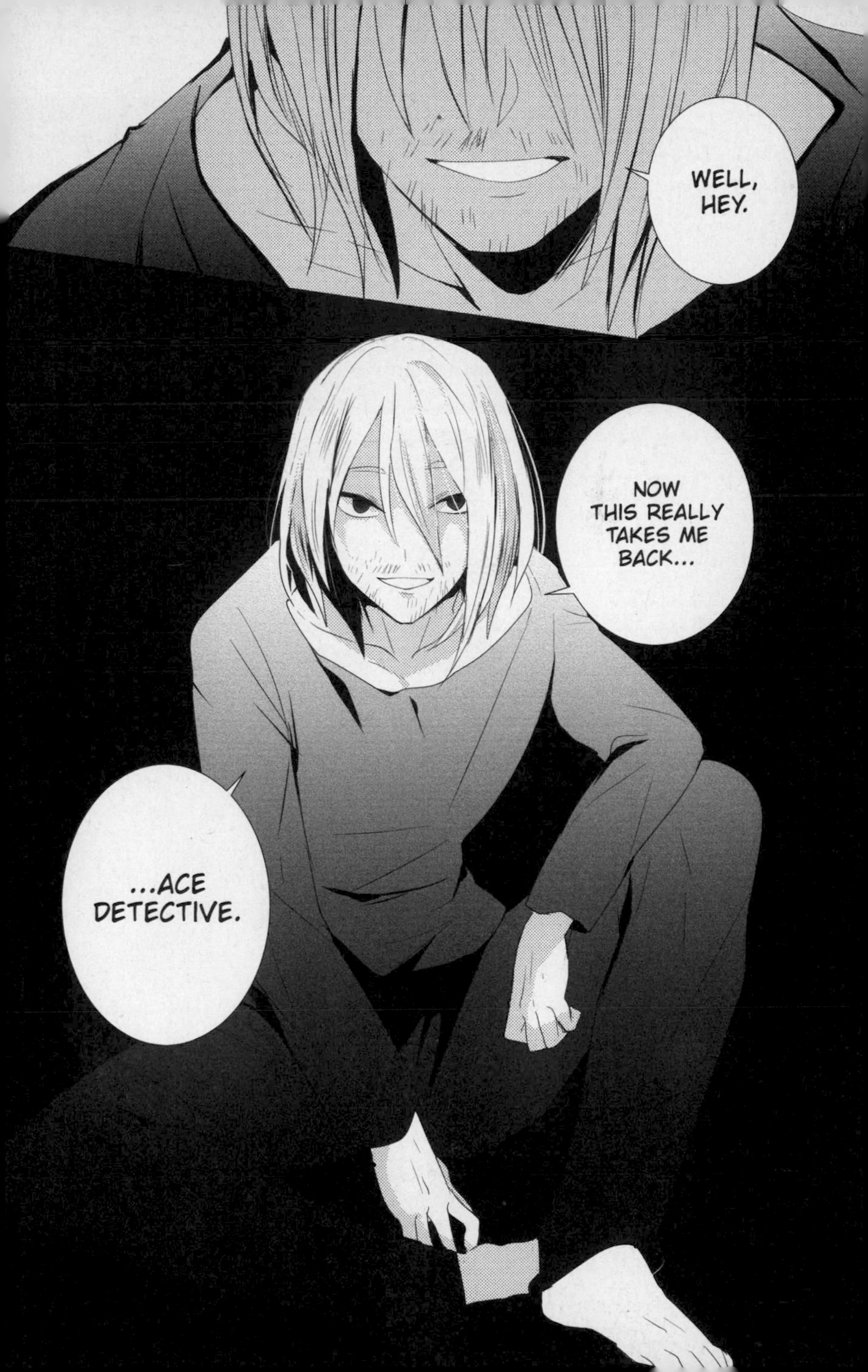
WELL, HEY.
NOW THIS REALLY TAKES ME BACK...
...ACE DETECTIVE.

The Detective Is Already Dead

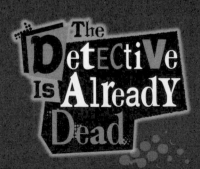

The Detective Is Already Dead

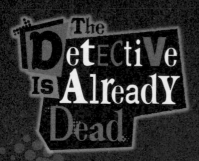

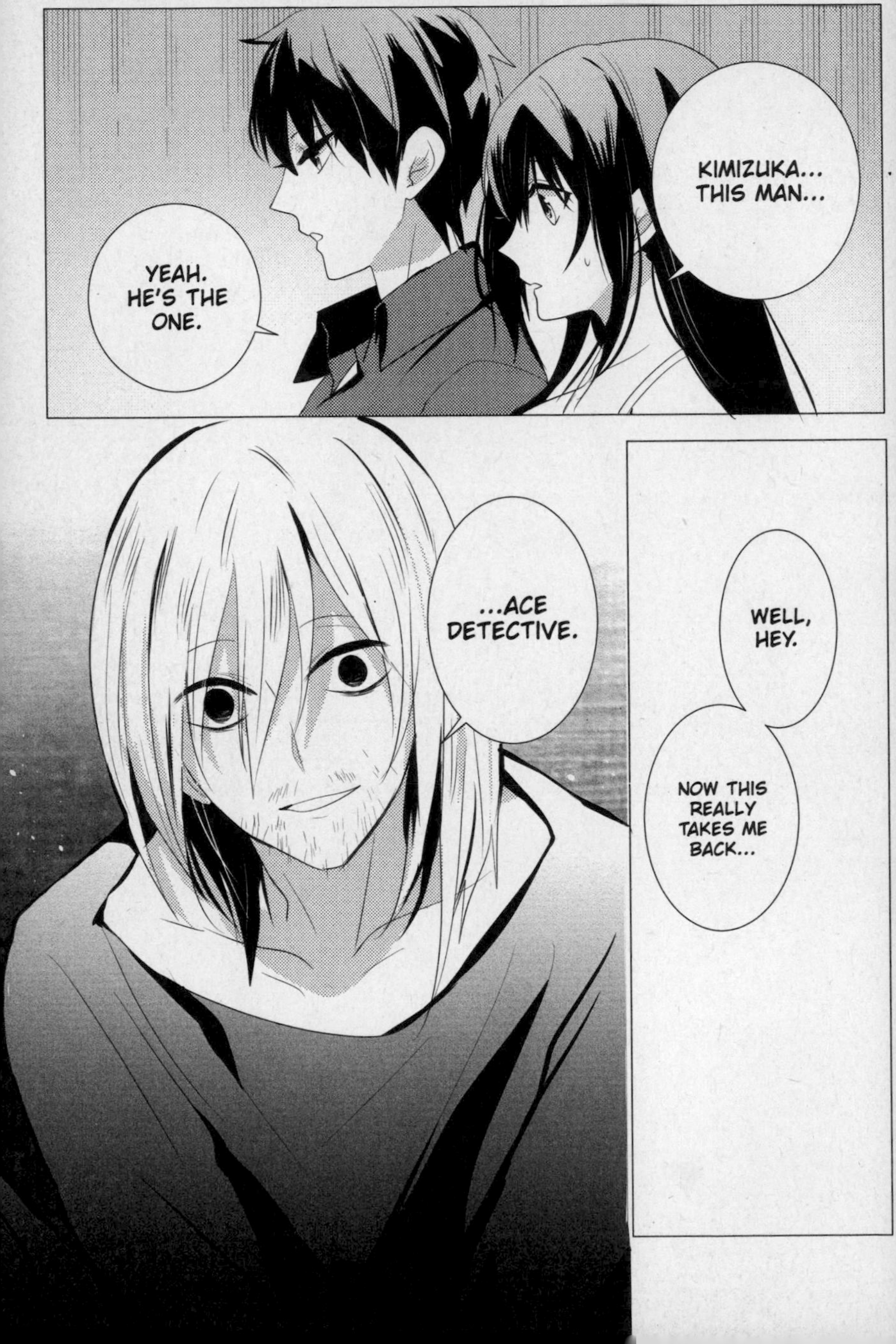
KIMIZUKA... THIS MAN...
YEAH. HE'S THE ONE.
WELL, HEY.
NOW THIS REALLY TAKES ME BACK...
...ACE DETECTIVE.

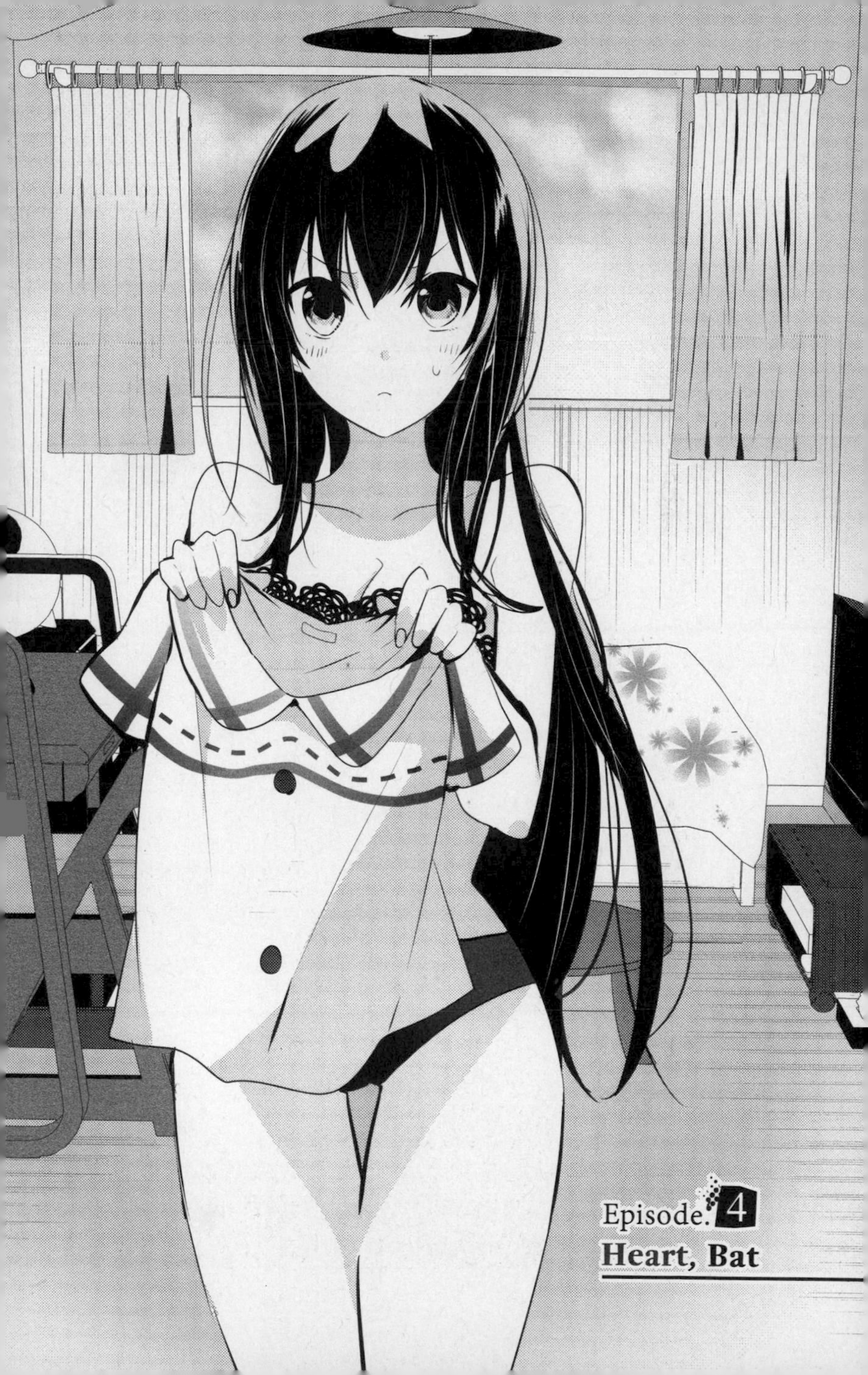
Episode. 4
Heart, Bat

I KNOW THIS JAILBIRD.

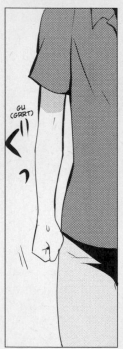

GU
(GRRT)

HIS ALIAS IS "BAT."

IF POSSIBLE, I NEVER WANTED TO SEE HIM AGAIN.

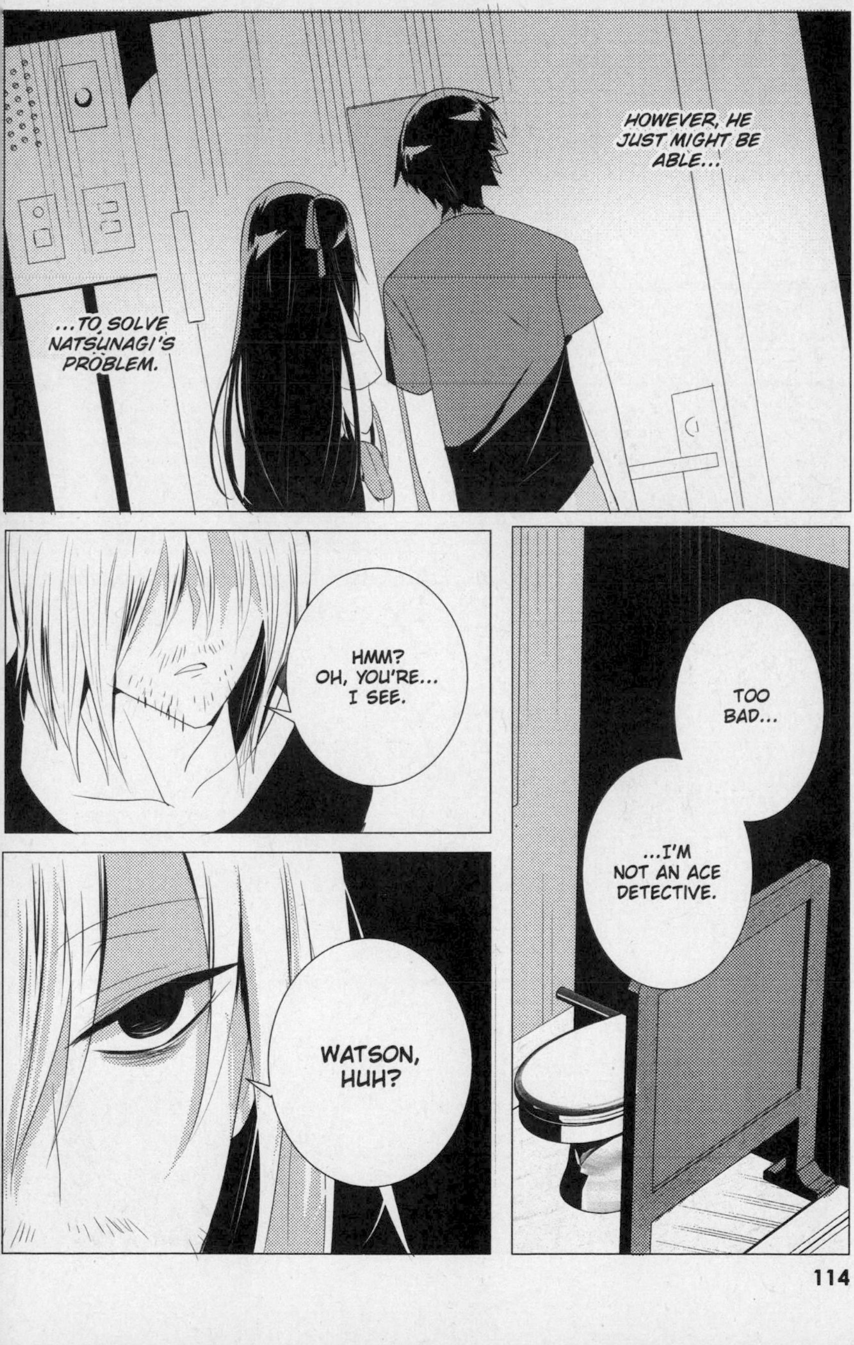
HOWEVER, HE JUST MIGHT BE ABLE...
...TO SOLVE NATSUNAGI'S PROBLEM.
TOO BAD...
...I'M NOT AN ACE DETECTIVE.
HMM? OH, YOU'RE... I SEE.
WATSON, HUH?

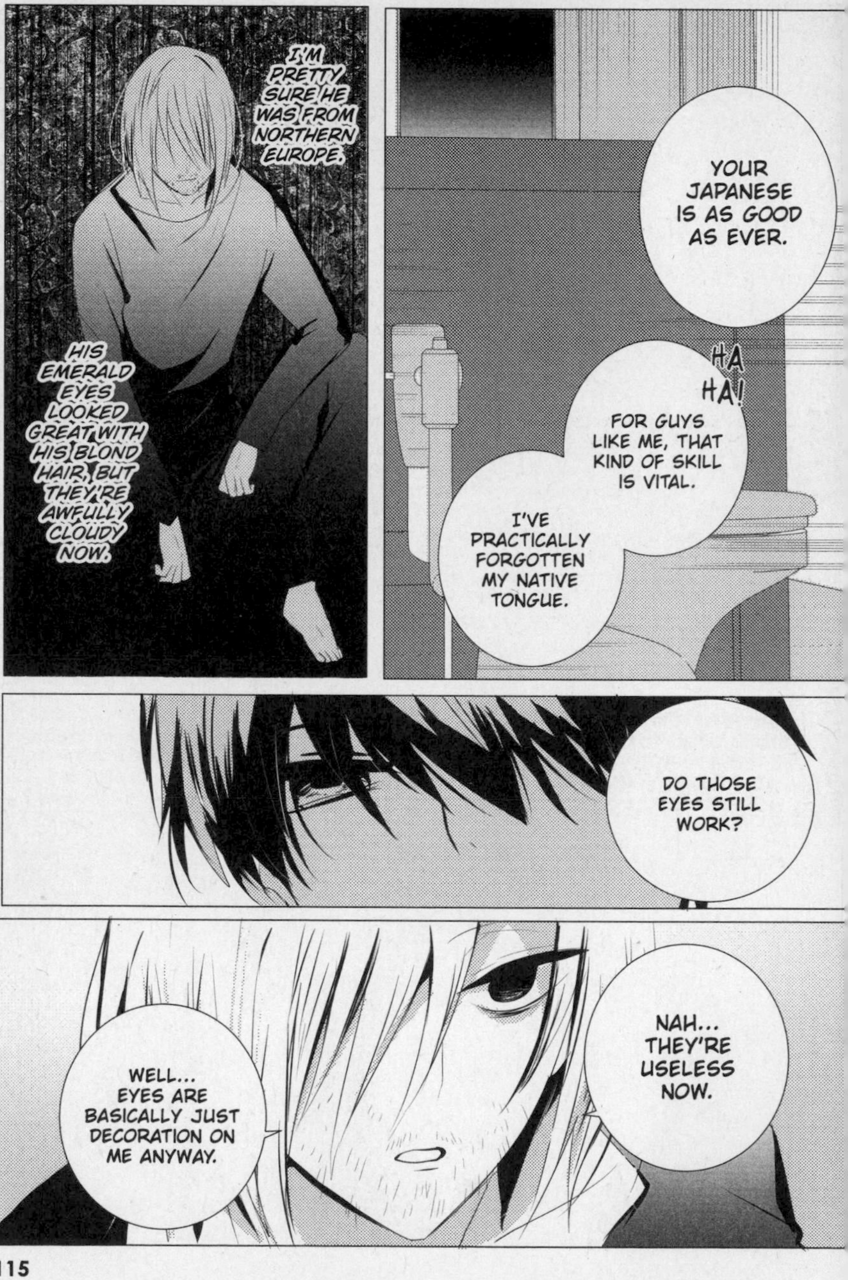
YOUR JAPANESE IS AS GOOD AS EVER.
HA HA!
FOR GUYS LIKE ME, THAT KIND OF SKILL IS VITAL.
I'VE PRACTICALLY FORGOTTEN MY NATIVE TONGUE.
I'M PRETTY SURE HE WAS FROM NORTHERN EUROPE.
HIS EMERALD EYES LOOKED GREAT WITH HIS BLOND HAIR, BUT THEY'RE AWFULLY CLOUDY NOW.
DO THOSE EYES STILL WORK?
NAH... THEY'RE USELESS NOW.
WELL... EYES ARE BASICALLY JUST DECORATION ON ME ANYWAY.

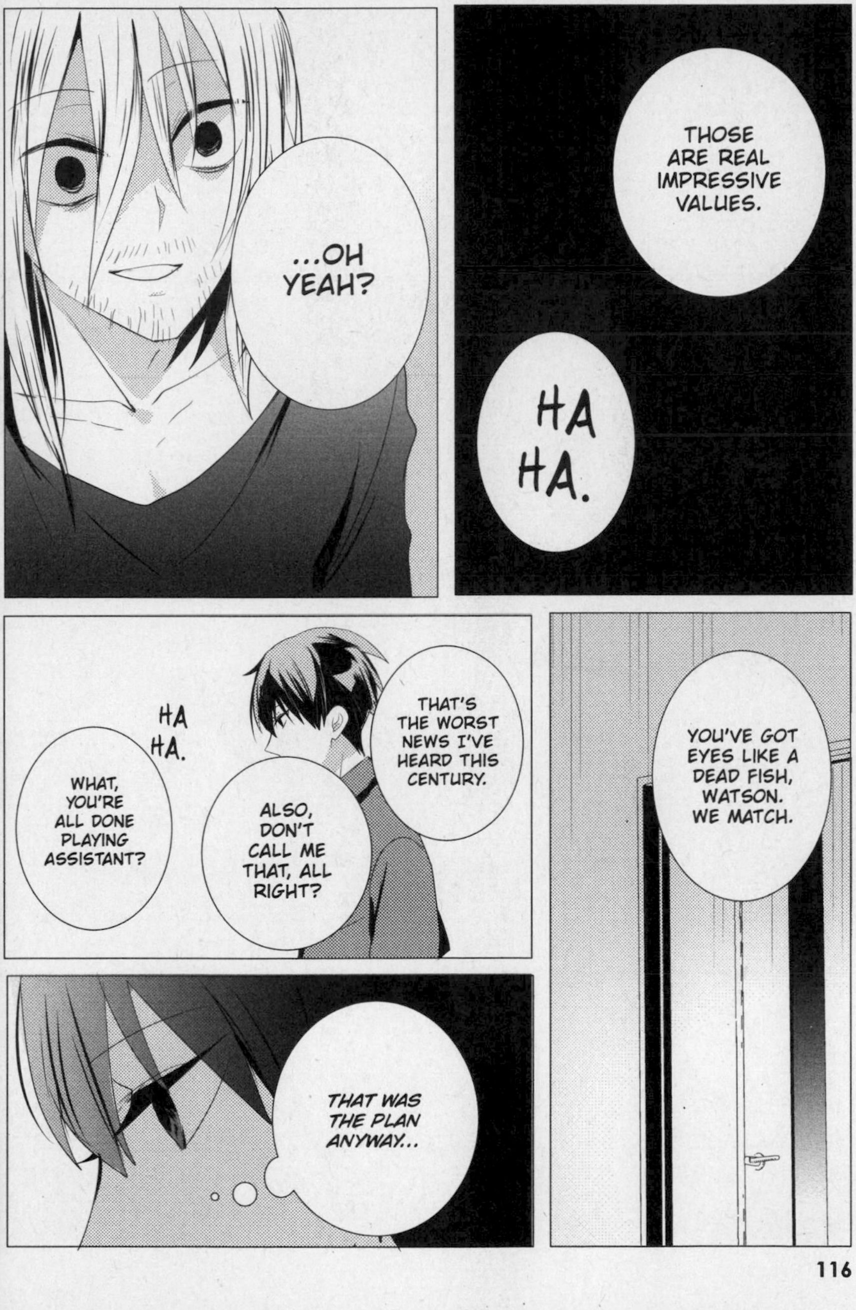
THOSE ARE REAL IMPRESSIVE VALUES.
HA HA.
...OH YEAH?
YOU'VE GOT EYES LIKE A DEAD FISH, WATSON. WE MATCH.
THAT'S THE WORST NEWS I'VE HEARD THIS CENTURY.
ALSO, DON'T CALL ME THAT, ALL RIGHT?
HA HA.
WHAT, YOU'RE ALL DONE PLAYING ASSISTANT?
THAT WAS THE PLAN ANYWAY...

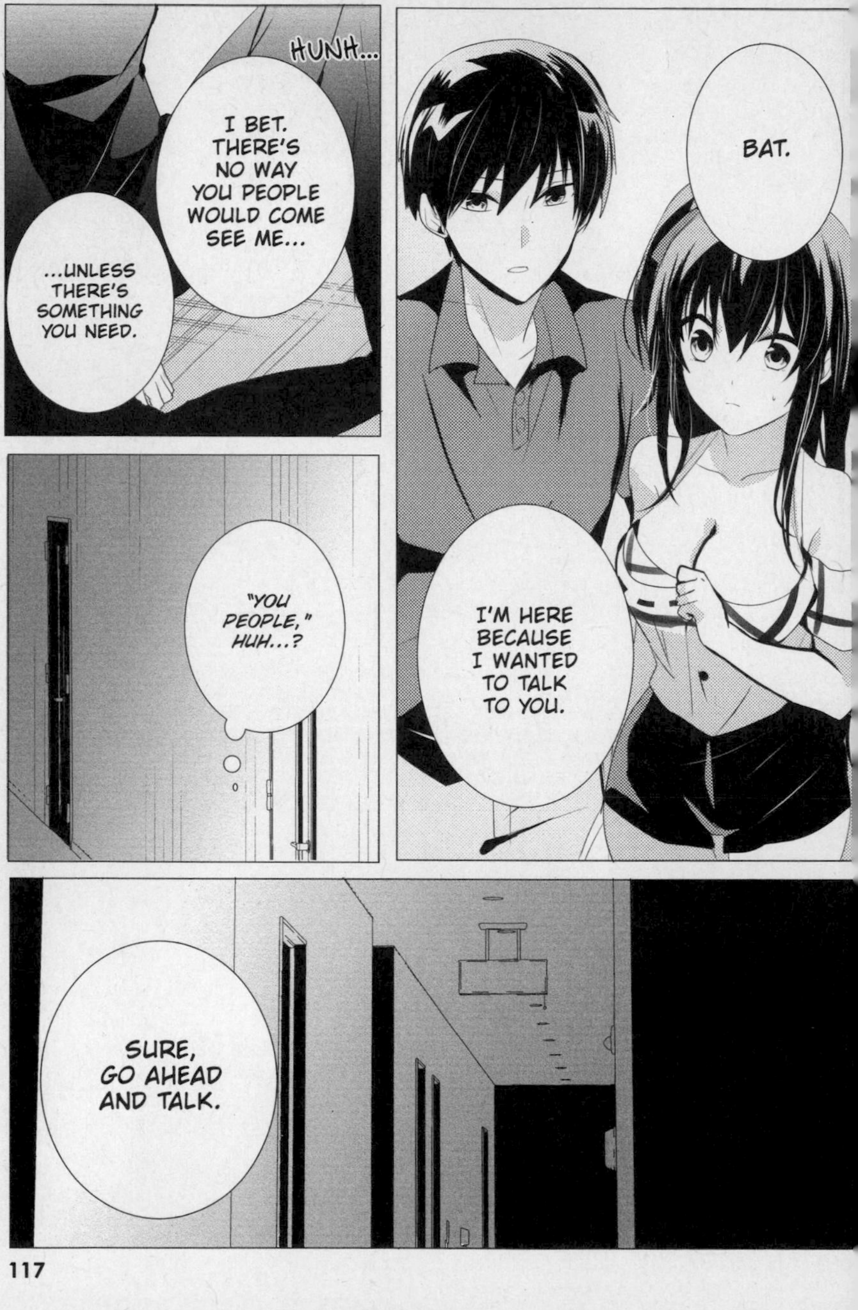
BAT.
I'M HERE BECAUSE I WANTED TO TALK TO YOU.
HUNH...
I BET. THERE'S NO WAY YOU PEOPLE WOULD COME SEE ME...
...UNLESS THERE'S SOMETHING YOU NEED.
"YOU PEOPLE," HUH...?
SURE, GO AHEAD AND TALK.

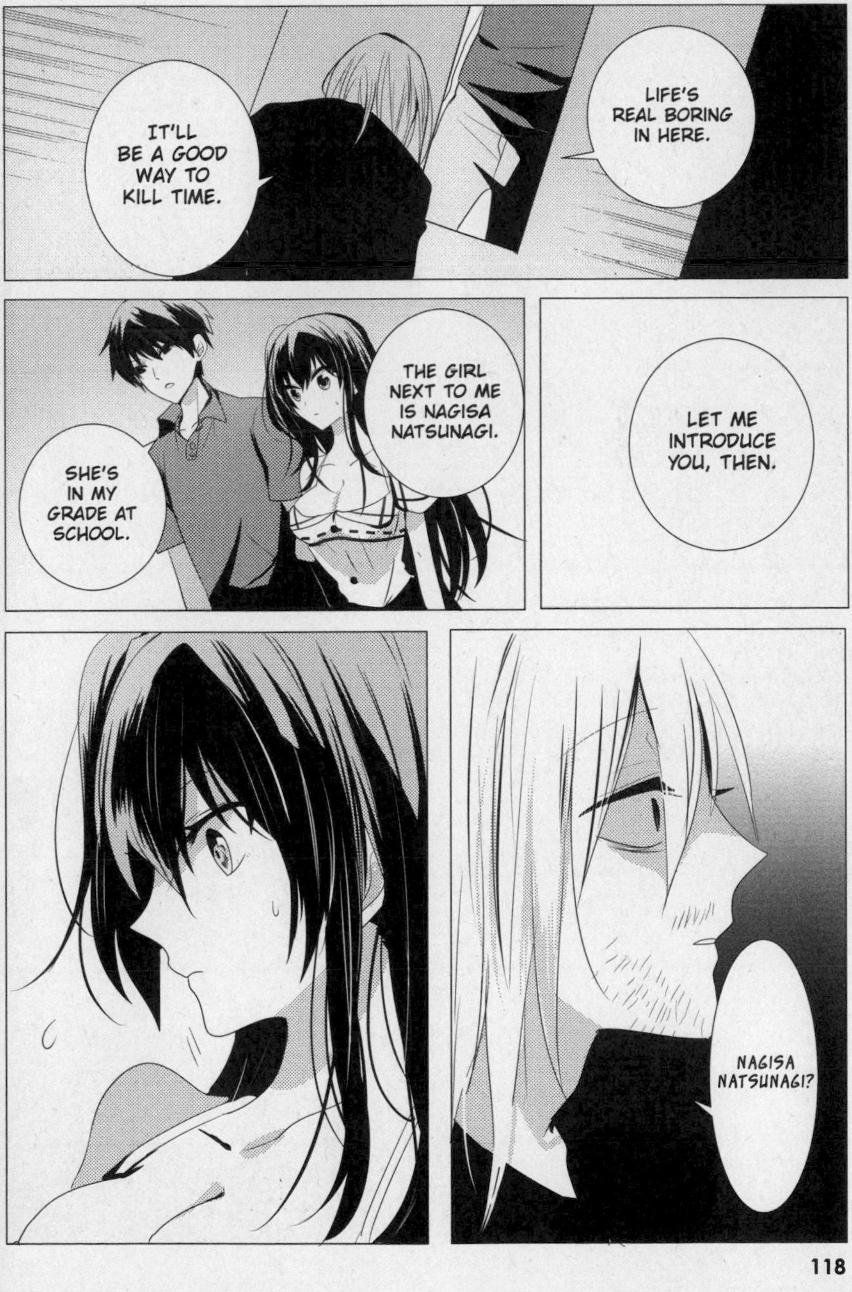
LIFE'S REAL BORING IN HERE.
IT'LL BE A GOOD WAY TO KILL TIME.
LET ME INTRODUCE YOU, THEN.
THE GIRL NEXT TO ME IS NAGISA NATSUNAGI.
SHE'S IN MY GRADE AT SCHOOL.
NAGISA NATSUNAGI?

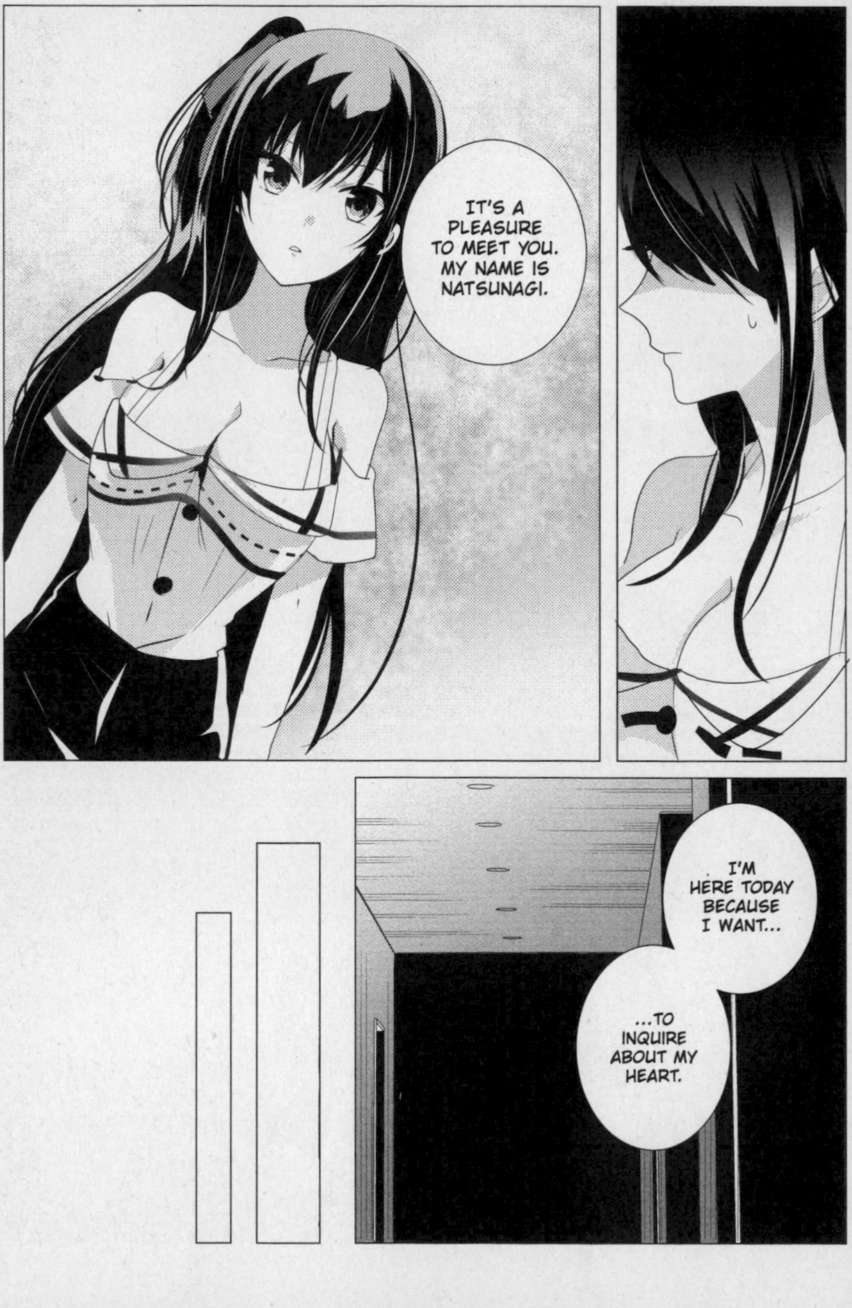
IT'S A PLEASURE TO MEET YOU. MY NAME IS NATSUNAGI.
I'M HERE TODAY BECAUSE I WANT...
...TO INQUIRE ABOUT MY HEART.

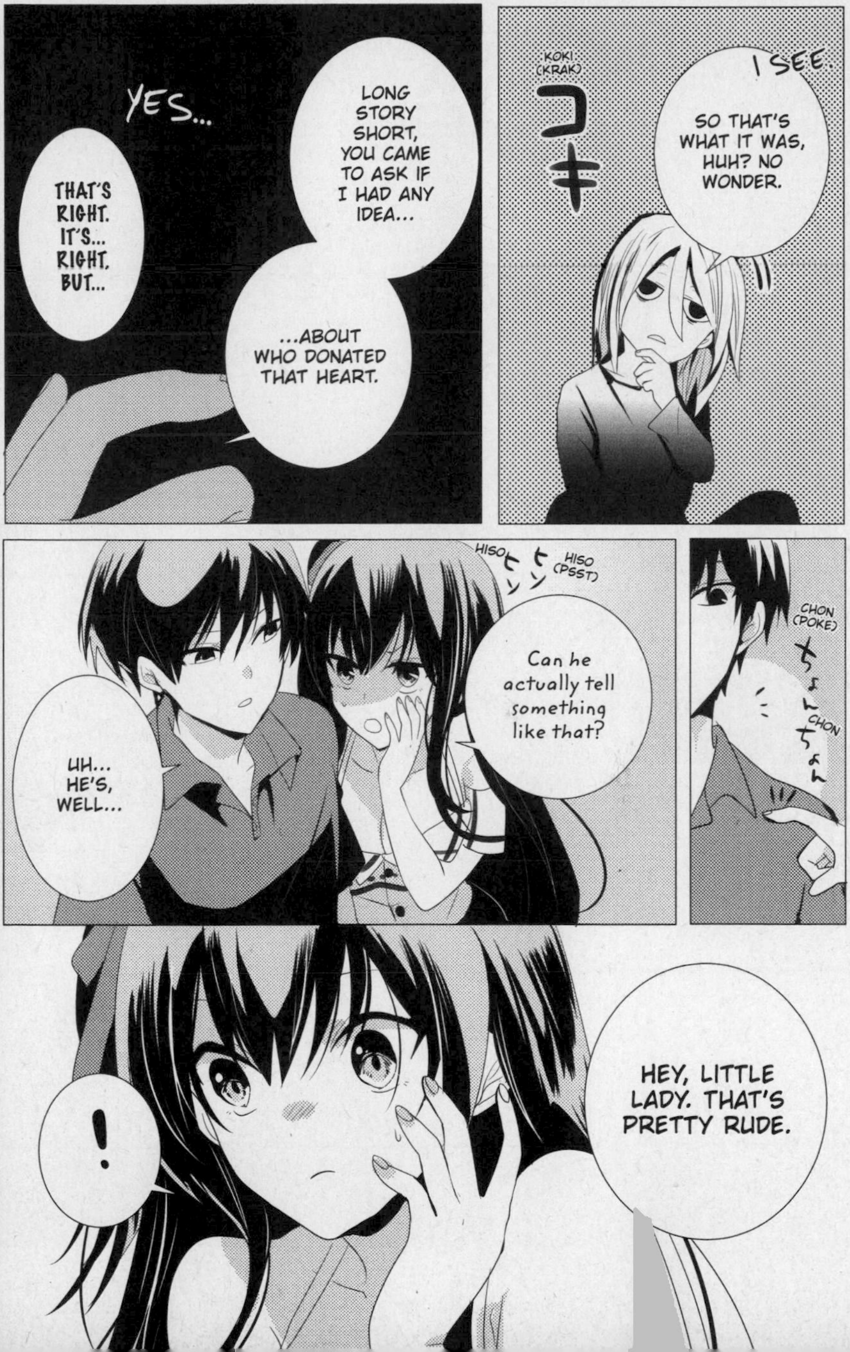
KOKI (KRAK)
コキ
I SEE.
SO THAT'S WHAT IT WAS, HUH? NO WONDER.
LONG STORY SHORT, YOU CAME TO ASK IF I HAD ANY IDEA...
...ABOUT WHO DONATED THAT HEART.
YES...
THAT'S RIGHT. IT'S... RIGHT, BUT...
CHON (POKE)
ちょん
CHON
ちょん
HISO (PSST)
ヒソ
HISO
ヒソ
Can he actually tell something like that?
UH... HE'S, WELL...
HEY, LITTLE LADY. THAT'S PRETTY RUDE.
!

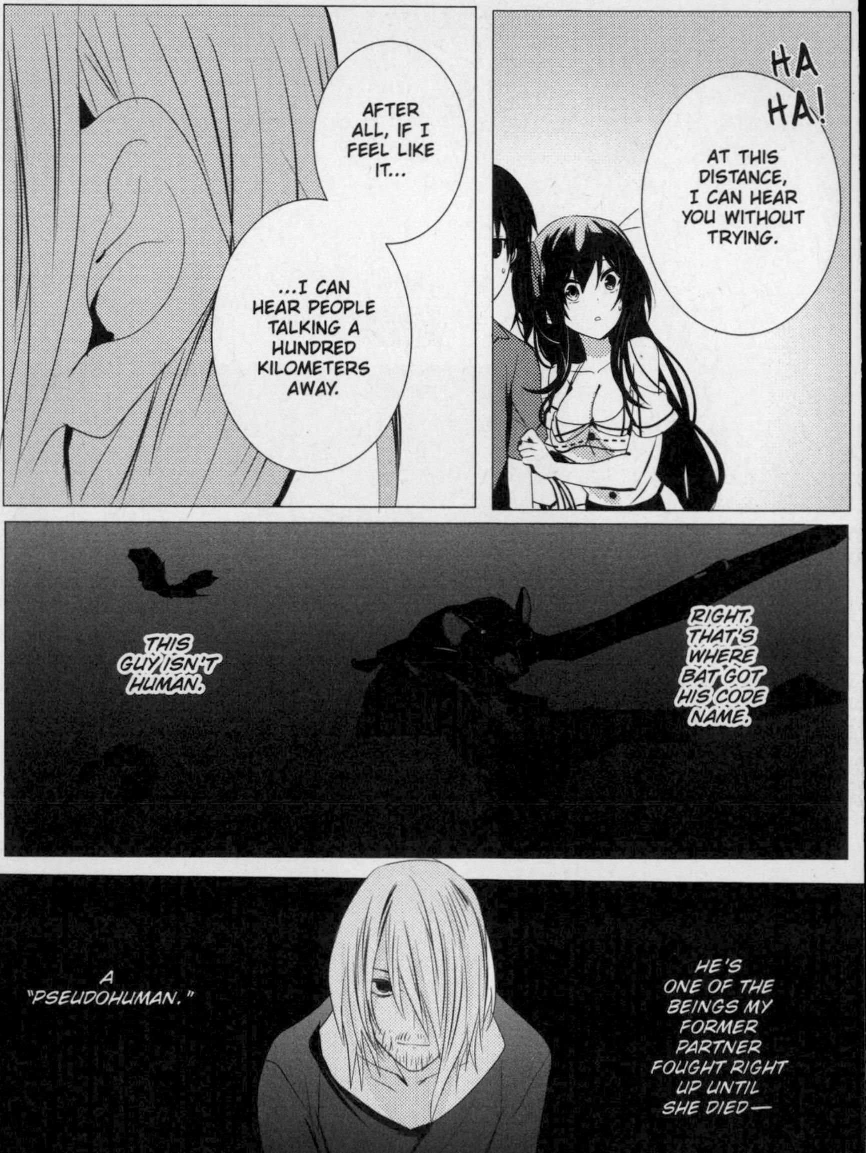
HA HA!
AT THIS DISTANCE, I CAN HEAR YOU WITHOUT TRYING.
AFTER ALL, IF I FEEL LIKE IT...
...I CAN HEAR PEOPLE TALKING A HUNDRED KILOMETERS AWAY.
RIGHT. THAT'S WHERE BAT GOT HIS CODE NAME.
THIS GUY ISN'T HUMAN.
HE'S ONE OF THE BEINGS MY FORMER PARTNER FOUGHT RIGHT UP UNTIL SHE DIED—
A "PSEUDOHUMAN."

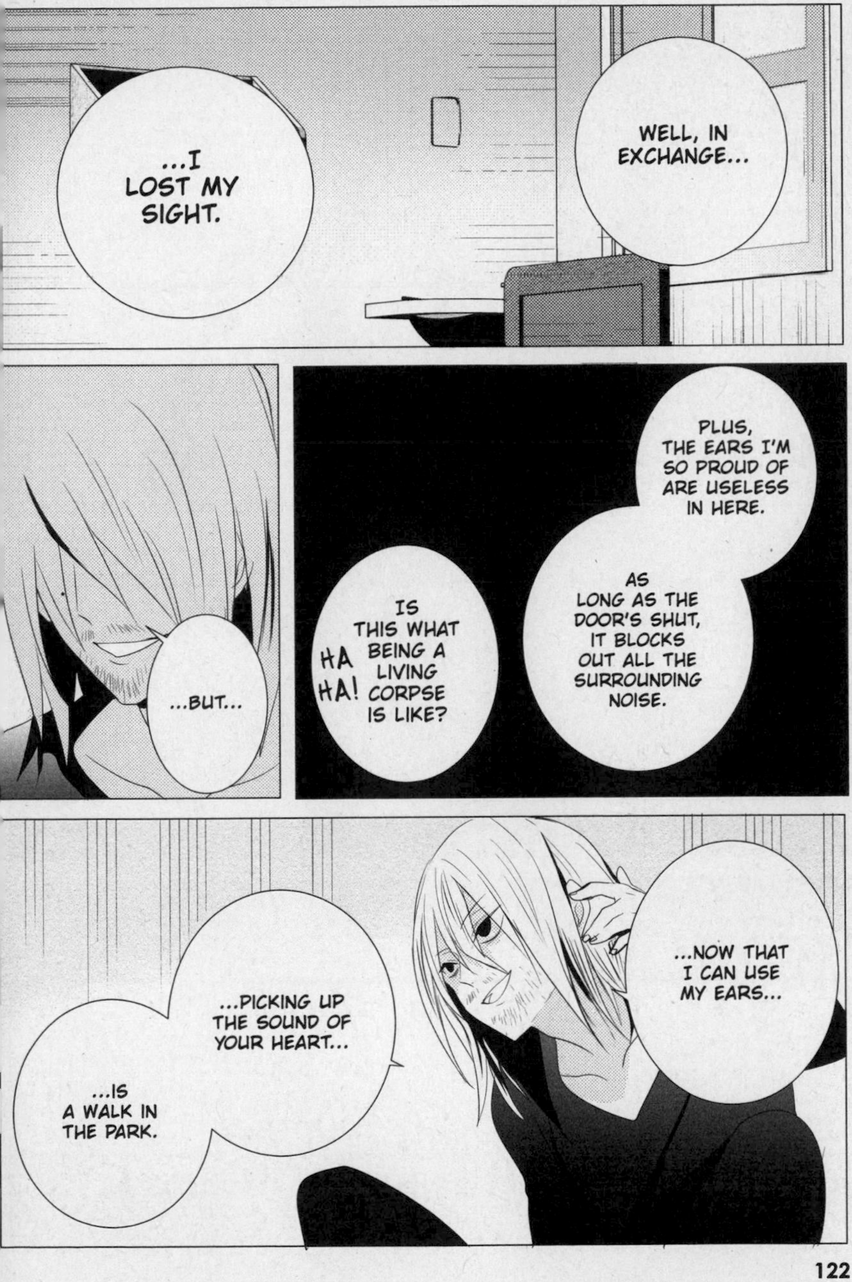
WELL, IN EXCHANGE...
...I LOST MY SIGHT.
PLUS, THE EARS I'M SO PROUD OF ARE USELESS IN HERE.
AS LONG AS THE DOOR'S SHUT, IT BLOCKS OUT ALL THE SURROUNDING NOISE.
IS THIS WHAT BEING A LIVING CORPSE IS LIKE?
HA HA!
...BUT...
...NOW THAT I CAN USE MY EARS...
...PICKING UP THE SOUND OF YOUR HEART...
...IS A WALK IN THE PARK.

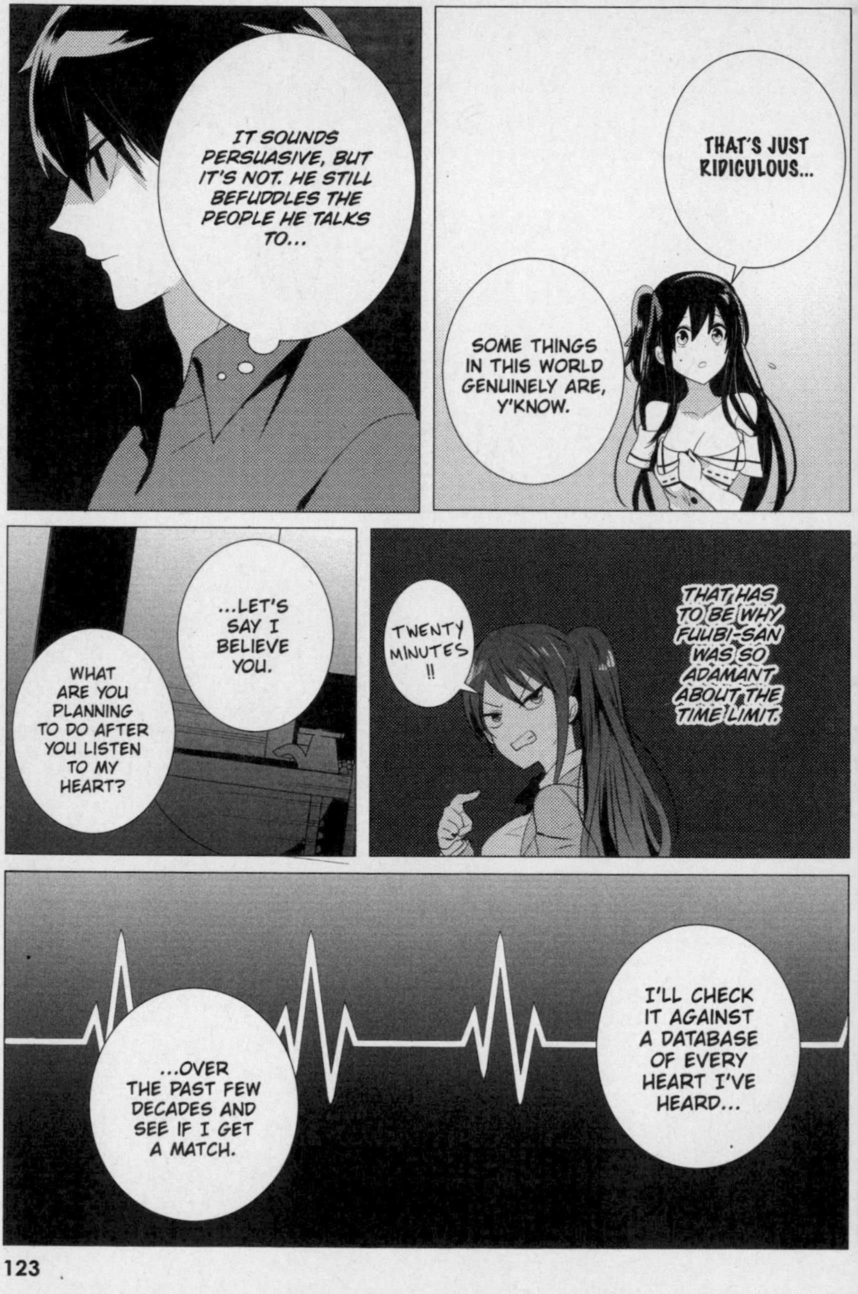
THAT'S JUST RIDICULOUS...
SOME THINGS IN THIS WORLD GENUINELY ARE, Y'KNOW.
IT SOUNDS PERSUASIVE, BUT IT'S NOT. HE STILL BEFUDDLES THE PEOPLE HE TALKS TO...
THAT HAS TO BE WHY FUUBI-SAN WAS SO ADAMANT ABOUT THE TIME LIMIT.
TWENTY MINUTES !!
...LET'S SAY I BELIEVE YOU.
WHAT ARE YOU PLANNING TO DO AFTER YOU LISTEN TO MY HEART?
I'LL CHECK IT AGAINST A DATABASE OF EVERY HEART I'VE HEARD...
...OVER THE PAST FEW DECADES AND SEE IF I GET A MATCH.

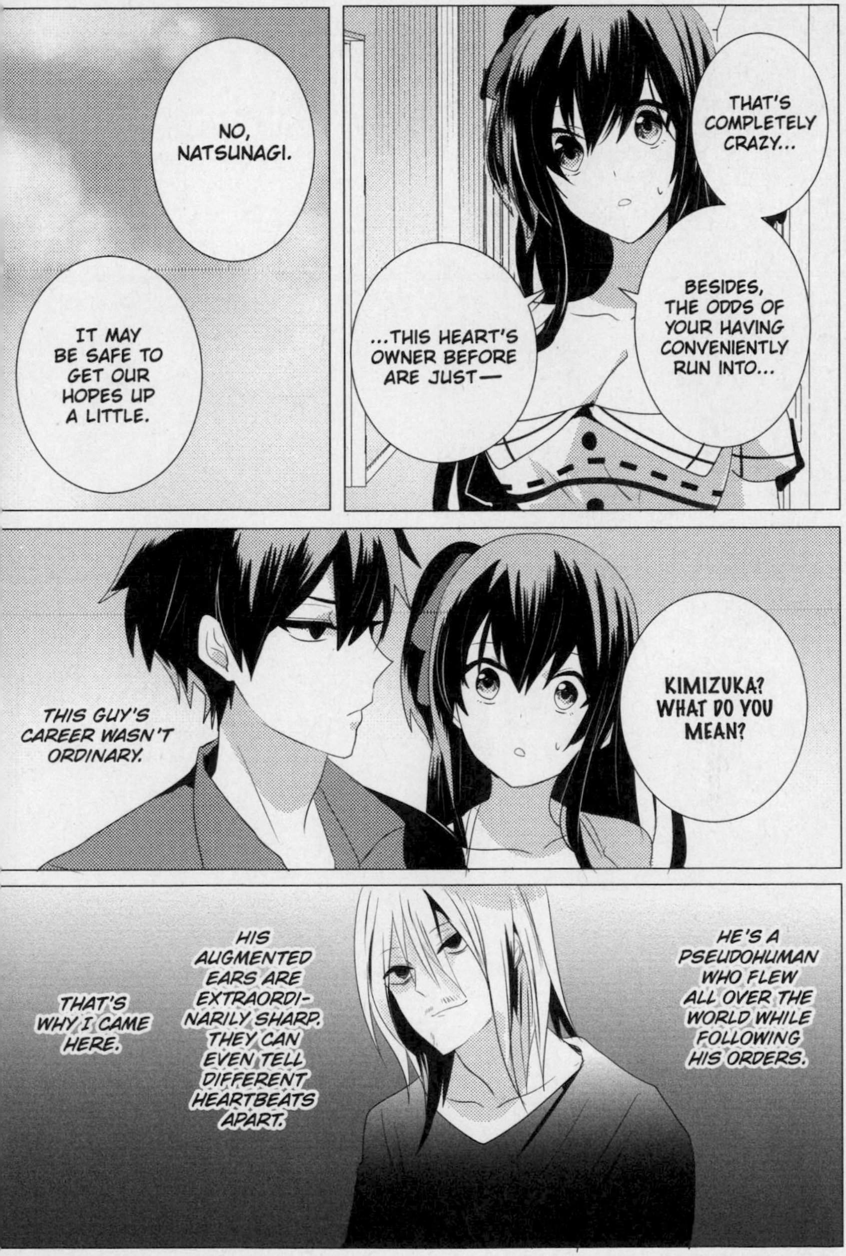
THAT'S COMPLETELY CRAZY...
BESIDES, THE ODDS OF YOUR HAVING CONVENIENTLY RUN INTO...
...THIS HEART'S OWNER BEFORE ARE JUST—
NO, NATSUNAGI.
IT MAY BE SAFE TO GET OUR HOPES UP A LITTLE.
KIMIZUKA? WHAT DO YOU MEAN?
THIS GUY'S CAREER WASN'T ORDINARY.
HE'S A PSEUDOHUMAN WHO FLEW ALL OVER THE WORLD WHILE FOLLOWING HIS ORDERS.
HIS AUGMENTED EARS ARE EXTRAORDI-NARILY SHARP. THEY CAN EVEN TELL DIFFERENT HEARTBEATS APART.
THAT'S WHY I CAME HERE.

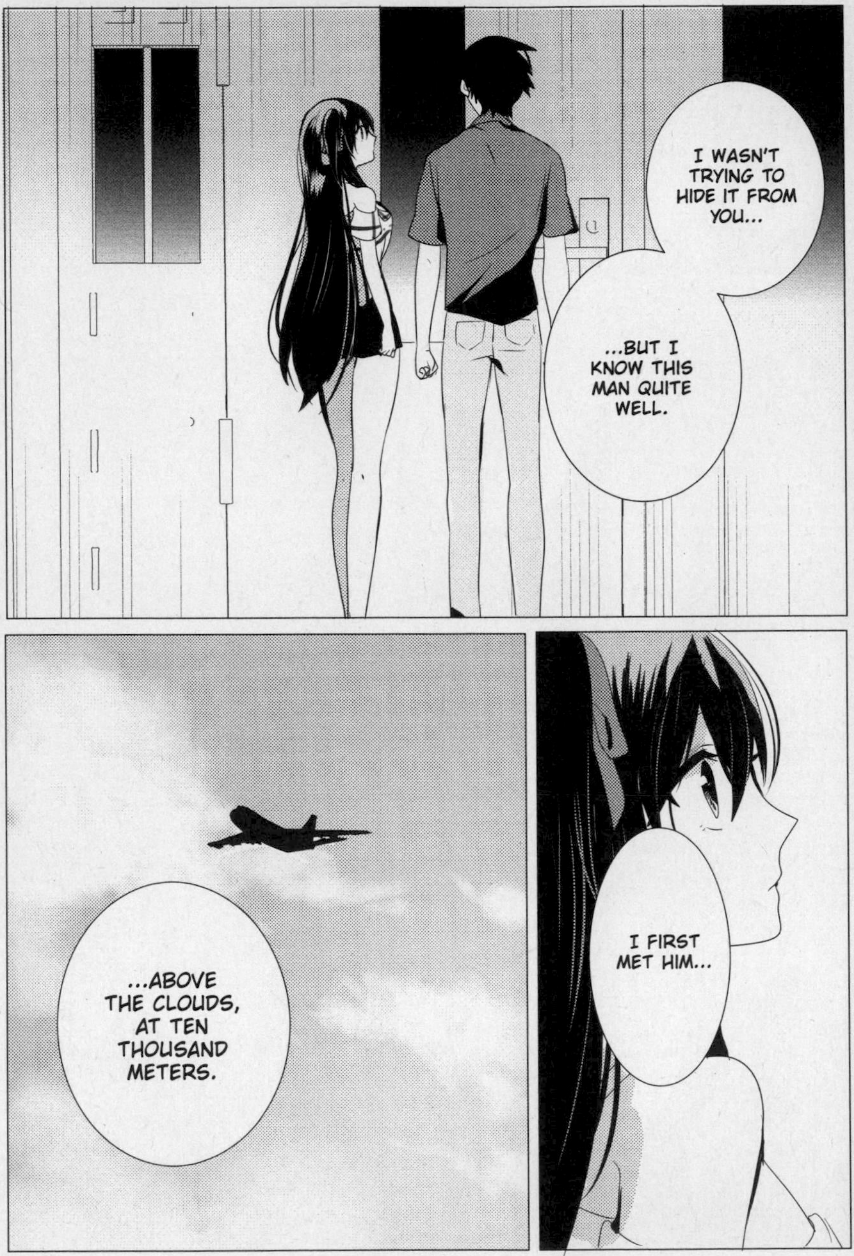
I WASN'T TRYING TO HIDE IT FROM YOU...
...BUT I KNOW THIS MAN QUITE WELL.
I FIRST MET HIM...
...ABOVE THE CLOUDS, AT TEN THOUSAND METERS.

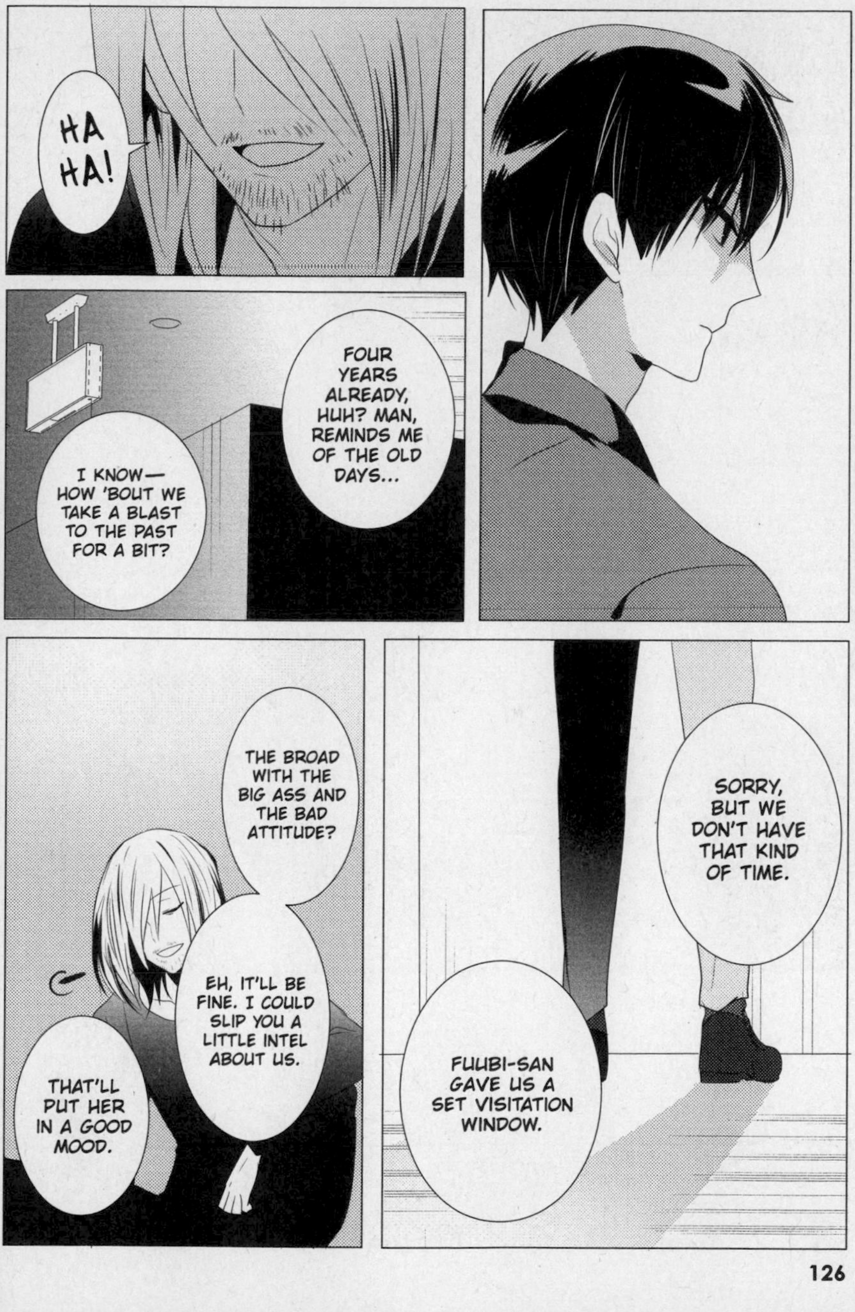
HA HA!
FOUR YEARS ALREADY, HUH? MAN, REMINDS ME OF THE OLD DAYS...
I KNOW—HOW 'BOUT WE TAKE A BLAST TO THE PAST FOR A BIT?
SORRY, BUT WE DON'T HAVE THAT KIND OF TIME.
FUUBI-SAN GAVE US A SET VISITATION WINDOW.
THE BROAD WITH THE BIG ASS AND THE BAD ATTITUDE?
EH, IT'LL BE FINE. I COULD SLIP YOU A LITTLE INTEL ABOUT US.
THAT'LL PUT HER IN A GOOD MOOD.

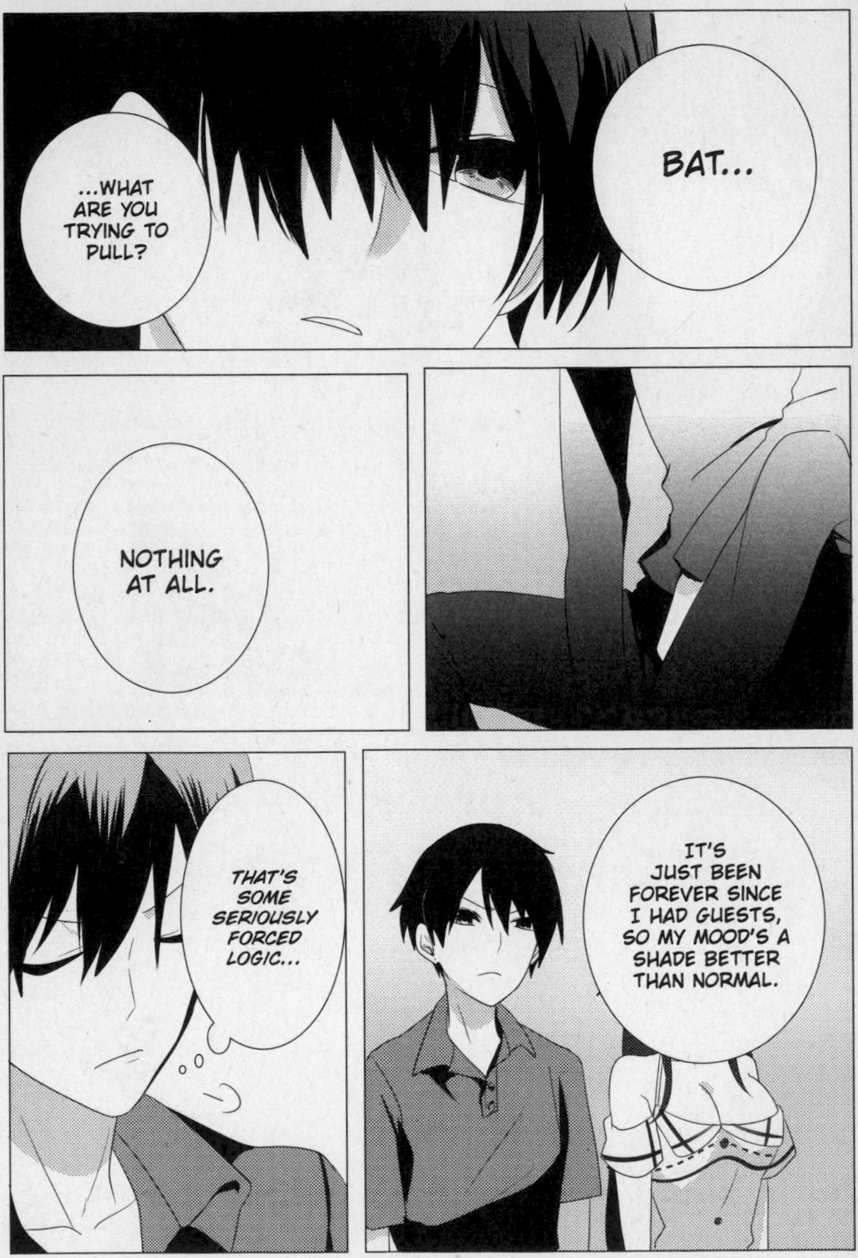
BAT...
...WHAT ARE YOU TRYING TO PULL?
NOTHING AT ALL.
IT'S JUST BEEN FOREVER SINCE I HAD GUESTS, SO MY MOOD'S A SHADE BETTER THAN NORMAL.
THAT'S SOME SERIOUSLY FORCED LOGIC...

SORRY, NATSUNAGI.

LOOKS LIKE THIS WILL TAKE A WHILE.

......

...LET ME TELL YOU...

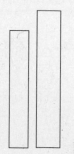

...ABOUT WHAT HAPPENED FOUR YEARS AGO.

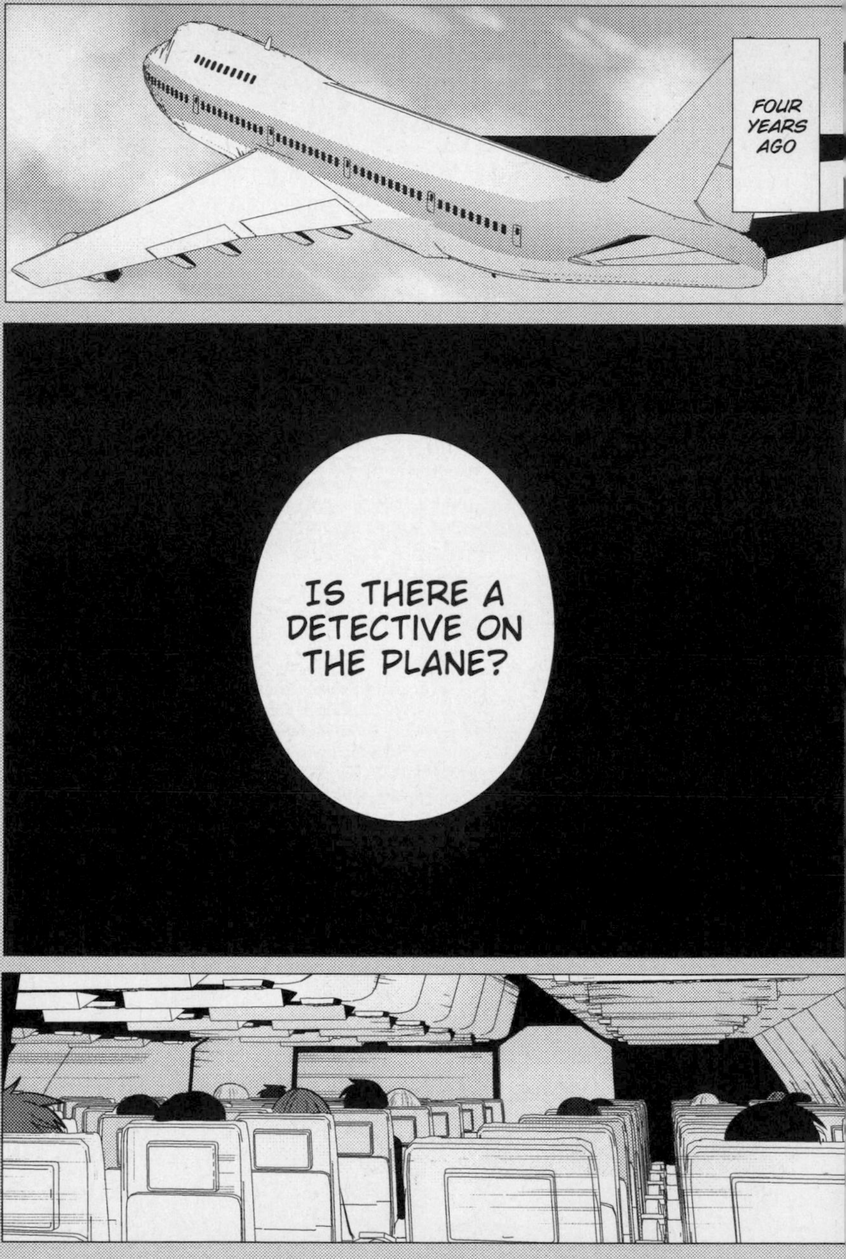
FOUR YEARS AGO
IS THERE A DETECTIVE ON THE PLANE?

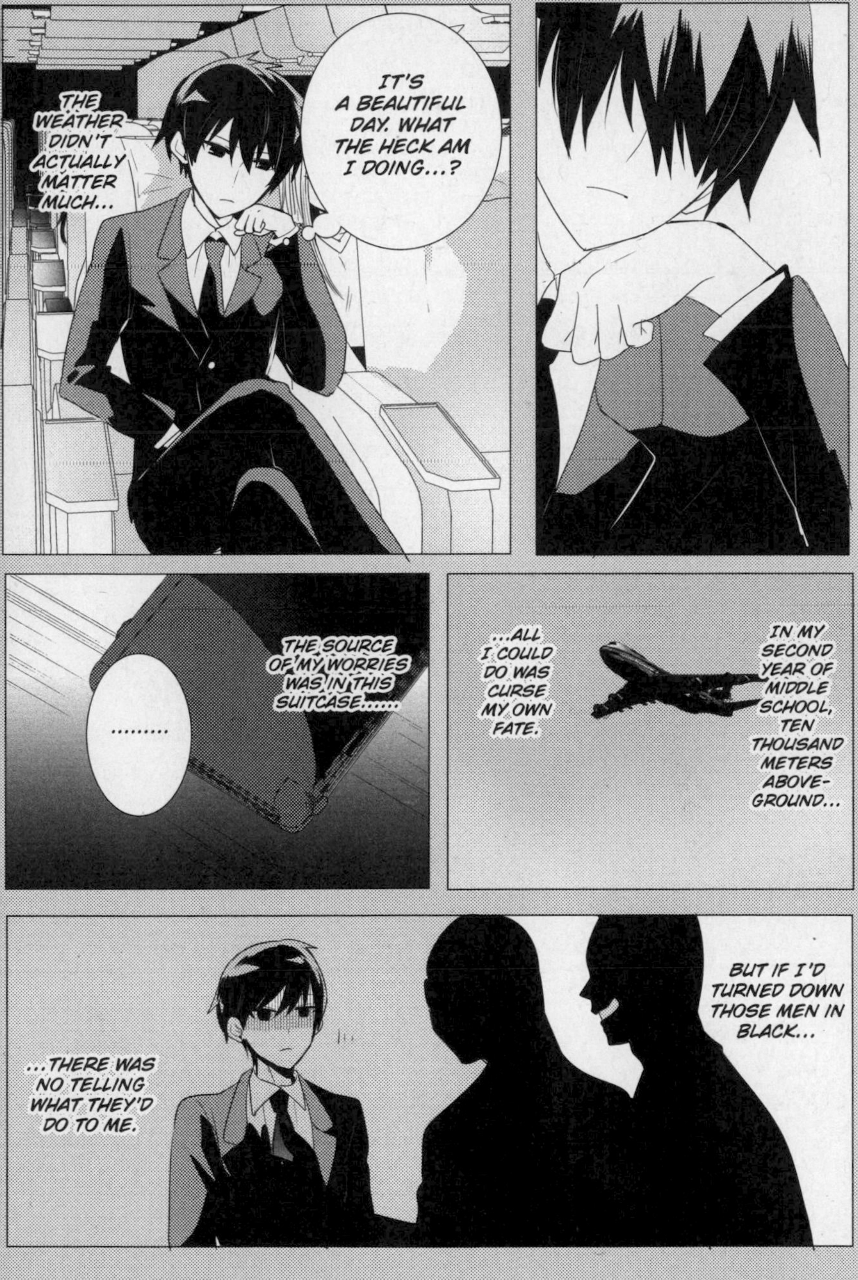
IT'S A BEAUTIFUL DAY. WHAT THE HECK AM I DOING...?
THE WEATHER DIDN'T ACTUALLY MATTER MUCH...
IN MY SECOND YEAR OF MIDDLE SCHOOL, TEN THOUSAND METERS ABOVE-GROUND...
...ALL I COULD DO WAS CURSE MY OWN FATE.
THE SOURCE OF MY WORRIES WAS IN THIS SUITCASE......
....
BUT IF I'D TURNED DOWN THOSE MEN IN BLACK...
...THERE WAS NO TELLING WHAT THEY'D DO TO ME.

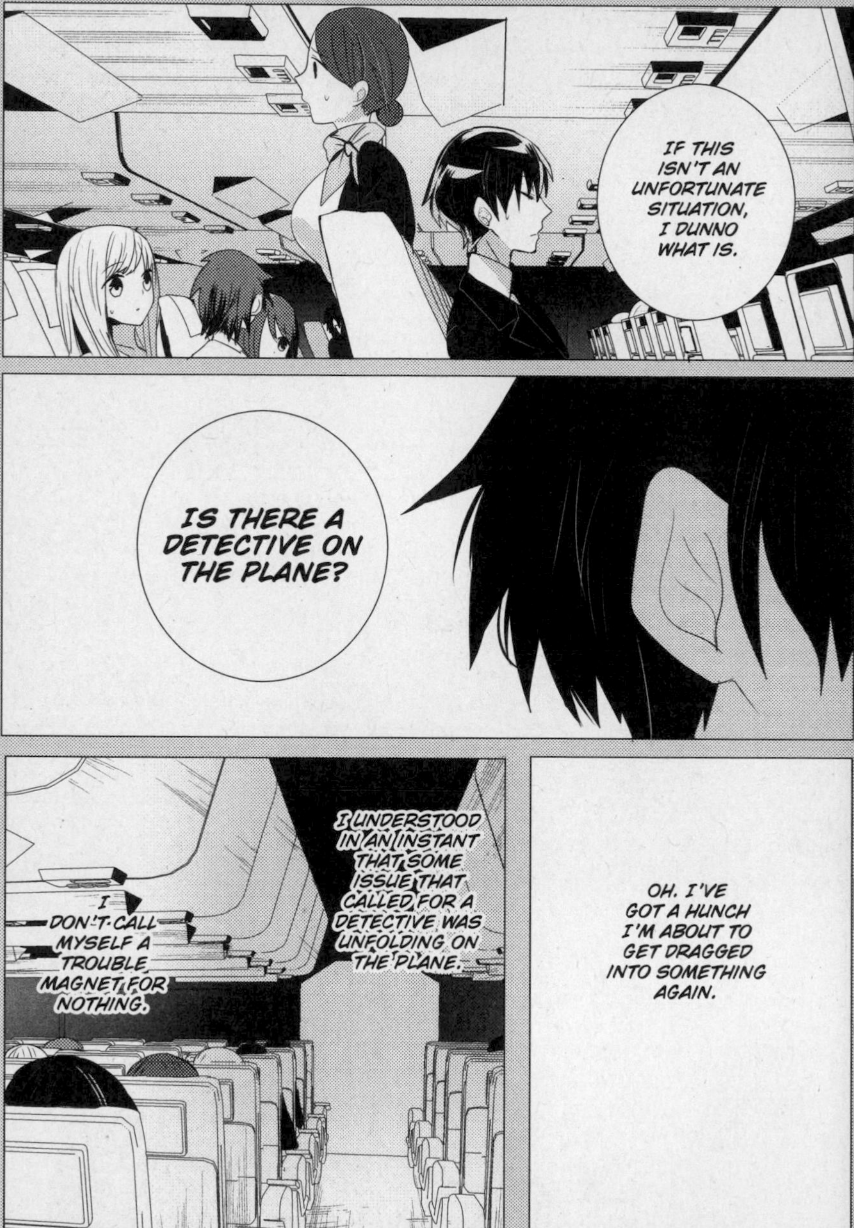
IF THIS ISN'T AN UNFORTUNATE SITUATION, I DUNNO WHAT IS.
IS THERE A DETECTIVE ON THE PLANE?
OH. I'VE GOT A HUNCH I'M ABOUT TO GET DRAGGED INTO SOMETHING AGAIN.
I UNDERSTOOD IN AN INSTANT THAT SOME ISSUE THAT CALLED FOR A DETECTIVE WAS UNFOLDING ON THE PLANE.
I DON'T CALL MYSELF A TROUBLE MAGNET FOR NOTHING.

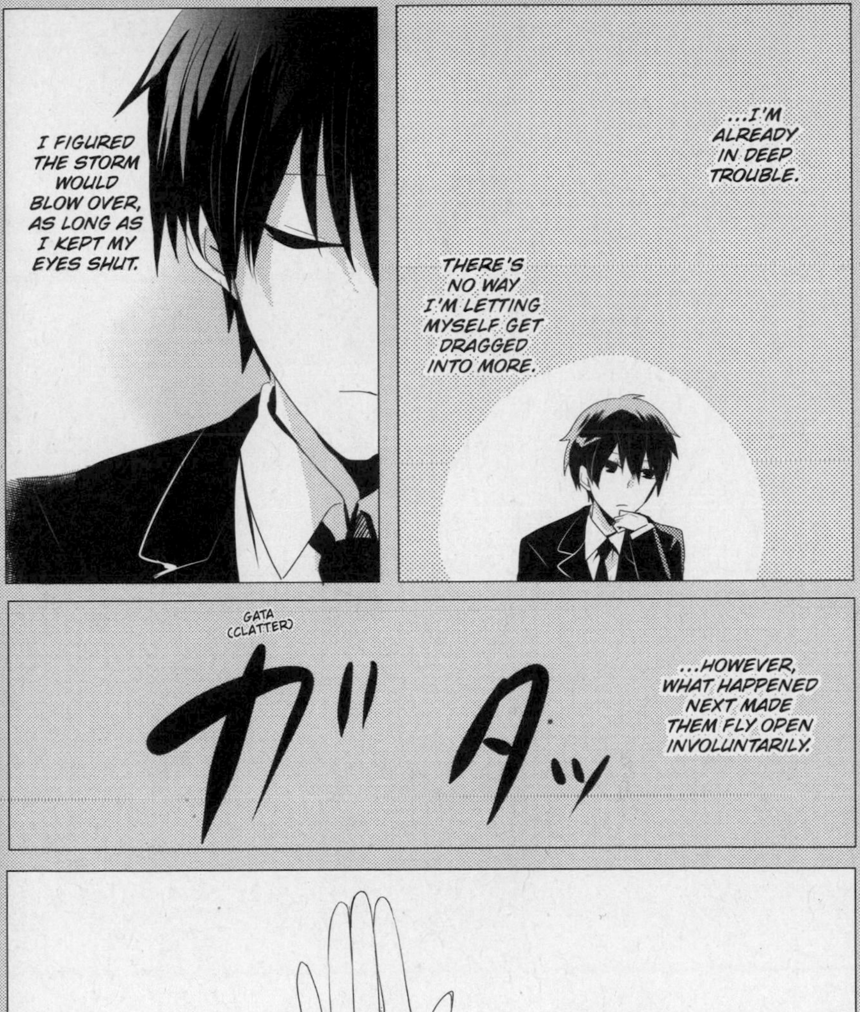
...I'M ALREADY IN DEEP TROUBLE.
THERE'S NO WAY I'M LETTING MYSELF GET DRAGGED INTO MORE.
I FIGURED THE STORM WOULD BLOW OVER, AS LONG AS I KEPT MY EYES SHUT.
...HOWEVER, WHAT HAPPENED NEXT MADE THEM FLY OPEN INVOLUNTARILY.
ガタッ
GATA (CLATTER)

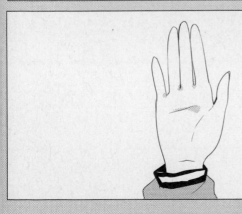

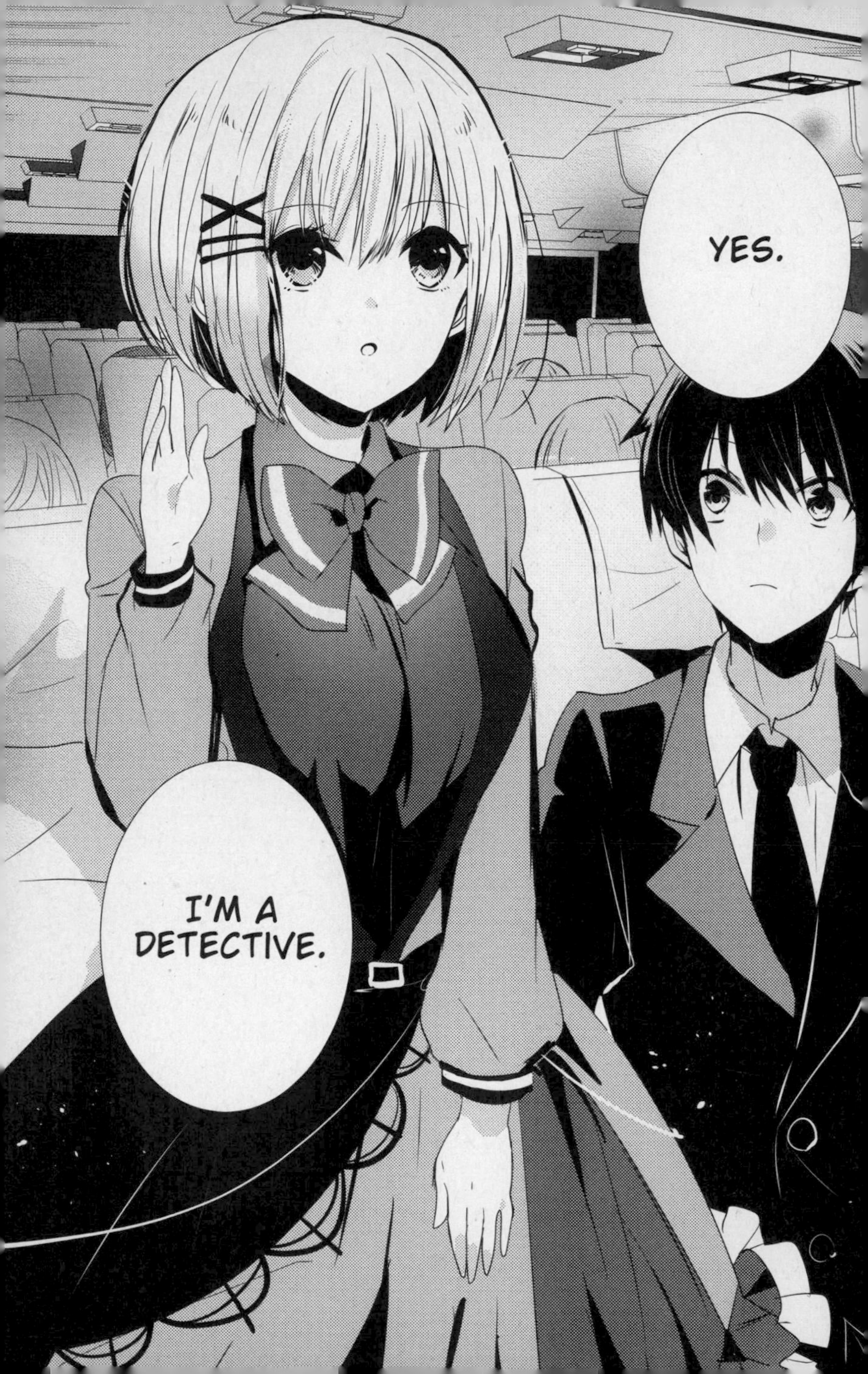
YES.
I'M A DETECTIVE.

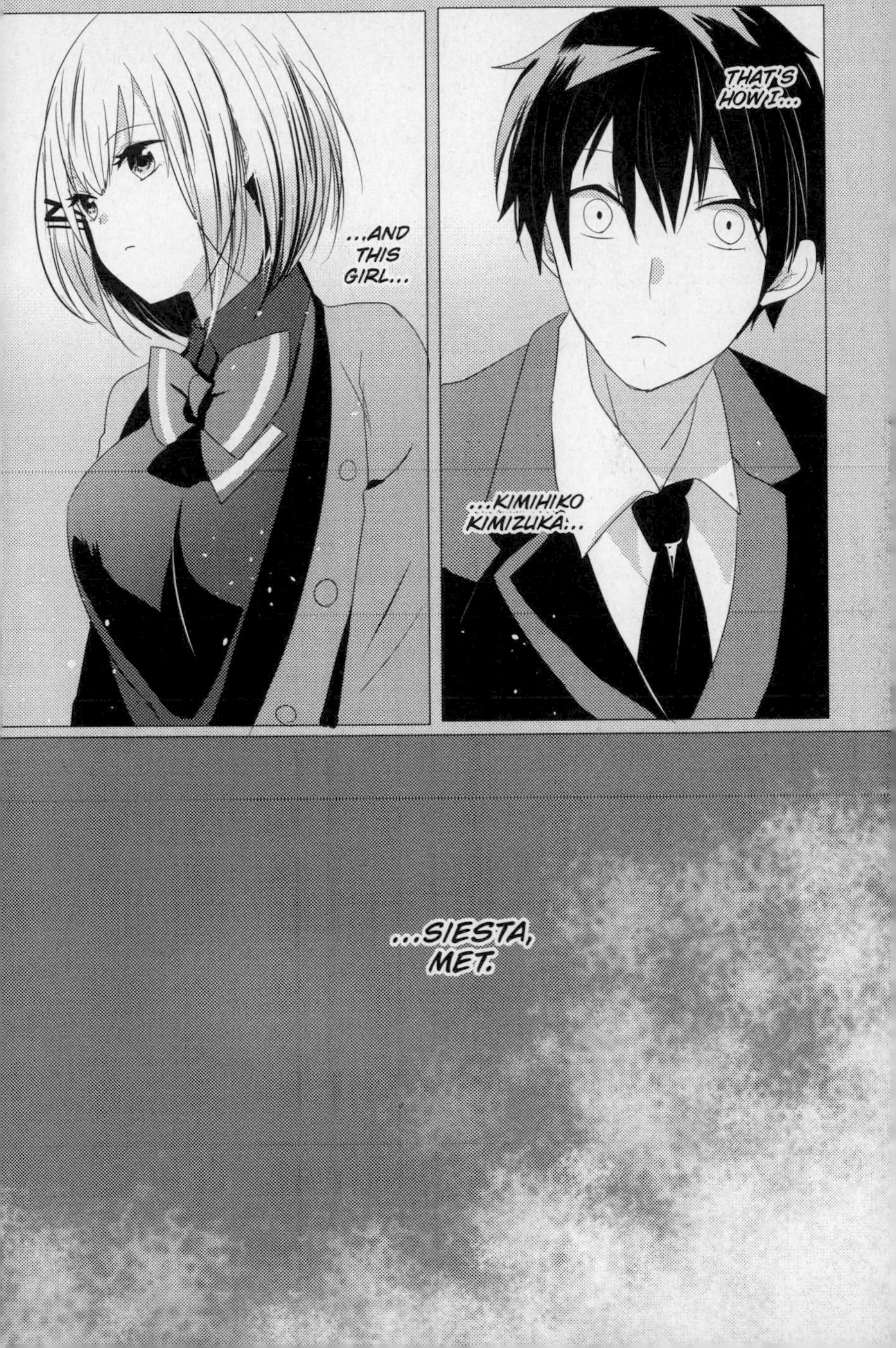
THAT'S HOW I...
...KIMIHIKO KIMIZUKA...
...AND THIS GIRL...
...SIESTA, MET.

The Detective Is Already Dead

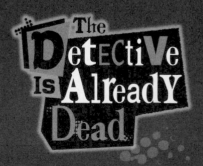

The Detective Is Already Dead

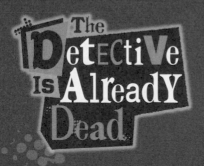

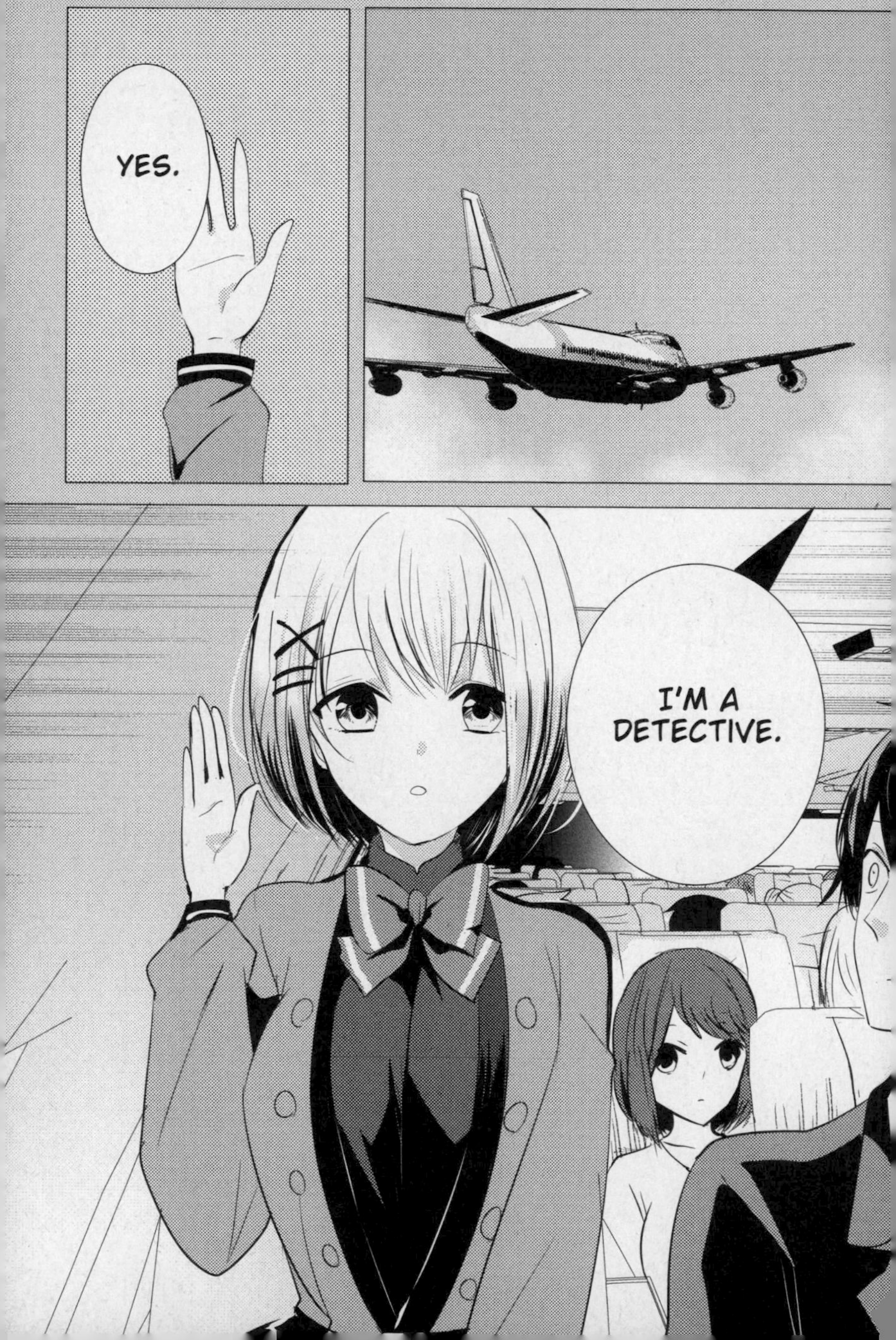
YES.
I'M A DETECTIVE.

Episode. 5
The Detective on the Plane

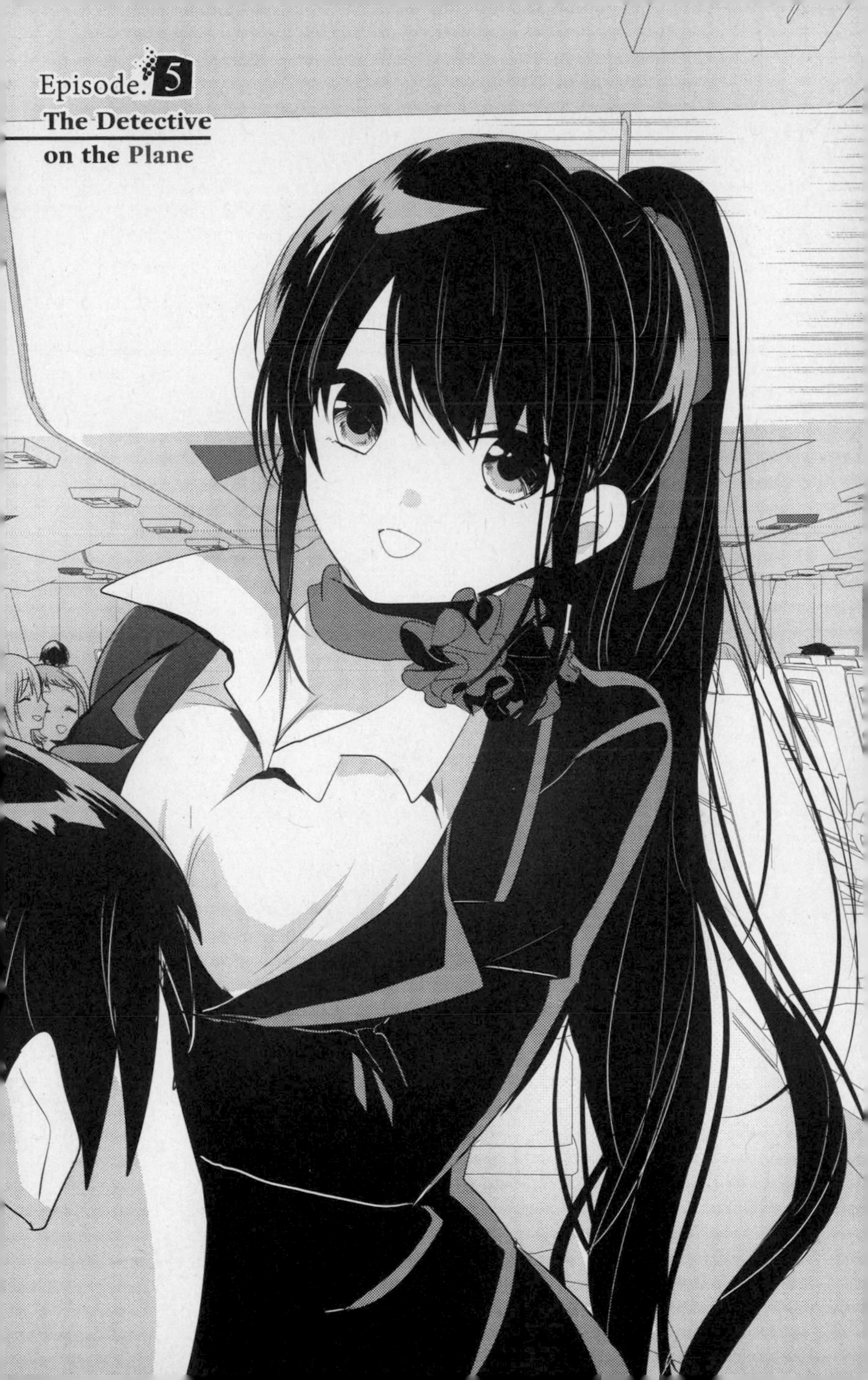

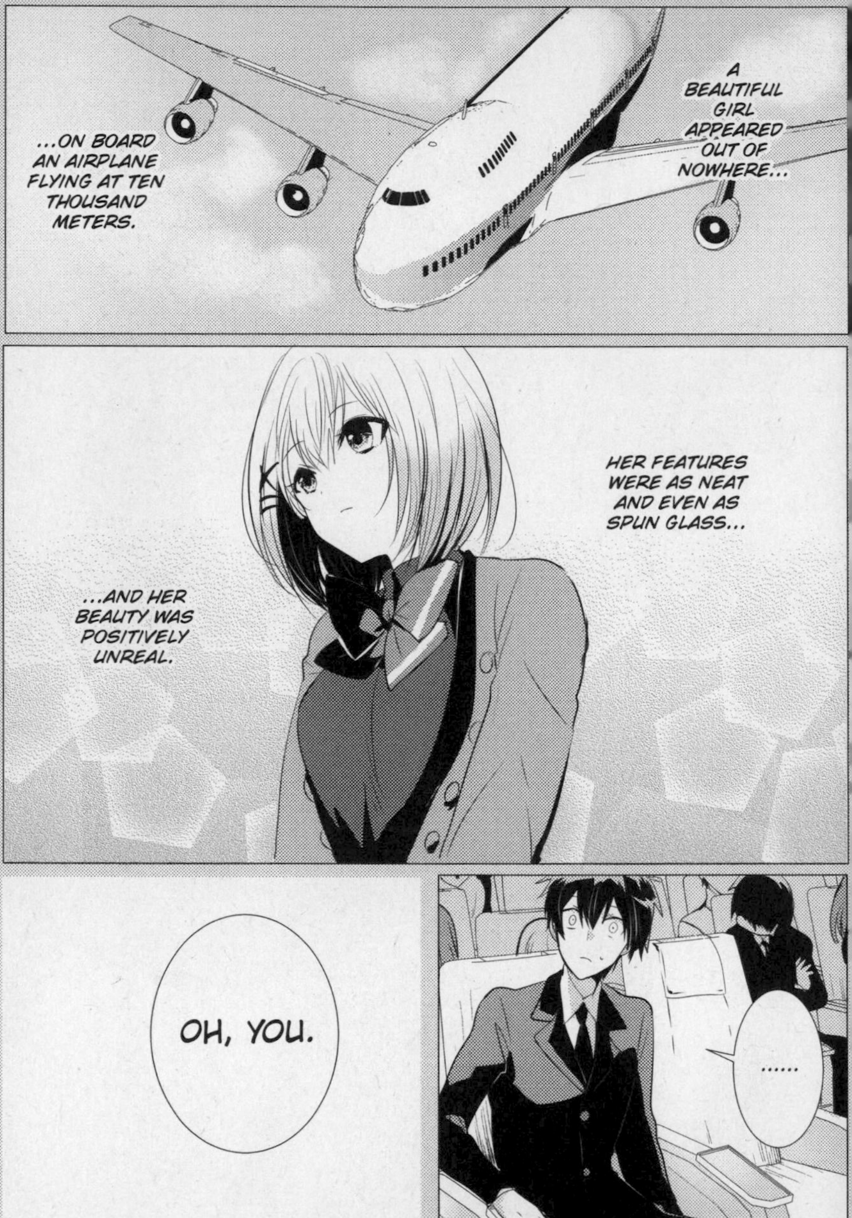
A BEAUTIFUL GIRL APPEARED OUT OF NOWHERE...
...ON BOARD AN AIRPLANE FLYING AT TEN THOUSAND METERS.
HER FEATURES WERE AS NEAT AND EVEN AS SPUN GLASS...
...AND HER BEAUTY WAS POSITIVELY UNREAL.
......
OH, YOU.

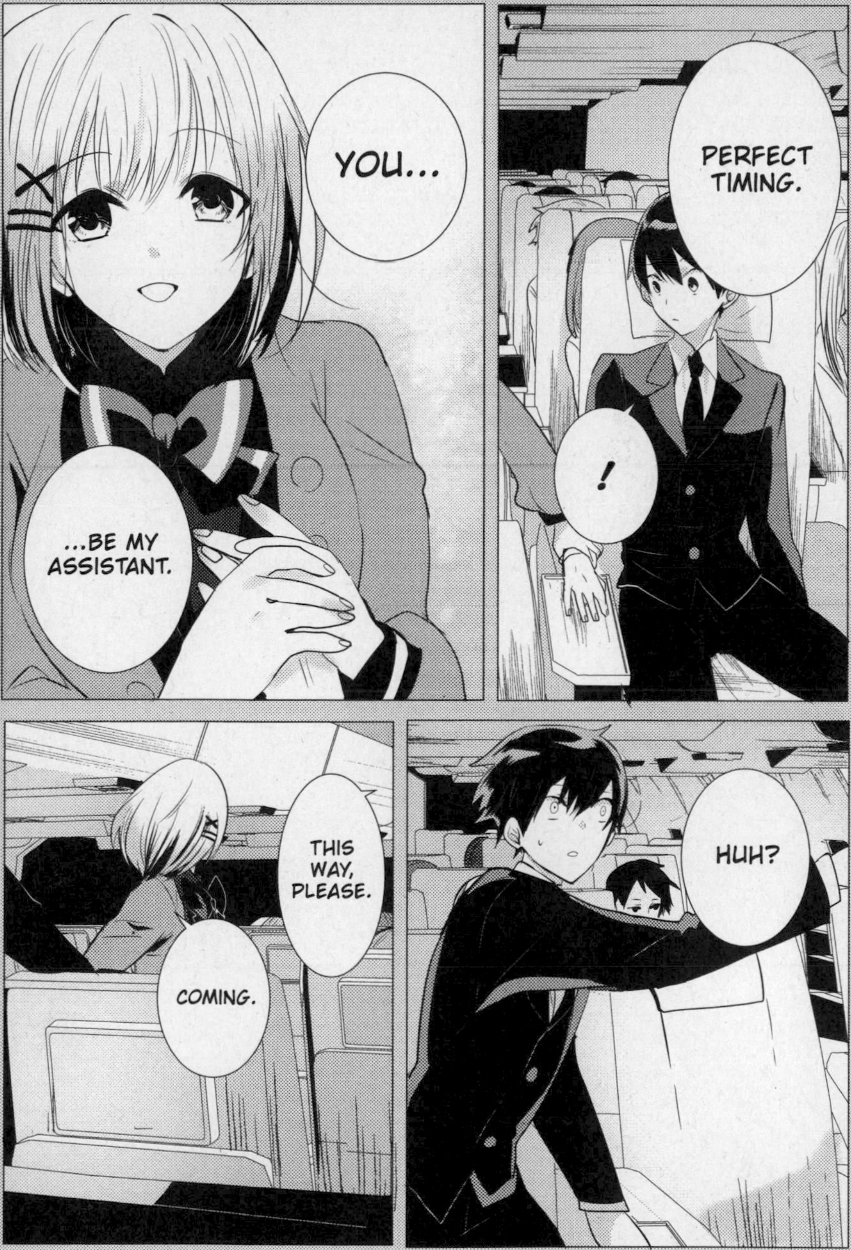
PERFECT TIMING.
!
YOU...
...BE MY ASSISTANT.
HUH?
THIS WAY, PLEASE.
COMING.

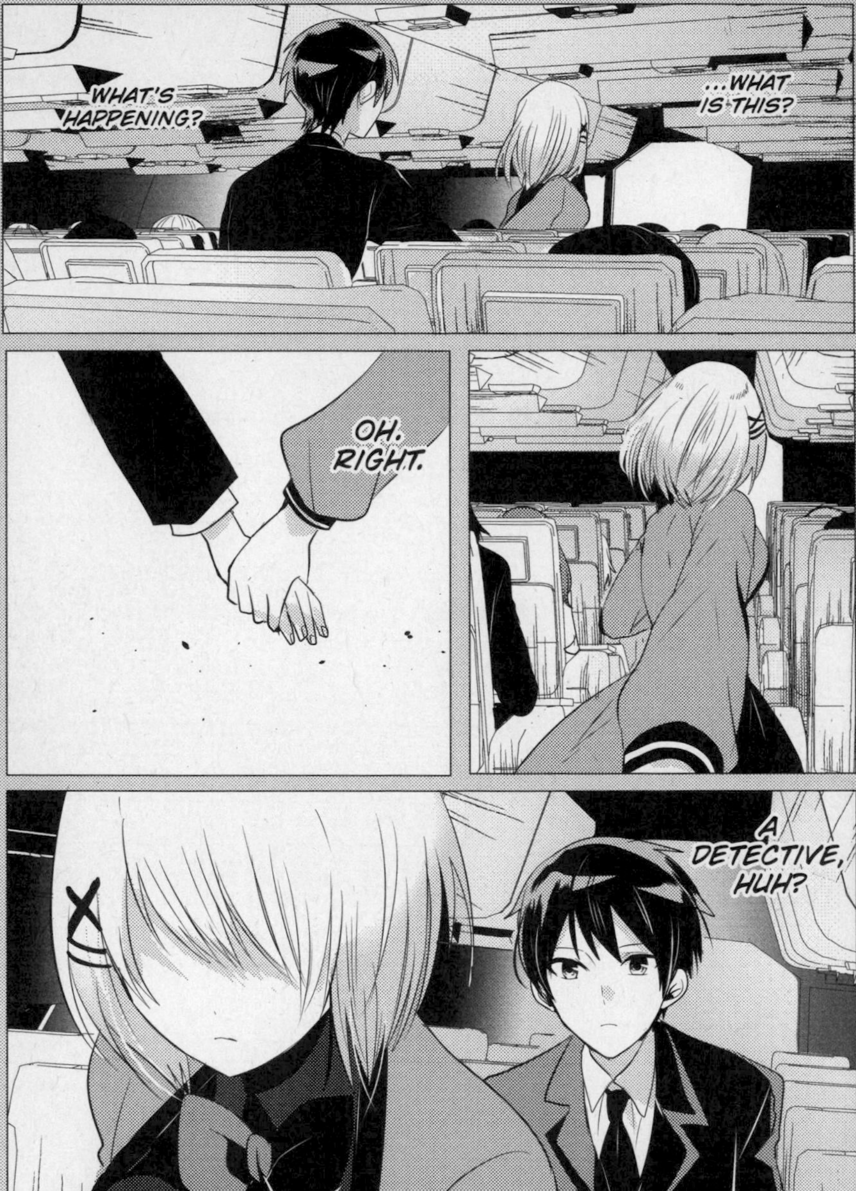
...WHAT IS THIS?
WHAT'S HAPPENING?
OH. RIGHT.
A DETECTIVE, HUH?

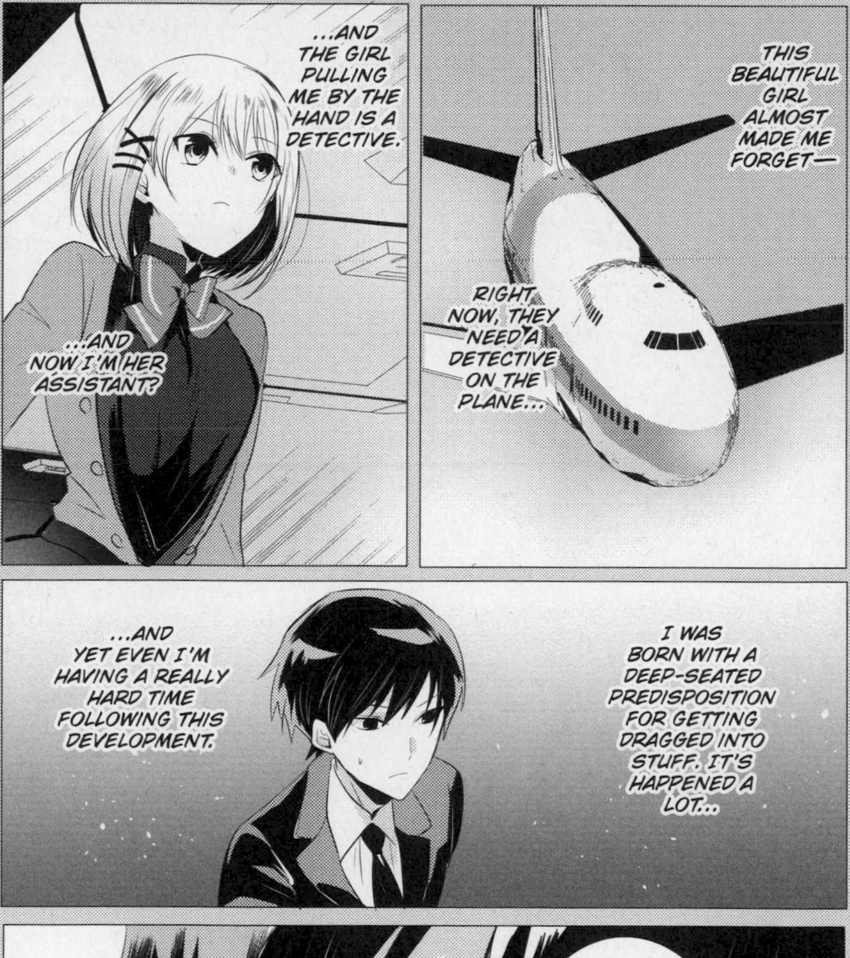
THIS BEAUTIFUL GIRL ALMOST MADE ME FORGET—
RIGHT NOW, THEY NEED A DETECTIVE ON THE PLANE...
...AND THE GIRL PULLING ME BY THE HAND IS A DETECTIVE.
...AND NOW I'M HER ASSISTANT?
I WAS BORN WITH A DEEP-SEATED PREDISPOSITION FOR GETTING DRAGGED INTO STUFF. IT'S HAPPENED A LOT...
...AND YET EVEN I'M HAVING A REALLY HARD TIME FOLLOWING THIS DEVELOPMENT.
SIESTA.

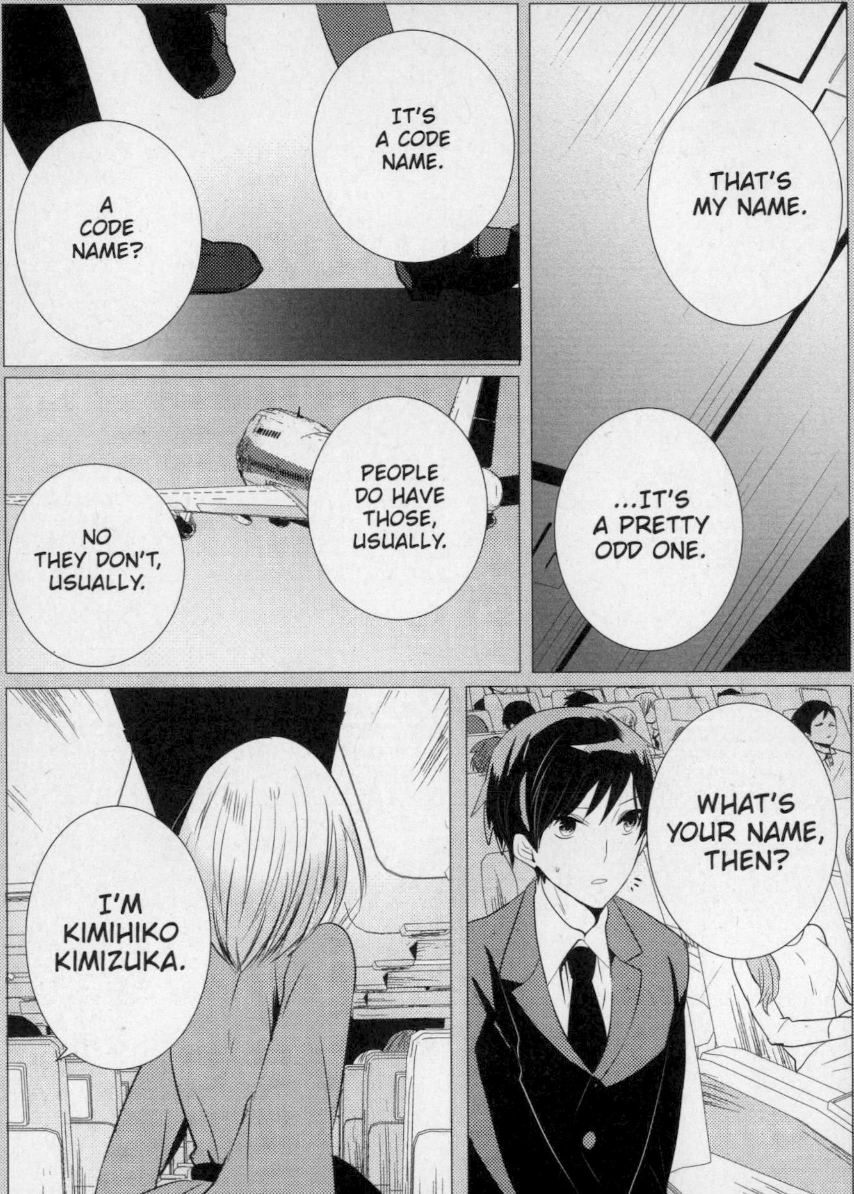
THAT'S MY NAME.
...IT'S A PRETTY ODD ONE.
IT'S A CODE NAME.
A CODE NAME?
PEOPLE DO HAVE THOSE, USUALLY.
NO THEY DON'T, USUALLY.
WHAT'S YOUR NAME, THEN?
I'M KIMIHIKO KIMIZUKA.

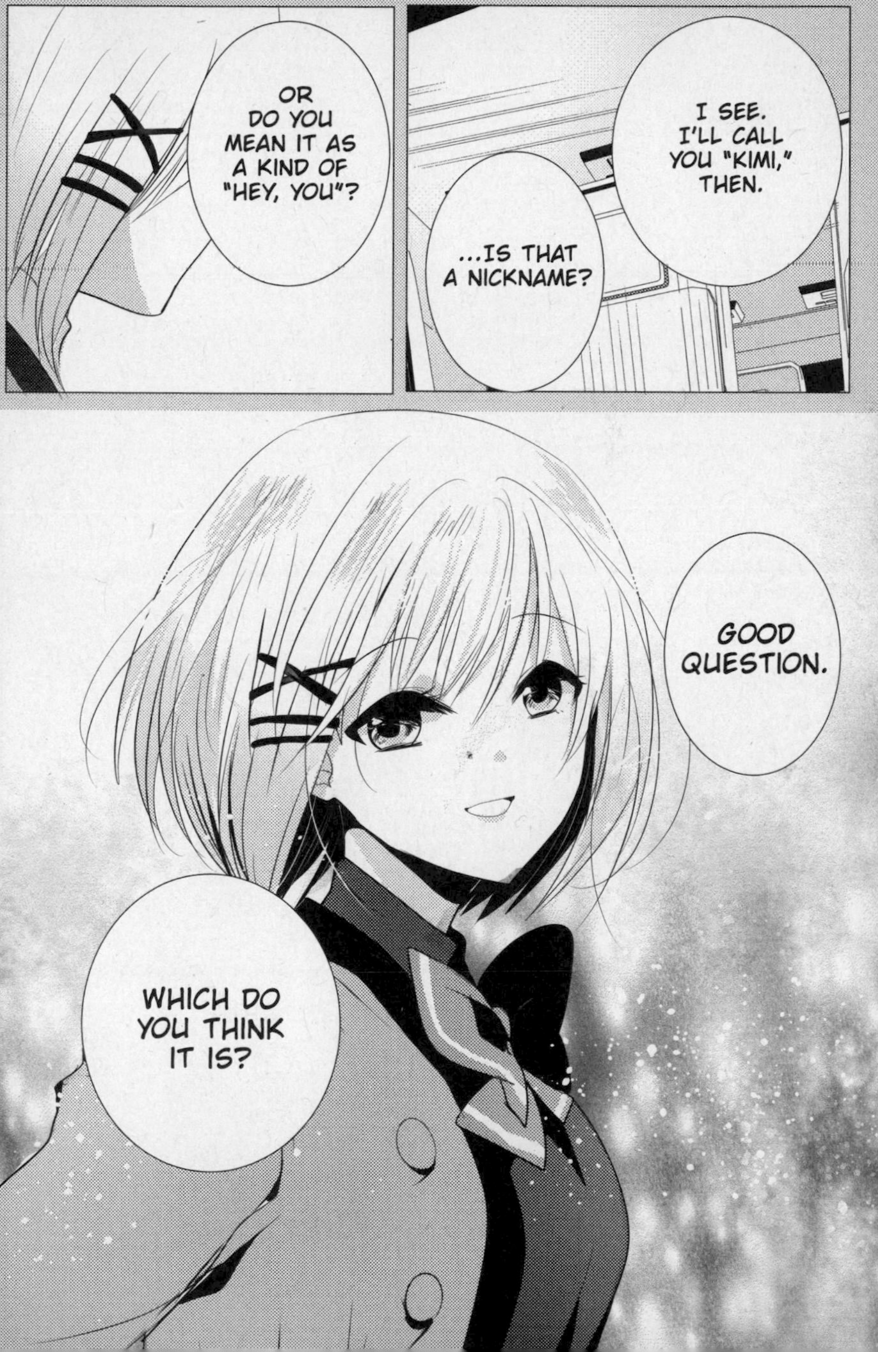
I SEE. I'LL CALL YOU "KIMI," THEN.
...IS THAT A NICKNAME?
OR DO YOU MEAN IT AS A KIND OF "HEY, YOU"?
GOOD QUESTION.
WHICH DO YOU THINK IT IS?

THIS IS NO TIME TO GET DISTRACTED BY HER SMILE...!

I'VE BROUGHT A DETECTIVE AND THE DETECTIVE'S ASSISTANT.

が
チ
ャ

GACHA
(KACHAK)

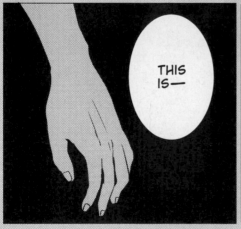

THIS IS—

!!

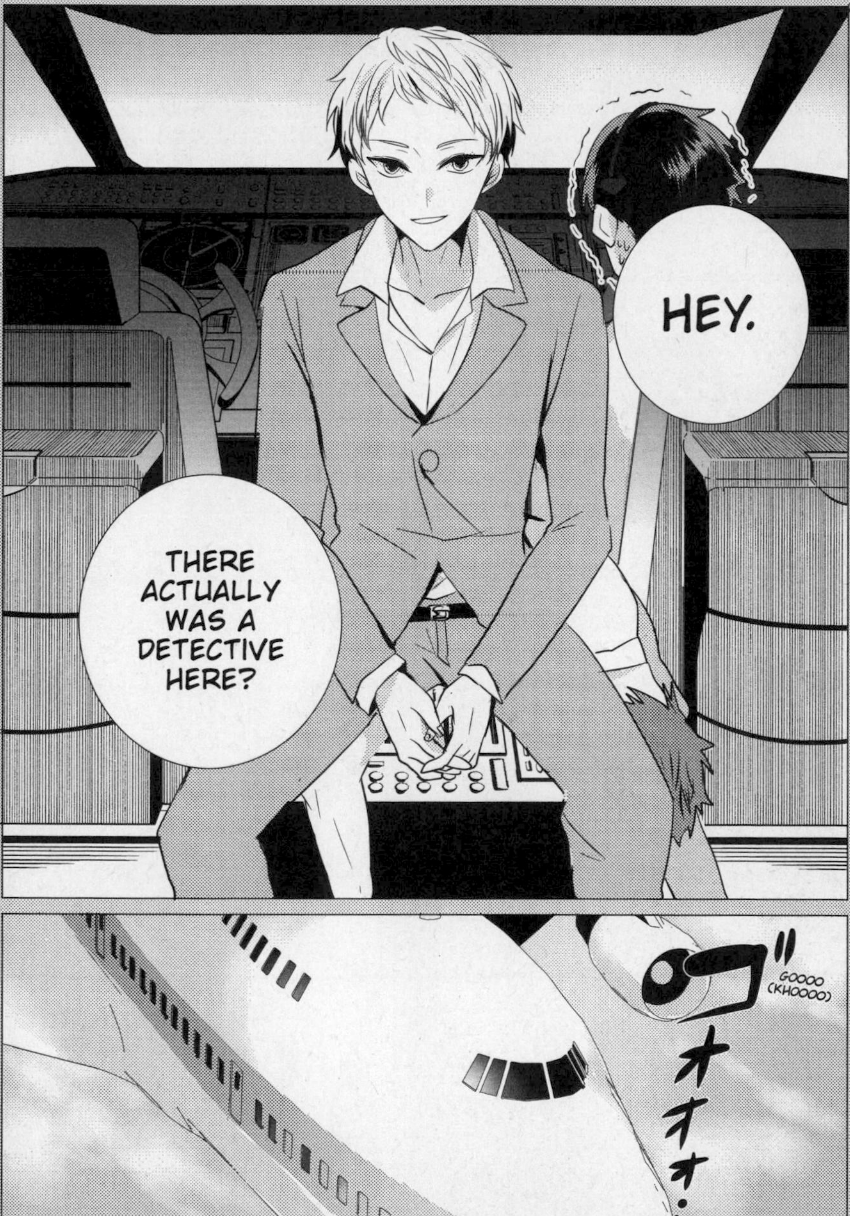
HEY.
THERE ACTUALLY WAS A DETECTIVE HERE?
GOOOO (KHOOOO)

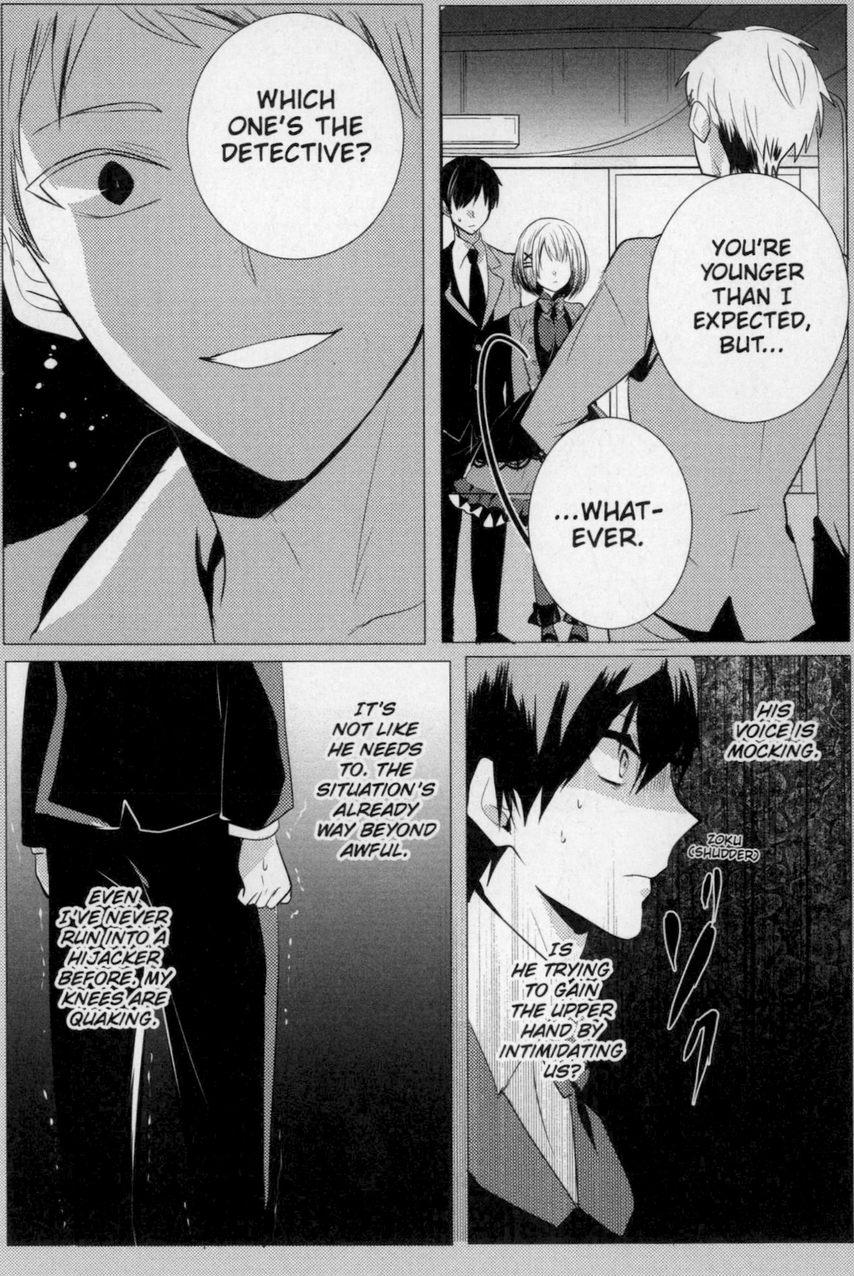
YOU'RE YOUNGER THAN I EXPECTED, BUT...
...WHAT-EVER.
WHICH ONE'S THE DETECTIVE?
HIS VOICE IS MOCKING.
ZOKU (SHUDDER)
IS HE TRYING TO GAIN THE UPPER HAND BY INTIMIDATING US?
IT'S NOT LIKE HE NEEDS TO. THE SITUATION'S ALREADY WAY BEYOND AWFUL.
EVEN I'VE NEVER RUN INTO A HIJACKER BEFORE. MY KNEES ARE QUAKING.

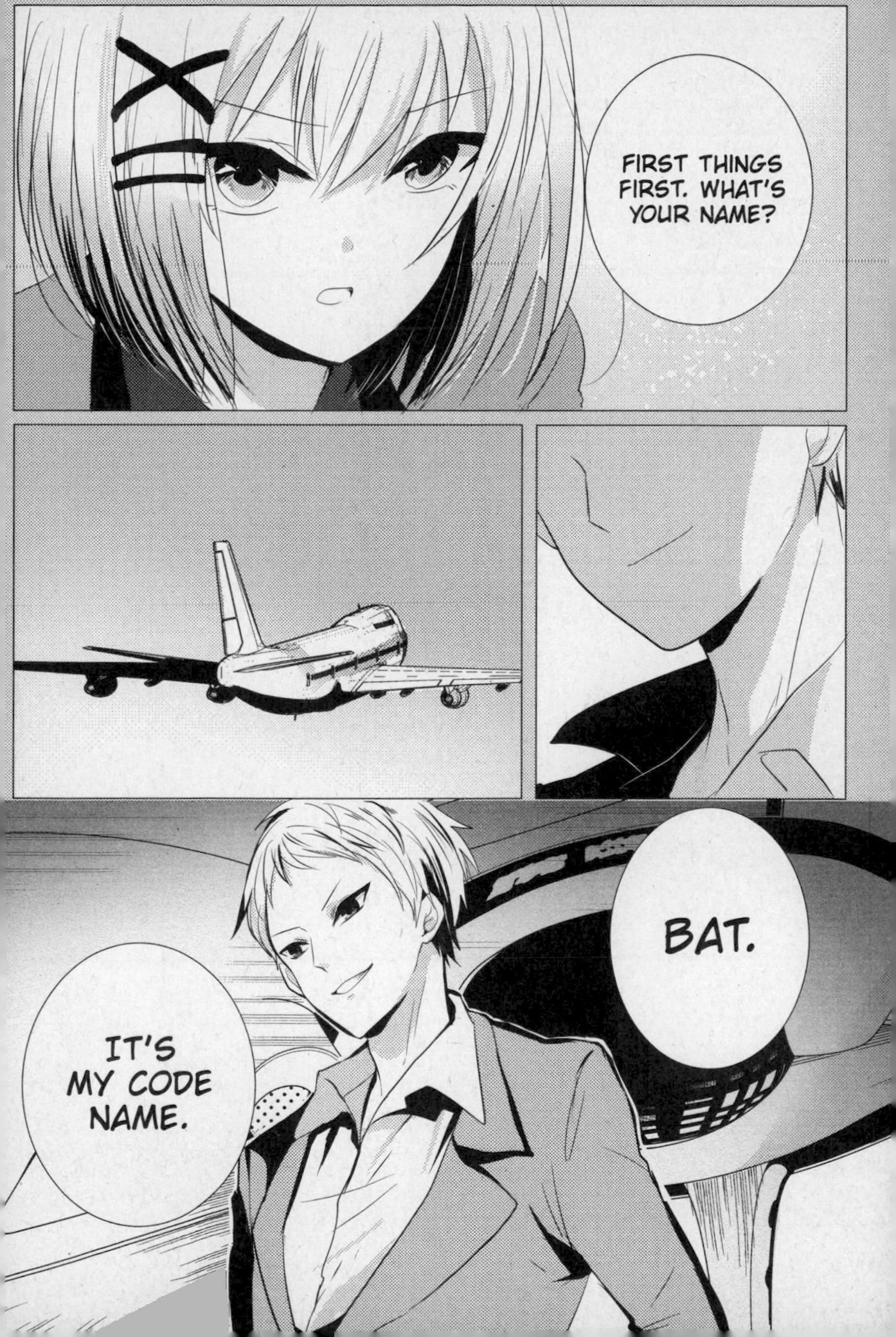
FIRST THINGS FIRST. WHAT'S YOUR NAME?
BAT.
IT'S MY CODE NAME.

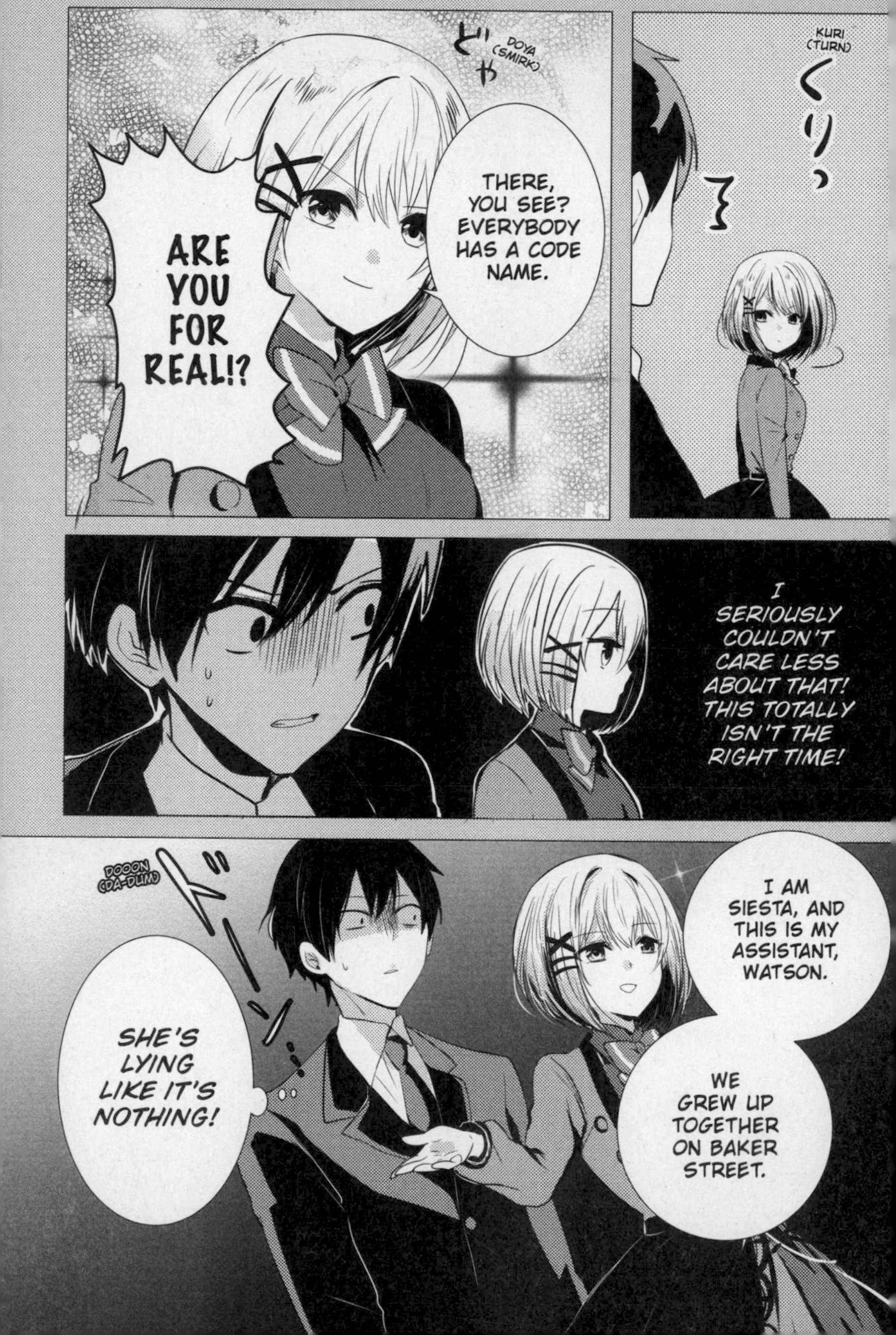
KURI (TURN)
くりっ
DOYA (SMIRK)
どや
THERE, YOU SEE? EVERYBODY HAS A CODE NAME.
ARE YOU FOR REAL!?
I SERIOUSLY COULDN'T CARE LESS ABOUT THAT! THIS TOTALLY ISN'T THE RIGHT TIME!
I AM SIESTA, AND THIS IS MY ASSISTANT, WATSON.
WE GREW UP TOGETHER ON BAKER STREET.
DOOON (DA-DUM)
SHE'S LYING LIKE IT'S NOTHING!

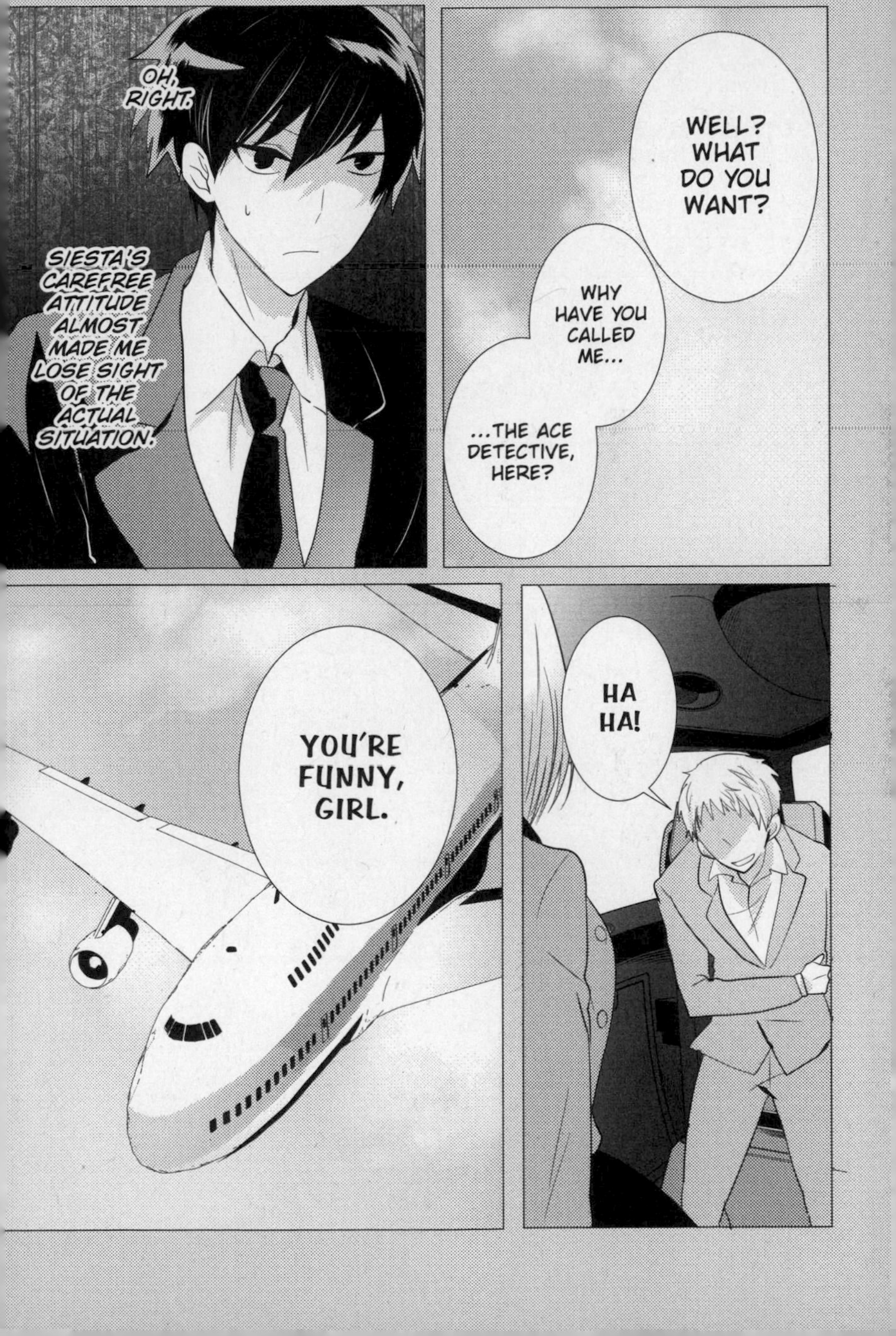
WELL? WHAT DO YOU WANT?
WHY HAVE YOU CALLED ME...
...THE ACE DETECTIVE, HERE?
OH, RIGHT.
SIESTA'S CAREFREE ATTITUDE ALMOST MADE ME LOSE SIGHT OF THE ACTUAL SITUATION.
HA HA!
YOU'RE FUNNY, GIRL.

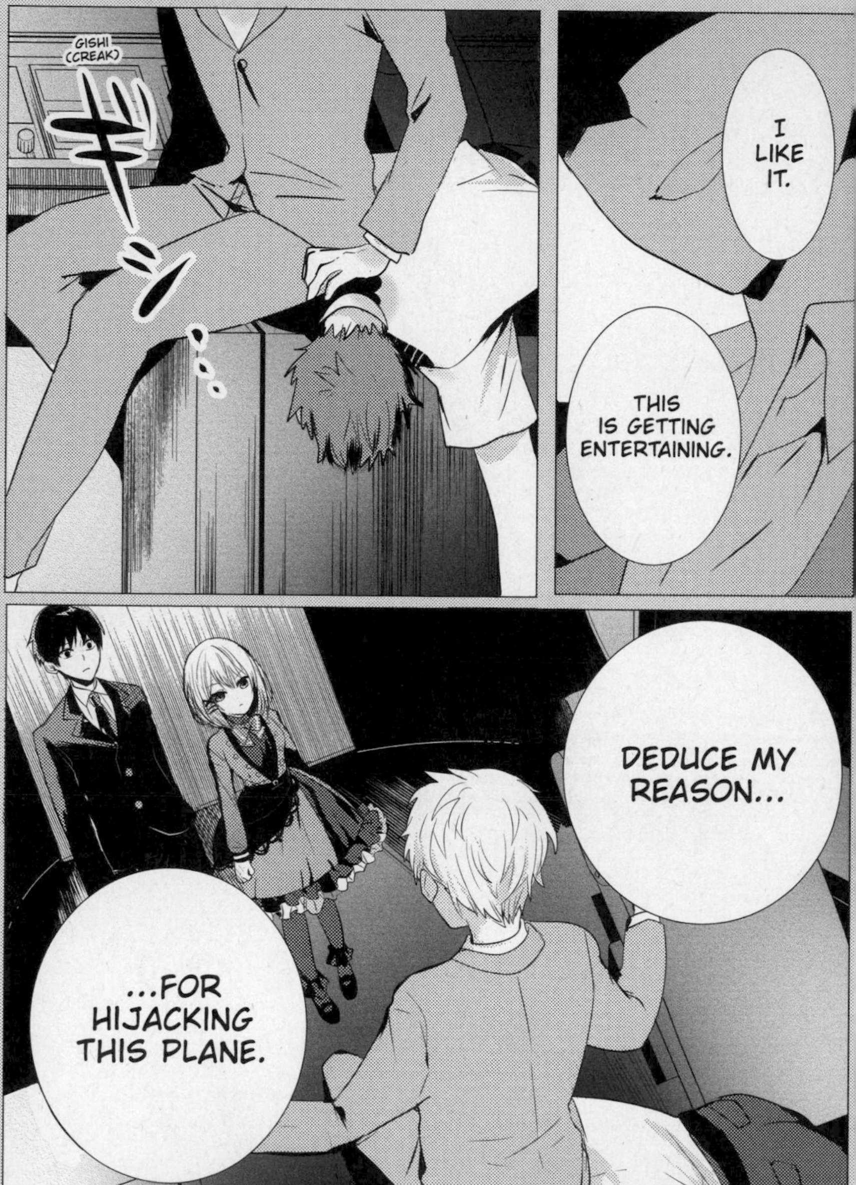
I LIKE IT.
THIS IS GETTING ENTERTAINING.
GISHI (CREAK)
DEDUCE MY REASON...
...FOR HIJACKING THIS PLANE.

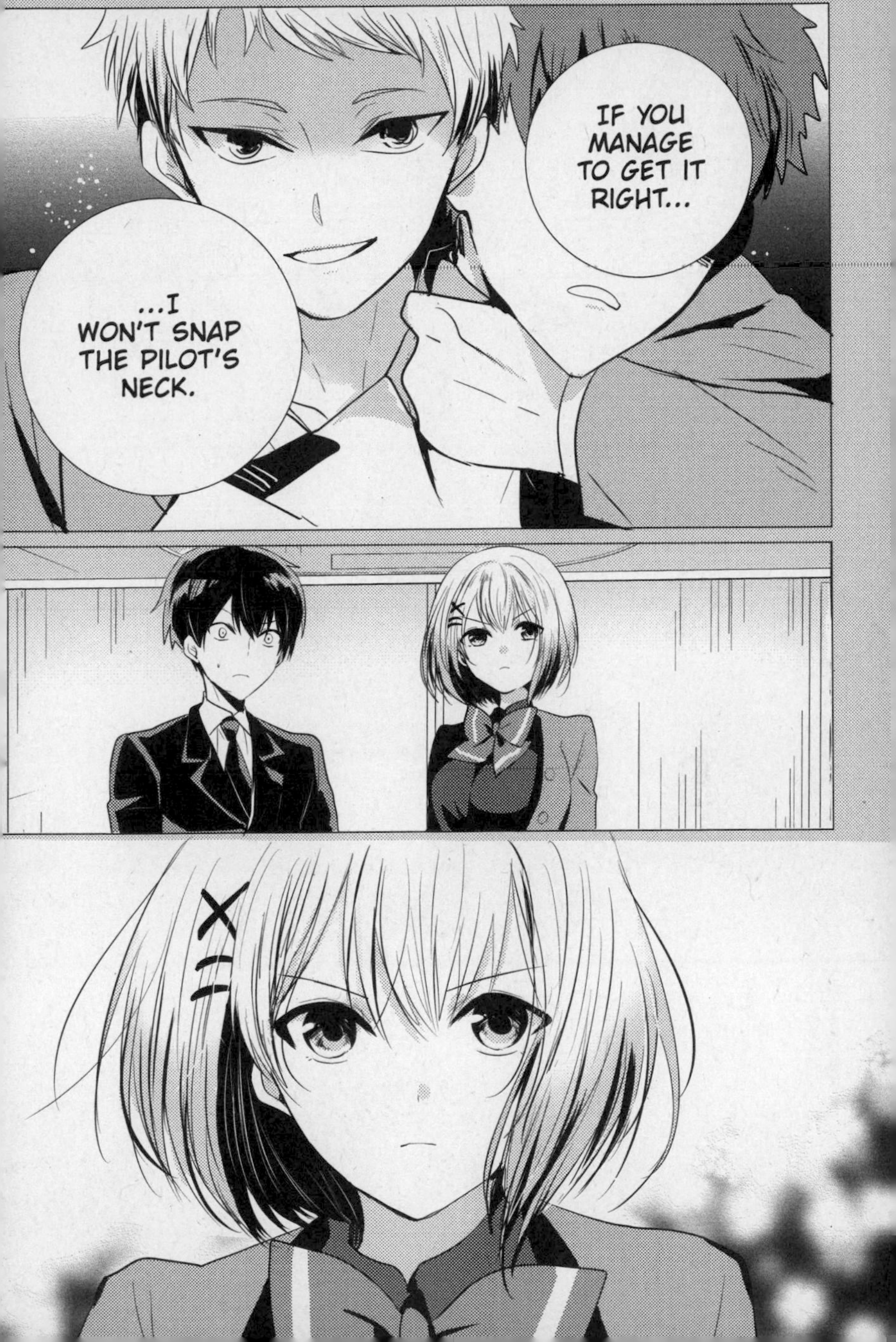
IF YOU MANAGE TO GET IT RIGHT...
...I WON'T SNAP THE PILOT'S NECK.

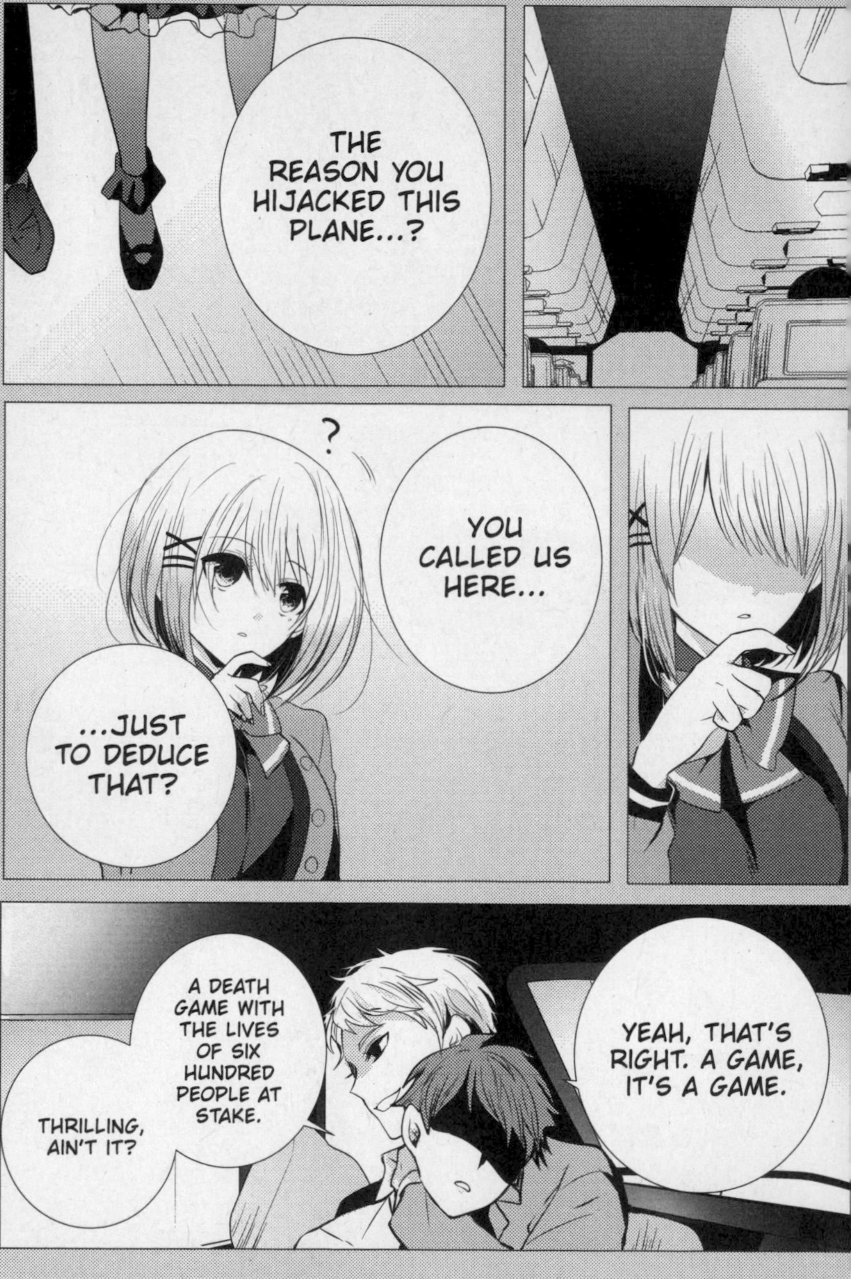
THE REASON YOU HIJACKED THIS PLANE...?
?
YOU CALLED US HERE...
...JUST TO DEDUCE THAT?
YEAH, THAT'S RIGHT. A GAME, IT'S A GAME.
A DEATH GAME WITH THE LIVES OF SIX HUNDRED PEOPLE AT STAKE.
THRILLING, AIN'T IT?

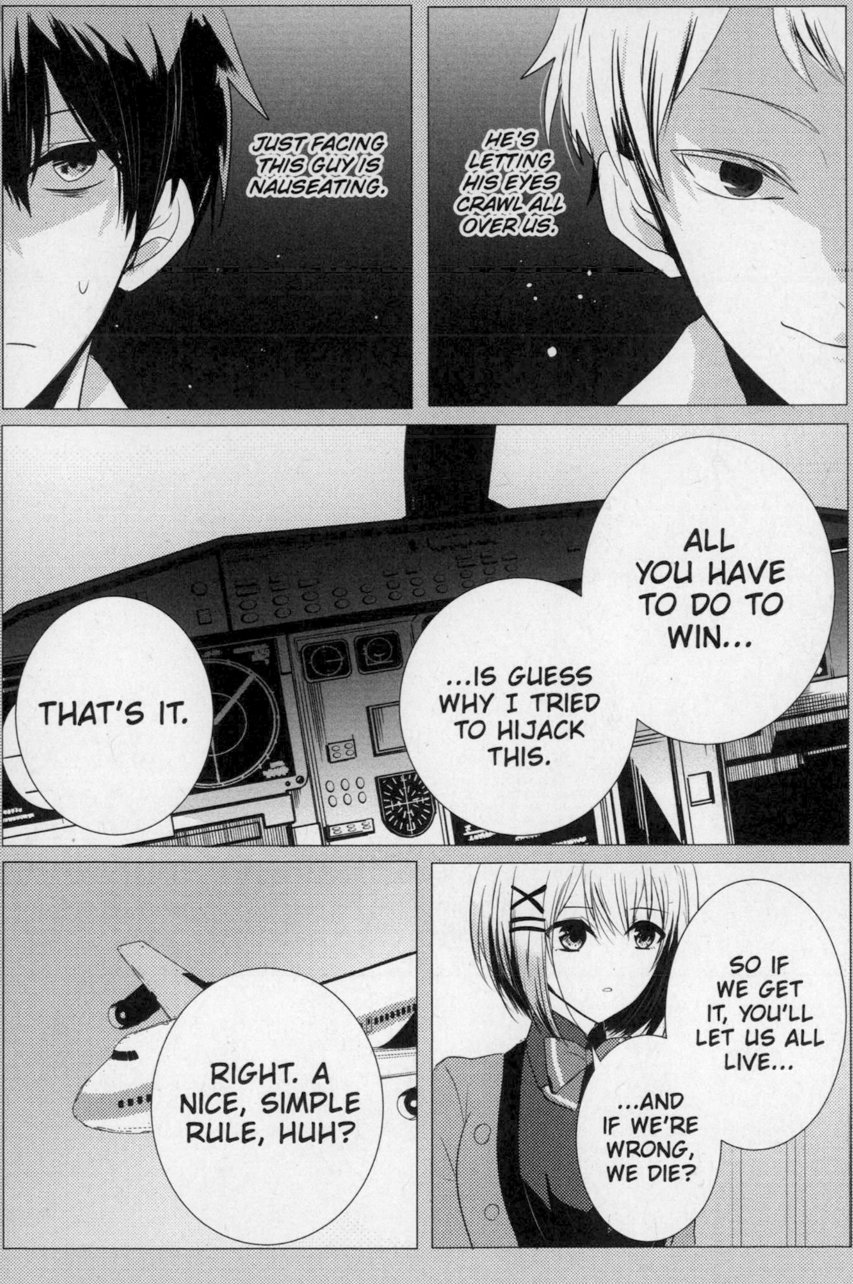
HE'S LETTING HIS EYES CRAWL ALL OVER US.
JUST FACING THIS GUY IS NAUSEATING.
ALL YOU HAVE TO DO TO WIN...
...IS GUESS WHY I TRIED TO HIJACK THIS.
THAT'S IT.
SO IF WE GET IT, YOU'LL LET US ALL LIVE...
...AND IF WE'RE WRONG, WE DIE?
RIGHT. A NICE, SIMPLE RULE, HUH?

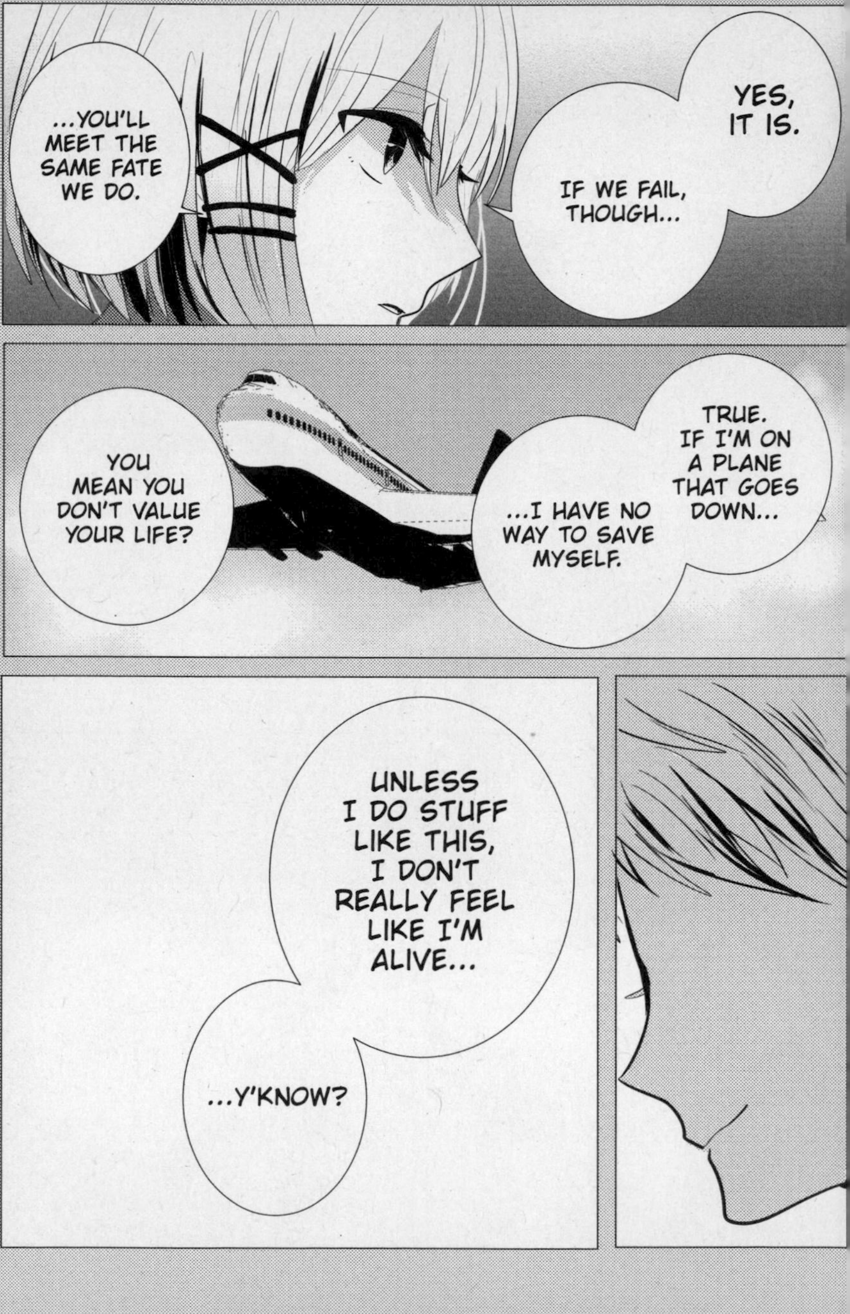
YES, IT IS.
IF WE FAIL, THOUGH...
...YOU'LL MEET THE SAME FATE WE DO.
TRUE. IF I'M ON A PLANE THAT GOES DOWN...
...I HAVE NO WAY TO SAVE MYSELF.
YOU MEAN YOU DON'T VALUE YOUR LIFE?
UNLESS I DO STUFF LIKE THIS, I DON'T REALLY FEEL LIKE I'M ALIVE...
...Y'KNOW?

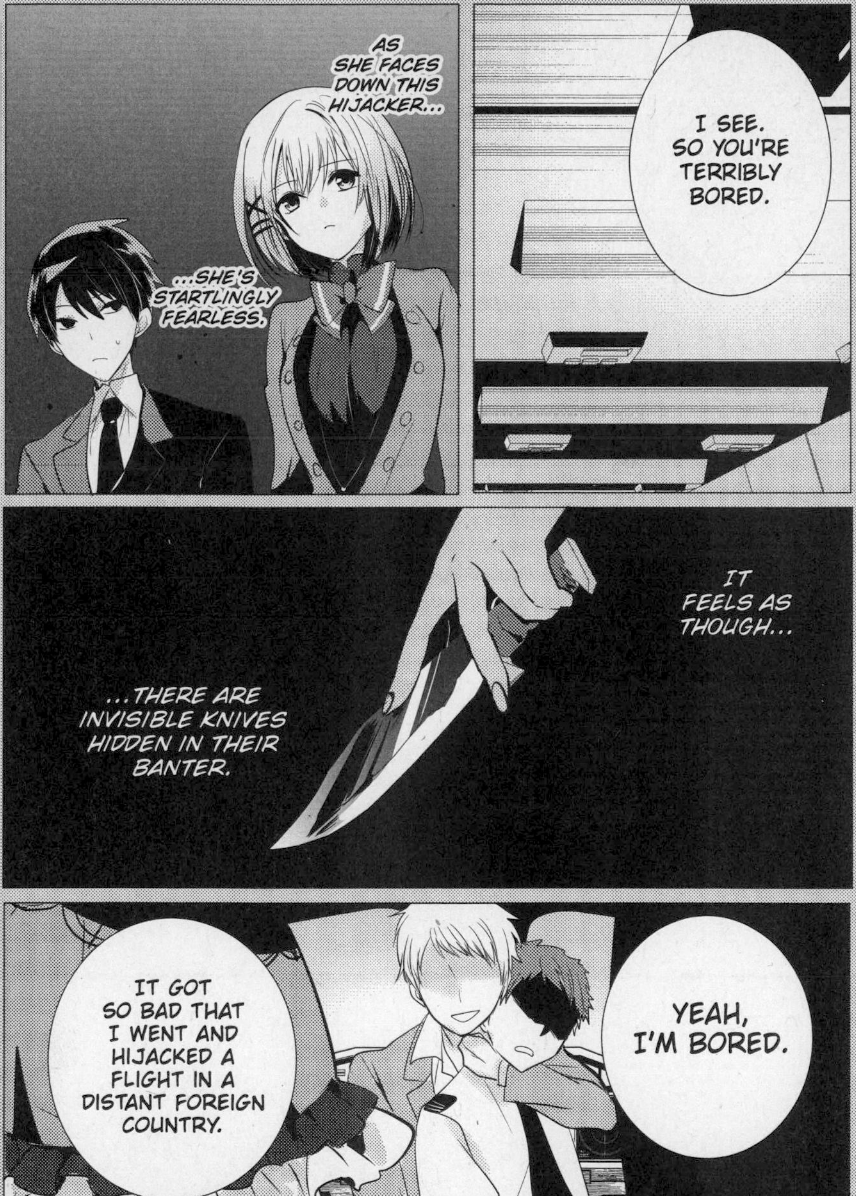
I SEE. SO YOU'RE TERRIBLY BORED.
AS SHE FACES DOWN THIS HIJACKER...
...SHE'S STARTLINGLY FEARLESS.
IT FEELS AS THOUGH...
...THERE ARE INVISIBLE KNIVES HIDDEN IN THEIR BANTER.
YEAH, I'M BORED.
IT GOT SO BAD THAT I WENT AND HIJACKED A FLIGHT IN A DISTANT FOREIGN COUNTRY.

ALL RIGHT.

THEN THAT'S THE ANSWER.

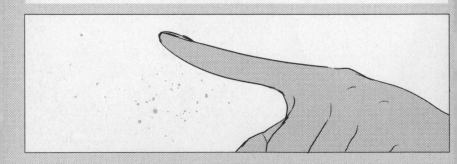

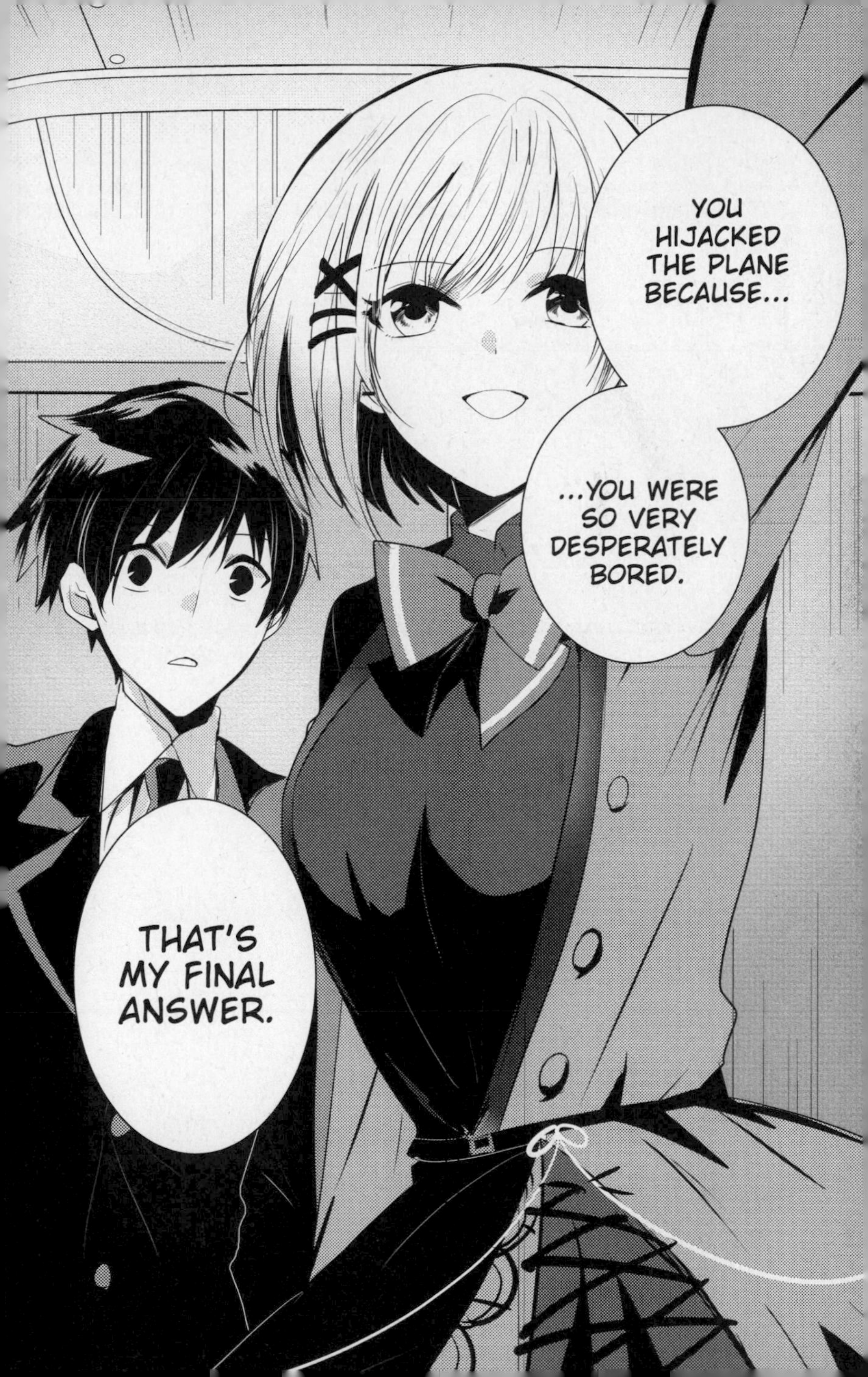
YOU HIJACKED THE PLANE BECAUSE...
...YOU WERE SO VERY DESPERATELY BORED.
THAT'S MY FINAL ANSWER.

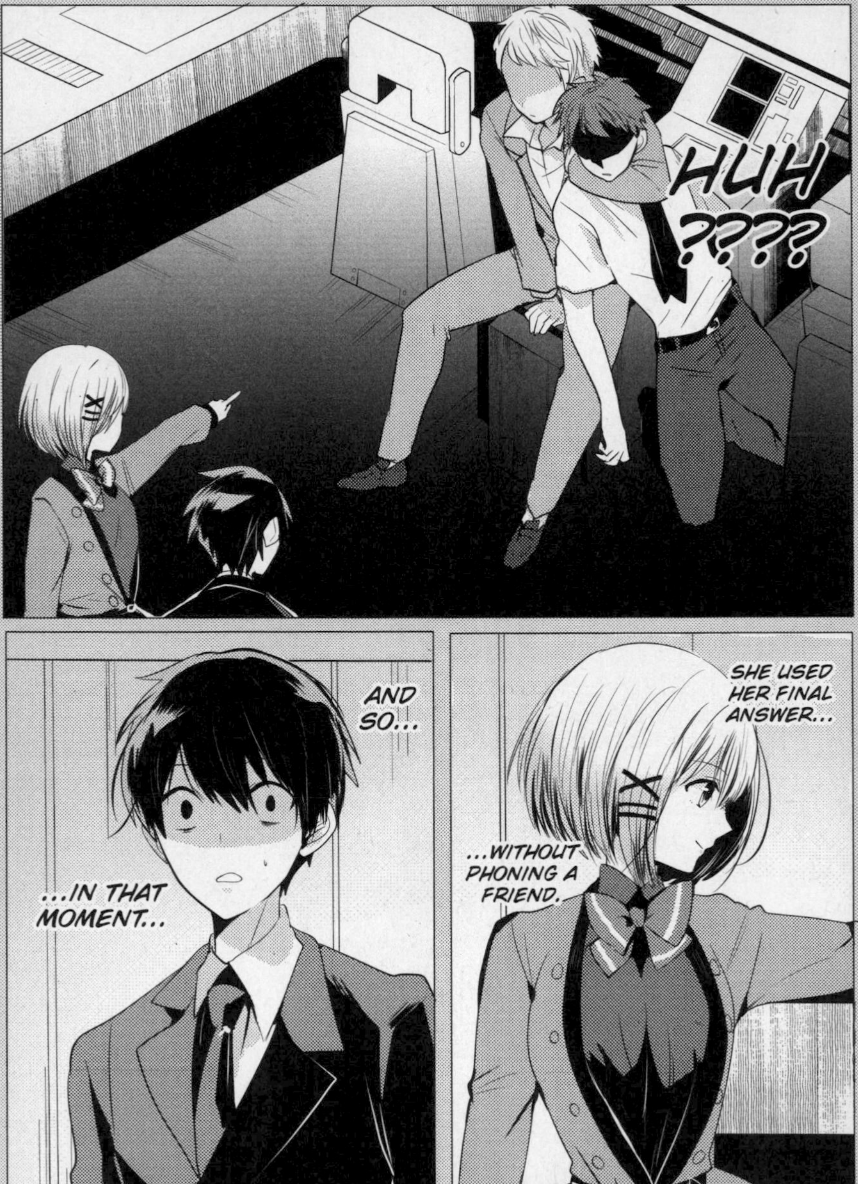
HUH ????
SHE USED HER FINAL ANSWER...
...WITHOUT PHONING A FRIEND.
AND SO...
...IN THAT MOMENT...

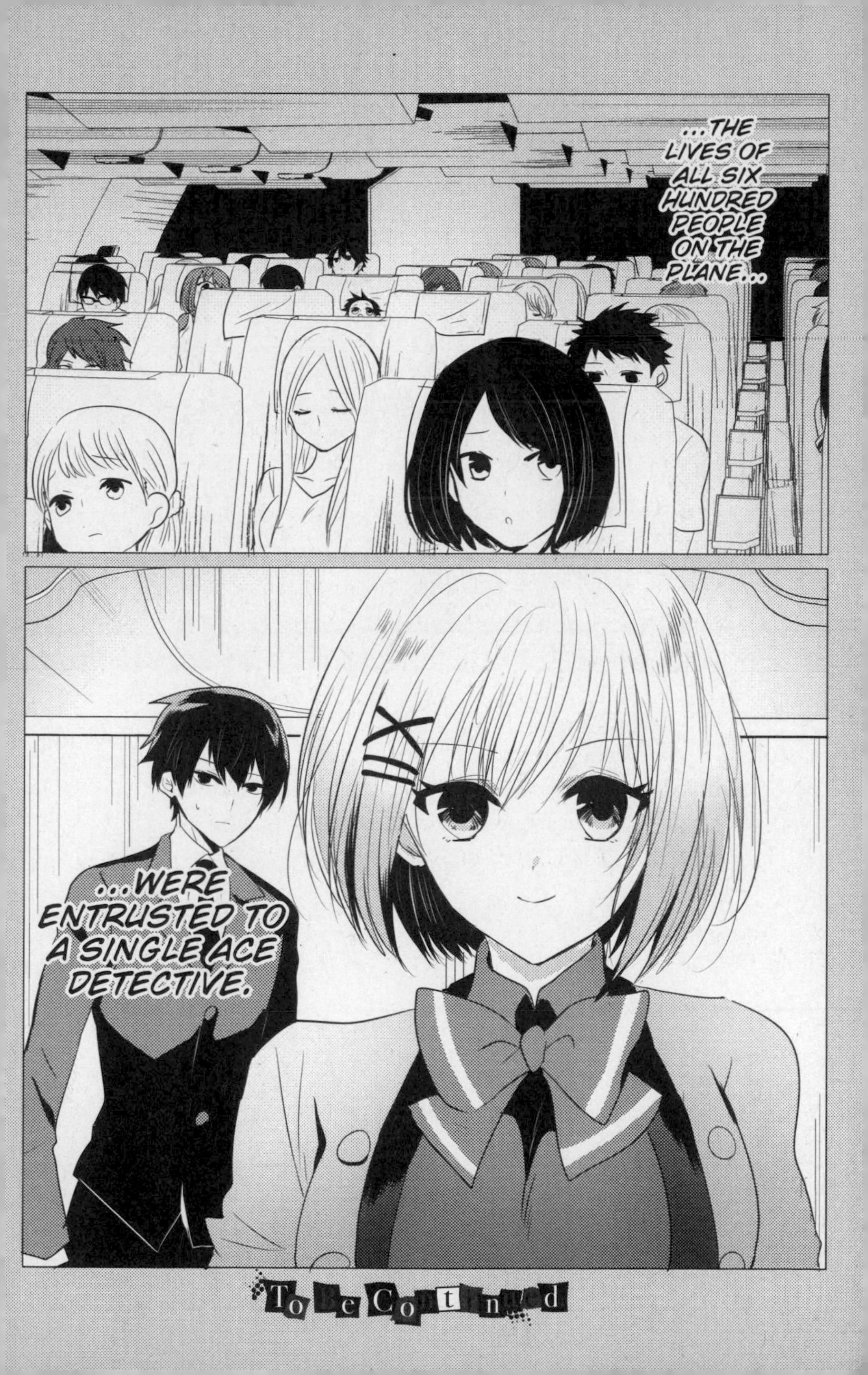
...THE LIVES OF ALL SIX HUNDRED PEOPLE ON THE PLANE...
...WERE ENTRUSTED TO A SINGLE ACE DETECTIVE.

To Be Continued

Translation Notes

Common Honorifics

-san: The Japanese equivalent of Mr./Mrs./Miss. If a situation calls for politeness, this is the fail-safe honorific.

-kun: Used most often when referring to boys, this indicates affection or familiarity. Occasionally used by older men among their peers, but it may also be used by anyone referring to a person of lower standing.

-sensei: A respectful term for teachers, artists, or high-level professionals.

no honorific: Indicates familiarity or closeness; if used without permission or reason, addressing someone in this manner would constitute an insult.

Page 144

Kimi: Siesta's nickname for Kimihiko is a play on words. Not only does it work as a nickname for both his family name and his given name, but it also has the same reading as the Japanese word for "you."

The Detective Is Already Dead

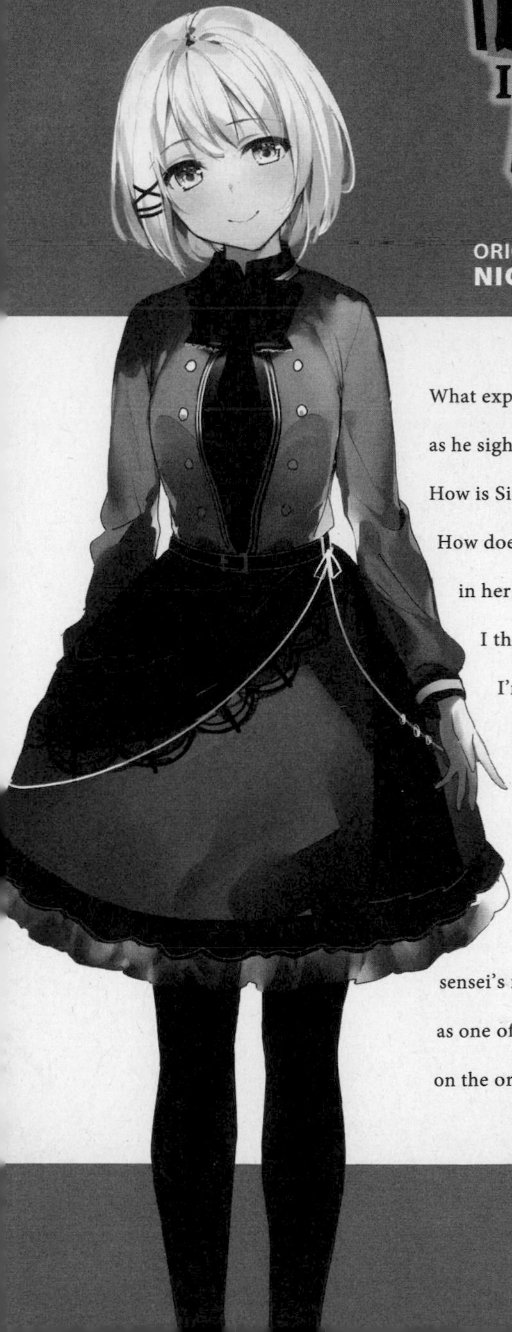

ORIGINAL AUTHOR COMMENTS:
NIGOZYU

What expression is Kimizuka wearing as he sighs, in this moment? How is Siesta teasing Kimizuka? How does Natsunagi's embarrassment show in her face when she yells at Kimizuka?

I think of things like that all the time while I'm writing the novels, but I'm really grateful that everything I've been imagining has been given a shape now. Long live Media Works!

(Also, Fuubi-san is incredibly cool...)

I hope to keep on enjoying Mugiko-sensei's manga version of *Detective* as one of its fans! I'll work even harder on the original novels too!!

The Detective Is Already Dead

CREATOR AFTERWORD: MUGIKO

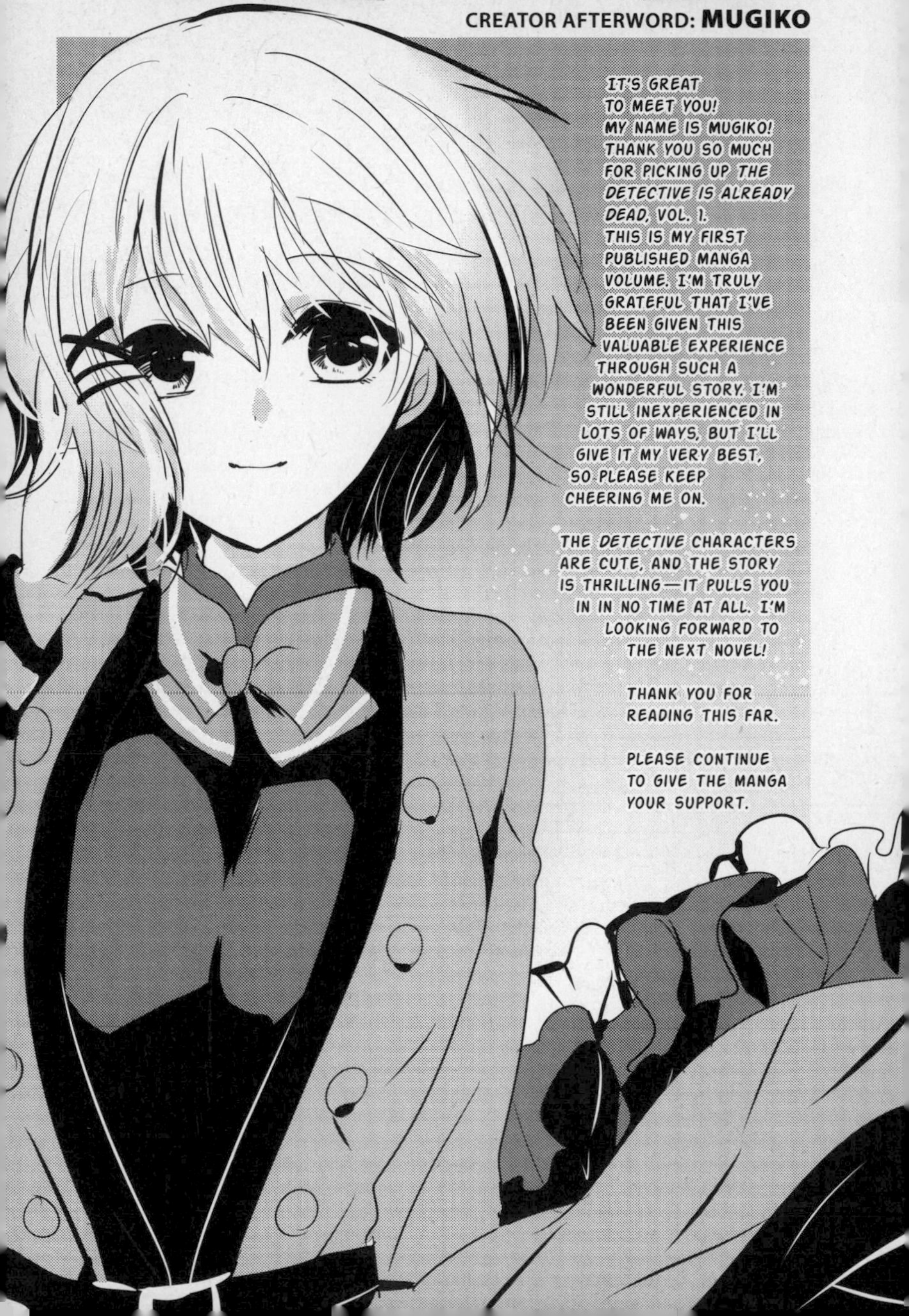

IT'S GREAT TO MEET YOU! MY NAME IS MUGIKO! THANK YOU SO MUCH FOR PICKING UP *THE DETECTIVE IS ALREADY DEAD*, VOL. 1. THIS IS MY FIRST PUBLISHED MANGA VOLUME. I'M TRULY GRATEFUL THAT I'VE BEEN GIVEN THIS VALUABLE EXPERIENCE THROUGH SUCH A WONDERFUL STORY. I'M STILL INEXPERIENCED IN LOTS OF WAYS, BUT I'LL GIVE IT MY VERY BEST, SO PLEASE KEEP CHEERING ME ON.

THE *DETECTIVE* CHARACTERS ARE CUTE, AND THE STORY IS THRILLING—IT PULLS YOU IN IN NO TIME AT ALL. I'M LOOKING FORWARD TO THE NEXT NOVEL!

THANK YOU FOR READING THIS FAR.

PLEASE CONTINUE TO GIVE THE MANGA YOUR SUPPORT.

Character Design **Umibouzu**

Translation **Taylor Engel**
Lettering **Chiho Christie**

TANTEI WA MO, SHINDEIRU. Vol. 1
©Mugiko 2020
©Nigozyu 2020
First published in Japan in 2020 by KADOKAWA CORPORATION, Tokyo.
English translation rights arranged with KADOKAWA CORPORATION, Tokyo, through Tuttle-Mori Agency, Inc., Tokyo.

English translation © 2021 by Yen Press, LLC

Yen Press
150 West 30th Street, 19th Floor
New York, NY 10001

Visit us at yenpress.com ❋ facebook.com/yenpress ❋ twitter.com/yenpress
yenpress.tumblr.com ❋ instagram.com/yenpress

First Yen Press Edition: October 2021

Yen Press is an imprint of Yen Press, LLC.
The Yen Press name and logo are trademarks of Yen Press, LLC.

The publisher is not responsible for websites (or their content) that are not owned by the publisher.

Library of Congress Control Number: 2021942345

ISBNs: 978-1-9753-3741-4 (paperback)
978-1-9753-3742-1 (ebook)

10 9 8 7 6 5 4 3 2 1

TPA

Printed in South Korea